MW00757942

I GET IT!
I FINALLY GET IT!!

I GET IT!
I FINALLY GET IT!!

Living With An Alcoholic, Memoirs

by
JO BINES

To order additional copies of this book, contact:
Xlibris LLC
1-888-795-4274
www.Xlibris.com
Orders@Xlibris.com
615648

TABLE OF CONTENTS

This work is dedicated to

MY GRANDCHILDREN

PROLOGUE

Friday Sept. 16, 2011 I had a Cat Scan in the morning. At 3:30 pm that very afternoon I was called by an oncology resident. I was told that I was to return to the hospital and register at 'Emergency'. The radiologist found an ascending aortic aneurism on the pictures, which is known to be fatal. After five hours of waiting and a cursory medical exam, I was sent home. An appointment has been made for me to consult with a thoracic-vascular surgeon on Tuesday. In the last twenty four hours my world has flipped over yet again. What was to be a routine bone scans to ascertain the whereabouts of the cancer I have been fighting for eleven years turns out to be another damn, deep 'pot hole' on this bumpy road I call 'my life'. I've been nagged by conscience to get back to writing this story

This is how I started eight months ago.

This is really hard to do. It is said that journalizing is cathartic, ridding one's self of demons. That it is liberating. One should not believe everything one hears on television. I just feel nauseated. There is a pain in my chest, a lump in my throat and tears running down my cheeks. My whole body is rigid. Is this a panic attack? It's taken me three years to sit down and write this story. I have tons of notes in many scribblers. I have to face the pain, the shame, the hurt, the frustration, the anger, the hate, the evil intentions, the loathing, the disgust and the blame. I was addicted to my love of my husband for forty years. I still am. Like a teenager, waiting for that phone call that never comes. It's hard to accept he just never was 'into me'.

It's easier to take the drug called 'Faking It'. Comments to myself like "I'm good!"
"Everything is fine thanks!"
"Well you know good days, bad days!"
"I'm getting by, it's just a matter of time!"
"No problems, don't worry be happy!"

Let me introduce myself. Let me introduce you to this fake. ME!

I'm 67 years old, mother of two daughters, grandmother of two granddaughters and two grandsons. In my youth I was a teacher. In middle age I was a sales administrator and service coordinator. I have been a cancer warrior for twelve years. I was the wife of an alcoholic for forty years. I have been a divorcee for five years. Well, legally separated, same difference, just less expensive. For the first time in my life I will be telling the whole truth. This is finally going to be all about ME! ME! ME!

This story is about unconditional love, about the spirit almost dying, about survival, about triumph, about self preservation, about courage, about endings and about beginnings about winning and just maybe about loosing.

This is for YOU and YOU and YOU, each and everyone of you dealing with your own realities right now as you read this. You know who you are.

I feel an unquenchable need to warn, to lift up the most weary among you and help you set a course. The partners of alcoholics are the most damaged, yet least recognized victims in our western society. It's time we speak out and bring attention and solutions to this ever so prevalent source of spousal and child abuse. Enough sweeping the problems under the rug. The walking on eggs shells and shushing everybody has to stop.

STAND UP and be counted. HOLD MY HAND and AWAY WE GO!

This story is real. I have nothing to hide anymore. My parents have died. His parents have died. If the living take offence, so be it. I do not feel the need to protect the 'guilty' anymore, not even myself. The names of the principle characters have been changed in order to protect their privacy.

CHAPTER 1

THE END

August 9, 10, 11, 12, 2007—Tulsa, Oklahoma.

That is what was written at the bottom in each little square of the calendar on the kitchen wall. My husband had written that there. The letters were so miniscule that one would hardly notice. But those words, repeated four times were a reminder and perhaps, in retrospect, a warning. My husband's name is Dick. It was a typical Saturday, in late June. Trudie had come by to go swimming with her baby girl. Her husband was working at the dealership, a couple of the neighbors were mowing their lawns. That was a noise that always annoyed me. The more powerful the lawnmower, the louder and more unnerving was the sound. I always mowed the lawns during the week. Weekends should be for peace and quiet. Today's society is not that way inclined. What am I saying? Men only have time to mow and take care of the lawns on the weekend or in the evenings. I keep forgetting I did the outdoor chores all the time during the week between 9am and 3pm. I wanted to free up the weekends so that I could spend time with my husband. What a joke! There in lies the denial. You see my husband was at the golf course every weekend, Saturday and Sunday, 7am to 5pm. Later I found out, five weekdays as well. Dad, that's what we called him when the kids were home or Papa when the grandkids were around, arrives by 5:30pm. Gets a drink (alcoholic) naturally. Dick never drank a lot of soft drinks or tea or many non-alcoholic beverages. Actually he had this daily beverage routine. Breakfast was apple juice and a coffee. Lunch was a couple of beers or whatever and the rest of the day hard liquor until bedtime. That could be midnight or later. I figured we were spending about $100.00 a week on alcohol. That was for our house consumption. Mind you I don't know for sure because Dick went to the store for that. The rest of the week booze was put on Dick's expense account. I have no idea what my husband did during the day. I presumed he was working. I was never privy to that information. I digress. But do you notice my preoccupation with alcohol.

Dick walked over to the diving board and dove in. He swam across the pool then he joined Trudie and me. He announced.

"I'm going on a trip to Tulsa, Oklahoma on August 9, 10, 11 and 12. Do you remember the guy in Ottawa that had given us free airline tickets to San Diego, a couple of years ago, when we visited your older sister? Well that's the guy who has planned this trip. There is a trade show and we'll do a bit of golfing. I asked

"Are the wives getting to go too? Like a spa trip while the guys work and play?" He answered

"Not this time".

THAT'S IT, THAT'S ALL, END OF DISCUSSION

Several weeks later I found an opened envelope addressed to Dick, on the dining room table, from a company in Ottawa. As usual I never looked at his correspondence, privacy! I placed it on the counter where he keeps his car keys to make sure it did not get lost. I presumed it was important. I'm such a conscientious wife. GAG!!!!

Dick never came to bed with me. We had separate rooms ever since I had had two mastectomies done, one in 2004, the other in 2006. So nothing was unusual when on the evening of the 8th of August, Dick yelled up from the family room, didn't even come to my bed to ask.

"Do you know where the suitcases are? I need to pack"

I said

"If you're old enough to fly to Tulsa, you are old enough to find a suitcase. Whatever you do, don't wake me up at four in the morning, to tell me you're leaving now."

You probably think I was being bitchy and you are right. I was so ticked that absolutely nothing was ever said about this trip and that as usual I was excluded from the 'secret life of Dick'. I felt nothing but bile in my throat that night. Well he would be gone for four days, no fights, no forced isolation. Anyways I had my birthday to get ready for. I was going to be 62 on the 14th of August and Carol and Ross, best friends from Montreal, were coming to celebrate. We had not seen each other for a whole year. I could hardly wait.

CHAPTER 2

SURPRISE! SURPRISE!

The next day, I was backing out the car and noticed my neighbor Johnnie walking up the street. I opened the window and yelled out

"John where are you going? Do you need a ride?"

"Sure my truck is in the shop"

I was always nervous with Johnnie. He was a 65 year old Italian, old guard. A chauvinist pig towards his wife and four daughters but a regular full time flirt with every other female. He had married his wife Rosa when she was fifteen. They came to Canada, from Sicily, when they were twenty and still had the heavy Italian accent forty five years later. They fought like cats and dogs. Wish I knew what they had been saying. But judging from the tone it wasn't nice. I guess it doesn't matter what language men and women use against each other. The aggressiveness always comes out in the tone and the 'LOOK'. Nasty looks always sound nasty. While I drove, he asked

"Did you hear from Dick yet?"

"No I didn't! Why do you ask?"

"Well the boys, my sons, said they keep watching the TV to see him but no luck yet"

"What TV? What are you talking about?"

"The golf game on TV, the Masters game. They were hoping to see Dick in the crowd walking along side Tiger Woods. Dick, when he was at their house working on the air conditioning, told my boys about his planned trip with a whole bunch of guys. Don't you watch it on TV?"

I had to do a super fast recovery. I was shocked and saddened and angry that my neighbor's middle aged sons knew the whereabouts of my husband but not I, his wife. Talk about embarrassing!

"No I haven't had time. Anyways the wives were not invited on the trip."

To that John replied

"Oh I know why, when I go out of town with all of my buddies on my tournaments we don't bring the wives. Men can be real animals!"

THAT'S IT, THAT'S ALL, END OF DISCUSSION

The subject then turned to trucks. I dropped him off at the garage. I got back from buying all the fixings for my birthday dinner with our friends from Montreal in four days. I put everything away and grabbed the phone.

I called my daughters.

"Do you know where dad is staying? Did you get a call from him? Do you know what he is doing in Tulsa? Do either of your husbands know where he is?"

"No Ma!" answer to all questions.

The oldest son in law said that he was actually 'bamboozled'. Isn't that the weirdest word. To this day, I think he was lying. He claims he is Dick's, his father in law's, best friend. Yet he did not know what Dick was doing? If Johnny's middle aged sons knew, I'm sure in my heart of heart Dick would have bragged to his buddy about such an opportunity. They are golf and pool and darts and renovation buddies. The Masters Golf would be to die for. Boast to the buds but hide from the wife! Do I sound suspicious? Damn straight I do! I am a traditionalist. In the family there is a hierarchy. Every culture has it. The oldest son in law is only eight years younger than us. This buddy, buddy arms around each others shoulders in the family photos and all that companionship just seems a bit peculiar to me, too chummy for my taste. There is a fine line and in my opinion that should always be respected. Oh I digress again. Where was I? There was no phone call from my husband for those four days. I kept busy and actually put him out of my mind. It was then that I realized that I really did not give a damn if my husband ever came back. I was actually content being alone. I was happy having a reprieve from the indifference or the confrontations. If you think you are paranoid or anxious or have a split personality. Yes Missy! You are right on all counts. All those symptoms are 100% valid. It's your survival mechanism kicking in all the frigging time. Don't be afraid! It's normal. You are not the crazy one!! But my God is it ever exhausting.

Actually the sheer terror of his return acknowledged to me that a 'last lap flag' had been put out on the track, regarding this marriage.

CHAPTER 3

ALL HELL BREAKS LOOSE

Brace yourself reader. The proverbial 'shit is going to hit the fan'.

August the 12th noon, the phone rings

"Hello! the eagle has landed, safe and sound. I'm in Ottawa, I'm on my way." I slammed the receiver down.

He walked in through the back door like always, 2pm.

"Hi, How are you?" to which I replied

"That is the dumbest question. How the hell do you think I am?"

He passes by me and into his bedroom. I follow him in.

"Where have you been?"

"I told you. You've known about this for weeks Tulsa, Oklahoma."

"I mean where were you staying. You haven't called in four days".

"Three and a half days" he replies with that condescending grin of his.

That wise crack just set me off, right then and there. It never failed. He corrected me on everything all the time, even in public. If I said something and if it was not 100% percent accurate he would interrupt me and take great pleasure in pointing out my error. I would say

"You know what I mean, who cares." He would reply

"If you are going to say anything then you should say it right the first time." We would all shake our heads, then I would proceed. I guess that would have been enough to shut me up but oh no, not me. I had to prove I was going to keep the floor and could not be put down.

Things changed a couple of decades later. I just stopped giving a damn and would continue talking over his criticism or eventually not bother continuing at all.

Back to the fight!

"What's wrong with you. Don't you see how awful that was. How hurtful? You could have called me!" he said

"I was only as far as my cell phone. You could have called me. Anyways there was a time difference of three hours. You always go to bed so early, and I didn't want to wake you up. Then I got busy and I forgot! Anyways I had left the itinerary on the dining room table ages ago. You just had to read it." I was becoming so frustrated.

"Good Lord the neighbor's sons knew all about this trip. You didn't mind bragging to them about it. But your own wife was not even worthy of a phone call to let me know that you had arrived and where you could be reached." He replied

"What is this, an inquisition? So what is it that you want now? the whole truth and nothing but the truth."

"Oh shut up. This is useless, I don't need particulars"

The aggressive tone and the snide look on his face chilled me to the bone. I could feel the current of evil wafting across the room. As usual it never occurred to me that he was probably loaded, wasted. One last ditch effort to seek some empathy for me and remorse from him. I continued

"Look at what you are doing to me, right now. I can hardly breathe and my heart is racing so fast I feel like it's going to jump right out of my chest and I feel like I'm going to throw up." To which he answered

"I have nothing to do with that. You are the one who is working yourself up into a dander, over nothing. Anyways what the hell are you going to do about it? Hey! Threaten to divorce me yet AGAIN!"

This blatant disregard for my feelings and total disrespect for me was incredible. There wasn't even any shame. That brick wall was impenetrable.

I think it was at that very moment, that a stone was rolled over the tomb called, our marriage.

I murmured,

"Your behavior has altered the course of our lives."

THAT'S, IT THAT'S ALL END OF DISCUSSION

He walked past me with his suitcase and went down to the laundry room and proceeded to wash his clothes. That was the first time in our life that my husband actually did his own laundry. Any dibs on the smells of those clothes? Now I understand why there are so many domestic shootings in the states. As God is my witness, had we had a gun in the house I would have followed him down to the laundry room and shot my husband dead then and there. It's called provoking someone physically or verbally to the state of momentary insanity. Honestly, our marriage had been teetering on the edge of a precipice for a long time, at least a decade. Sunday August 12th, 6pm, I was pushed right over the chasm. Instead, I ran to my bathroom and vomited my guts out. I did not come back out that evening. The next day, my husband left for work just like every other Monday, as if nothing ever happened. I began to get everything ready for our friends' visit. They were due in around 3 pm. My daughters and their children dropped in for a swim and a visit. The grandkids were in heaven swimming along with their Labrador. Everyone was having a great time. I had prepared a great Atlantic salmon dinner and everyone was pleasant. The next morning after breakfast as I was serving coffee by the pool, my girlfriend yelled out.

"There is someone at the front door".

My husband goes and returns with a dozen long stem yellow roses and a ladies golf hat. The color yellow was always my favorite. My husband was trying to impress by giving me my usual birthday present, yellow roses. They are my favorites, a symbol of friendship. How ironic! I was 64 years old that day. So I gave Carol the hat since she was the golfer lady, not I. I brought the roses into the house. My girlfriend was so excited for me. I just felt like screaming. I'm nauseous just thinking back on it.

The two husbands were chatting by the pool. My husband said

"Ross, I got us a tee off for 10:30am today".

"Thanks Dick but if I go golfing with you I won't get to see Jo and that's why we came here for the girls' birthdays. Carol and I have to leave after noon."

"Oh too bad!"

Dick walked out through the yard gate and went golfing. Honestly I was happy alone with Carol and Ross. I never mentioned a word of my problems. It would have been inappropriate. She's had Parkinson for several years and her husband has been her primary care giver. We were going to have a good time. She and I are warriors. We 'GET IT'. Even though Cancer and Parkinson are two totally different diseases the psychological stress is the same. Carol staggered into the pool and is having fun with her dog. I thought she could be drowning and her husband says

"Don't worry I'm keeping an eye on her she has to come up for air, like everybody else does".

Finally, he convinced her to come out because they had to get ready to leave. By this time because of all the excitement and exercise she was all twisted up like a pretzel and the tremors were pronounced. Out come the meds. In the privacy of the upstairs guest room her husband got her out of her wet bathing suit and dried her off. Ross then got her dressed and brushed her hair. She turns out as glamorous as always. I helped him pack up the car. He then proceeded to groom and brush the dog because he didn't want a stinky wet dog travelling in the back seat of the car, all the way to Montreal. Then they were off. I was so lonely and so sad. It was then, after watching Ross take care of his wife and acting as a true, caring partner, a good husband and friend that I realize that I was not going to live with my schmuck any longer.

CHAPTER 4

PLANNING MY FUTURE

Well when the Healer, the Lover of the two, the Giver, the Fixer Upper and at an emotional level 'the hand that feeds your heart' dies than
"WATCH OUT".

I had asked Dick a long, long time ago after another bout in the ring.
"Why did you marry me anyways?" he answered
"Because you were strong and I wouldn't have to take care of you!"

I took that as a compliment in those days. They were so few and far between. Let's face it, anyone with an ounce of brains in their head knows "You never corner an ALPHA FEMALE"

That inner strength of mine was going to pay off. After forty years instead of taking care of two, I was going to just take care of one.

The day after my birthday I phoned our lawyer and asked him for the name of a family law attorney. Our attorney was shocked. He said

"I have known you and Dick for over ten years and you do love each other. Couldn't you try and resolve this through counseling. Honestly, there must be a way. You've been fighting cancer for that long and honestly the stress of filing for divorce and legalities involved would not be a healthy option for you right now."

Understand, I did not give him the particulars of the event that took place. After all he was also my husband's lawyer for business issues. It was no one's business except my soon to be family lawyer. She could advise me on what to say and to whom and what to keep to myself. This is a truth I must warn you about. I learned it the hard way. A serious confidence was broken by my eldest daughter and our relationship has been weakened ever since. Never forget. It's kind of like a poker game. You have to keep your hand close to your chest. I thanked our lawyer for his concern and said

"Please, just give me the name of a lawyer."

"This lady is really good she has a lot of experience and I know you would prefer the expertise and perspective of a woman"

I called my new lawyer's office and explained everything over the phone to her assistant. The assistant is kind of like a screener. She was going to pass it on to the attorney who would make a judgment and call me the following day to confirm whether or not she would take on my case. Boy! reliving all of this is so hard. I feel nauseous again and I'm shivering. The point I'm trying to impress you with, is

"This is no game, not just a flirtation with the concept of freedom. It is serious business that can bring you a great deal of deep pain and sorrow. So make sure you are ready to leap in the abyss, alone".

The only good thing about being at the bottom of the well or at the beginning of a long, pitch black tunnel is

"Look, there is a glimmer of light at the top or at the end. I like to think that it is the halo of a guardian angel glistening at dawn".

The lady lawyer called back the next morning and explained to me the process. An initial fee of $4500. was to be paid. That amount would either be increased or decreased depending on how much time had been spent on this litigation. She booked an appointment for two days later and in the meantime I was to write a synopsis of our forty years living together, concluding with why I thought I needed to be legally separated from this man, my husband. This, along with the check indicated to her the seriousness of my intent. If you expect any lawyer to be all empathetic and emotionally vested with your plight, DON'T. It's a business and when in a meeting or on the phone, you are on the clock. The meter is running. They are called billable hours. Remember the Grisham law novels, well that part is true, not fiction.

That evening my two adult daughters took me out for my birthday dinner. I was into day three of my project, shaken but determined. I told my girls what I had done. They were stunned because this was happening so fast. They recovered and said.

"We're not surprised but why did it take you so long?"

To which I replied without any hesitation.

"In '92 Dad had moved to Ontario I stayed behind in Montreal because my salary was higher and we really needed the money. I moved in '93 and all I wanted to do was keep close to my family. Then there was a DUI, a real reason to make the leap. Then grandchildren were being born and I really wanted to help there and my family really distracted me. Having my little ones was like falling in love all over again. They filled a huge void. I was helpful to my daughters and felt useful. Then the excuse of all excuses in 2000, CANCER. When you're doing battle with breast cancer, three surgeries, sixteen rounds of radiation, six months of chemo, hair loss, big like a blow fish all in eight years, there is no room to think of 'matters of the heart'. By the time I filed for separation I had already had three reoccurrences of cancer. On the weekends or a couple of days a week, I in my naivety, would of thought of us as a close, extended family. My daughters would probably argue that point. Rightly so! But they can write all about that in their own book. My daughters and I, in true Montreal style, closed the restaurant. Our city is small. People, literally, chow down from 5 to 6:30pm and are gone. We hung out till 11pm. The cook and the two waiters were satisfied with the healthy tip. Rare treat Northern Italian cuisine and several Brazilian coffees. It's probably weird to you but I actually had a lot of fun at this birthday party. Putting everything on the table early in the evening helped us get over it, put it aside and get down to more interesting conversations. My daughters have serious, busy careers so I always found their work interesting and I was proud of them. We three rarely had the opportunity to hang out alone. The youngest was designated driver. She has the patience of a saint. She was worried about my emotional state and was on stand by. My husband was snoring when I got back home.

The meeting with my lawyer went well. We covered strategies. We agreed I was not to tell him anything, no advance warning. I was too afraid of what he would do to me if we had to hash it out before it went official. My anxiety levels were high enough as it was. A letter was to be delivered to his place of employment. In it my lawyer would also provide the opportunity for him to contact her in the event he could not find legal representation and she would provide him with three names. Unfortunately I could not get rid of him from our house. The law provides that shared domicile be available, if required, until final decree of legal separation has been recorded in the courts. I was really scared about that. I knew I was in good hands legally but I was scared of his vile temper. I hardly spoke to my husband except to tell him that his supper was ready in the oven. He probably figured I would come out of my funk like I always did and smooth things over for us. His life never skipped a beat. He went to work, went golfing and did everything else in between, whatever that was, as per usual. One evening he brought home the application for renewal for my Canadian passport to fill out because ours were going to expire in November. My reaction was

"What ever makes you think I would ever want for us to travel together until last month's episode is cleared up." His response was

"Oh! Just stop talking about it!"

Note, he never made a single effort to brooch the subject of my anger towards his behavior or attitude. He would have thought, she'll come around. She always does. His indifferent behavior is based on quite a lot of experience, from his adolescence, his university failures, his jobs. He had a lot of experience at dodging bullets. His paramount goal in our marriage was to deflect any criticisms and accept no responsibility what so ever for any actions of his. Ever!!

It was at this time I was starting to get the sneaky suspicion that Dick probably liked our arrangement, A 'marriage of convenience' Gee! I believe in those also. Especially the kind, where the husband does his thing but the wife gets to use all his credit cards and travel and shop and dine etc. etc. A mutual understanding to stay out of each others business as long as things are discreet and everyone is provided for. Ours was pretty one sided. My husband did his thing. I had been paying for myself and our kids for over 30 years. I had a fulltime job. I was financial partner and full time household domestic, cook, and groundskeeper for forty years.

Man! the guy had it 'made in spades'. My eighty year old girlfriend (former boss lady in the 70s) said of me a couple of years ago.

"I never thought you of all people could be such a sucker".

CHAPTER 5

REALITY CHECK

I did mention before to keep things on the QT when you are filing for separation. This sounds contradictory. What I do suggest is confide in a doctor, nurse, friend, sister, someone you trust will be on your side. Someone who would be a good listener. Let's face it everything that is going to come out of your heart is going to be huge. Keep a journal, hide it, write all of your fears and uncertainties. Select a keeper of your memos to yourself. Maybe you could write on separate sheets of paper and hand them into your friend. Let them save them in a manila envelope for you, for future use if needed. Maybe this should be started before the end, whenever you think there is something out of sync, something you feel is going really off kilter. You often talk to yourself about troubling things that are happening. So write them down. I wish I could be sure about this but honestly I'm baffled most of the time when it comes to relationships between men and women. Go with your gut, I guess. I'm not too keen on using the internet because every man and his dog can get to your private writings. Believe me, if the police come to your home or if you appear in court, you better have some written data and a witness who can vouch for your honesty in these dealings. The 'she said, he said' concept is useless in legal matters.

The next two or three weeks were spent calling a couple of very close friends and my sisters trying to reconcile all this in my mind. My girlfriend, Stella of forty years couldn't get over how radical this was. She always thought everything was fine with us. We always seemed to get along. She had never seen us fight together. Discuss sure, argue sure, but those were in political discussions or on social issues.

"You were both able to carry on a conversation that used to leave me out on the side. I just couldn't keep up with you guys. You were always hot for each other. Look at all the renovation, building projects you both seem to thrive on. Maybe you should start one of those together again."

She was from Florida and we only got together once a year. She noticed on that summer's visit I was a lot more jumpy and edgy. Now she knew why. She had no idea things were so bleak and was disappointed I had not confided. She was afraid I might be having a nervous breakdown. We talked long distance every other day through this mess. She was there for me, far away physically but very close emotionally.

I cannot emphasize enough and I will continue to bring it up, the depth of shame and, embarrassment a person such as myself feels at the very thought of confiding ugly happenings in one's private life. There is such a feeling of failure. Let's face it we do not want to bother anybody because we truly think, with a lot more hard work, things will work out for the better. More than anything, we cannot admit to ourselves that this person we are totally committed to and have vested interests in for our future and that of our children does not feel the same way about us. What we have not yet realized is that the hard work needs to be shared by the two partners. One person is not going to get the job done. You know the book and the movie 'He isn't into you'. Well nobody wants to admit that. Yes DENIAL, based on self preservation. Nobody wants a broken heart or spirit, defeat, aloneness. I can assure you I don't remember there ever being that in any fine print when I took my wedding vows. Another close friend's first husband, whom I had never known, was an alcoholic also. He died in his fifties of sclerosis of the liver. She confided in me the signs that are so commonly found in that type's behavior. It started to make more sense to me now. She uses the word OBLIVIOUS to best describe the person's demeanor. The definition is, unaware, unconscious of, unmindful, disregardful, insensible, insensitive, distant, removed, unconcerned, unfeeling, detached. Do you remember yourself, all on your own, all those nights crying, sobbing. The kids were deep in sleep in the other bedrooms. Do you remember all those words you came up with to describe the attitude displayed by that man you loved unconditionally. Check out 'oblivious'. There they are.

Are you starting to get it? What I want you to remember the most is the FEAR we have of his coming home and more than likely having a hissy fit and waking up the kids. How many times have we laid there silent, not moving while we heard him rummaging through the refrigerator. We hardly ever really slept did we? You could take a lot of his crap but you sure as hell did not want him waking the children. No one should ever have to live like that. This is mental ABUSE. Like being in a war zone, gorilla warfare, waiting for the enemy to strike. And strike they do.

Another good meeting I had at the time of my crisis, besides that with the lawyer, was the get together I had with our family physician. I felt really weird, health wise and needed a consult. We had him as our summer GP since 1988, at the time of our younger daughter's near fatal boating accident. Guardian angels do abound. You better believe it. I confided in him while he handed me wads of tissues. He listened carefully and never interrupted. Then he said.

"Look I shouldn't say this because I am also Dick's physician and we do play golf together once in a while but",

A pause that seemed like an eternity to me. I could tell he was really choosing his words carefully.

"Dick has always seemed to be a very self-centered man. Now we have to figure out how to help you through this. I'm not going to dissuade you. What was done to you this time and how it was done was thoughtless and disrespectful. I'm sure this sort of thing is not the first time. It's just the first time you share with a doctor. Mostly, I'm concerned about these symptoms of yours, nausea, dizziness, rapid heart palpitations, ringing in the ears, seeing stars, the feeling that you are going to pass out."

I was dumfounded to think that I actually could have an ally in our family GP. He continued.

"This physiological experience is not related to the cancer you have now. This is as serious. This is a classic anxiety attack. If these reoccur there is a very high likelihood of your having a stroke. What I need for you to do is after the papers are served to Dick you have to do everything in your power to get him to move out of the house. You cannot afford any more confrontations and your lawyer can handle all the rest of the stuff." I asked

"Can't you call her and counsel her that this is your advice to her as our family doctor?" I almost begged

"No I cannot. If he refuses to go and you and your lawyer decide to go to court to have a judge pass judgment that he has to leave than I will gladly appear as a witness for your case. You can have your lawyer call me if she needs any confirmation of my opinion."

Oh my God. Such a hard emotionally, topsy turvy, upside down I am going to vomit feeling.

"I want you to call the office anytime for another chat. You say your sister wants you to go on anti-depressants. Do you want a prescription?" I answered

"No, not yet, I'm too tired to figure out all the stuff about anxiety drugs. I have enough to deal with. I think I need my wits about me, not for my thinking process to be dulled in any way."

"OK! Instead I would like for you to consider psychological counseling for the cancer and this divorce. Call me when you are ready. I can't force you but you need an objective, professional to help you walk through these minefields."

Monday the 17th of September was the day that the letter was to be delivered to my husband's office. My younger daughter came by to spend a few hours. She wanted to be with me in case things went really bad, to get me out of the house if need be. She had lived with us on and off, as an adult woman between university and different career locations. She had witnessed some of the more violent confrontations and had been a victim of several herself. So we were bracing ourselves for the worst. My eldest daughter had called a few times during the previous weeks to find out how things were developing with the lawyer. I found that kind of odd because she usually would mostly email every four weeks or so. I had told both daughters on the Friday that the lawyer's letter was being delivered on the Monday. The phone rings at 2pm. My husband was calling to check on the furnace repair guys. I fond that odd also because he never called home during the day. He sounded casual, distant, disconnected. I asked

"Did you not get a lawyer's letter this morning?" He replied

"It took me by surprise! I've left messages at three lawyers that I know. I won't know what to do until I get their professional advice"

Hang up.

Trudy and I went over some possibilities for future plans. They had thought that perhaps they could buy the house from us. It was big enough for me to still stay there and I could help out with my grand daughter. She was a good kid. It's a terrible thing for even an adult child to have to deal with such a chaotic process as parental break-up. Our daughters were in their mid 30s. I think what I regret the most is her having to assume the position of protector for her own Mom. But in retrospect, considering the verbal and mental abuse she had and I had put up with from him, I think she was just as anxious to get her father out of my life as I was. We decided to ease up on any plans yet and go through the legalities first. I explained that I had done my homework and that I did have enough investments through my inheritance to take care of my costs of living for quite a while yet.

I couldn't look at her anymore without tears of frustration streaming down my face. I was ashamed and guilty even with her. It was time for her to go home. She had her own family now. That had to be the priority. Just a couple of hours later Dick calls again. Wow! twice in one afternoon, wonders never cease (just kidding). You do learn to develop a sense of humor after having survived all the drama. My husband asked

"Did you defrost anything for dinner?"

"What? Yes of course. Why?"

"I'm having supper at Marie's (eldest daughter) house. She invited me"

"Shouldn't we go over this legal letter?"

"No, I'm waiting for a lawyer to call"

"Are you coming here to sleep?"

"If you don't want me to, I can sleep at Marie's." I answered

"Get here before 7:30pm ring the front door bell."

At that time my husband had not noticed that I had removed the front and back door house keys from his keychain a couple of days before. You see he never had to let himself into the house or any of our places before because I was always home where I was supposed to be. I always got home first from work or babysitting or appointments or whatever and always had the back door unlocked. Why the big deal about the keys, you might wonder. Well I wanted to have control over something. Since I never knew, in my forty years when he was going to be coming home or in what condition, for that matter, I wanted to insist on the fact that there would only be one point of entry and that was the front door and the time would be ETA before 6pm or the door would be locked on him. He could just get himself a motel room. If he started a hassle at the door I was in my right to call the police stating marital dispute. Now that the letter had been served I had more access to protection than I think I ever had before. Under the law he had a right to inhabit the marital domicile. The rules of this cohabitation had to be established by us, especially me if I could swing it. In a way I was glad I had all this help available out there. Even though it was from strangers, at least they knew how this hardball game was played. I sure as heck will not ever in a million years have to walk this path again.

My husband was on time, I turned on the porch light and unlocked the door and stepped back, just in case. He came in carrying a small toiletry bag men use for their shaving things. I asked
"What is that for?"
"I brought it in case I was going to sleep overnight at Marie's."
"I don't understand, you just got the letter this morning and you never came home during the day. When did you pack it?"
"Last night, Sunday night she called and told me I was going to get a letter of your filing for legal separation, at my office today. If I wanted to I could stay over at their place."
I was stunned, a very private confidence broken by the eldest, going to take care of her daddy. Just like, when she was fifteen years old, the first time we separated. What was even more shocking is that Dick was going to lean on her now as a confidante and have her soothe this transition for him. Another crutch, if not the wife, in the absence of a girlfriend on the sidelines, why not the eldest daughter and his best buddy, her husband. The seasoned manipulator strikes again, 'clever as a fox'. What a coward! Maybe it was her way of hoping, that if she were to take him in, he would finally, after all these years, approve of her and appreciate her. I can't even be bothered speculating anymore. Only she knows why she did not let us handle this ourselves without her meddling. I'm too tired now to try and fix it. It's really ironic that two years later he told me he thought our eldest daughter was 'a flake'. So sad luckily I never told her that. What did I have to gain? These are 'loose, loose' situations. What is even more strange is the eldest, two years later, filed for legal separation from her husband and borrowed my legal document to use as reference. I tell you my whole world, as I knew it, was unrecognizable.

Back to the tale. Instinctively my need to protect my family took precedence. I said

"You can't go and crash on the daughter's futon in the basement. The grandkids should never be exposed to their grandparents' problems. They don't have the capacity to understand this mess.

"What is Papa doing in the bed downstairs? Where is Nana? What would you answer?"

In passing, I must say that a year later my nine year old granddaughter happened to say to me, when I was driving her back from school,

"Nana I know why you and Papa don't live in the same house anymore." 'Why is that honey?'

"Because you guys had fights all the time. I didn't like that."

"Well honey I promise you, you won't have to see that anymore, ever."

From the mouths of babes, don't forget that kids don't miss a trick. I then realized that what was normal behavior between us, husband and wife fighting every day, arguing, bickering had become such a bad experience to our grandkids. Of that I am truly ashamed. Sorry my dear beauties.

There was no more contact or talking that night. We each went our own separate way to our bedrooms.

Days went by, no conversation at all. My husband would be in by 6pm. He ate downstairs in the family room and watched T V. I had dinner upstairs in the living room. Two rooms lit by the glow of color televisions, not a single light on in the house. Very much like a bat cave would be dark, silent, cold and dank. To this day I have a sneaky suspicion that my husband was waiting for the final hurrah! I get to do all the hard work on this also. I took care of everything else, why not this separation. If his relationship meant anything to him at this point, surely he would say something, do something, react, act. It was like 'bring it on'. Finally his jailer was going to release him from prison. After our girls had flown the coop, he always had this joke he loved to share with everybody.

"The kids are gone. The dog has died, the cats have died, the fishes and the turtles have died. Now there is just the wife and me."

Quote Martin Luther King, "Free at last, Free at last. Thank God almighty we're free at last."

The sad thing is, it was the truth. He had finally been unburdened. Now Glory be! The wife was going to cut him loose and she would be gone too. Eventually, the man tells me he has a lawyer. He had to call my lawyer to get the name. I guess his huge network of friends just copped out on him. Oh! where are your buddies when you need them most? Hey, bar fly buddies are only useful in the fun times. When the going gets tough, they scatter like rats on a sinking ship. His lawyer happens to be a lady also. She gave him the first consultation free because he hadn't had a chance to clear some of his investments yet to pay her full fee. Boy was he ever ticked when he found out the cost. HA!HA!

CHAPTER 6

LET THE GAMES BEGIN

Now I'm starting to sound a little bit cocky because I can actually see the sliver of light at the end of the tunnel. I hate our living arrangements. I want him out. His very presence makes me sick to my stomach. But my lawyer explains to me that if I want him out I have to petition the court judge to render a call. That takes a court date which could take eight weeks and still the judge may not necessarily rule in my favor. So wait it out. He has a right to shared domicile. I was not going to leave my house because that creates another problem. It would suggest that I have the ways and means to live outside of the domicile, which is true but we don't want anyone to know that. Also he gets to hold on to the property and to stay there because he claims he can't afford to move out. It's all about legal strategies. Hey! I don't care what people say about lawyers. When they think they are holding a royal flush, let them do their job. Their job is to win for you.

"Hang on" I keep telling myself, the wheel of justice turns slowly.

One evening Dick wanted to talk to me. We got into a discussion. He said his lawyer had suggested we go to counseling. I said

"Mine did also ask if counseling would be helpful for a reconciliation? They have to do that. The courts are to conclude that all options have been considered and that separation is the last resort. There was no way as far as I was concerned. I know damn well how to sustain a marital relationship. I have done it for 40 years. I could counsel anybody on patience and compromising. I was a pro." He then offered

"Well do you want me to get you a cleaning lady? Would that make you happy?"

"Our problems go a lot deeper that my being able to use the help of a cleaning lady. Where do you get such asinine ideas? I have a better idea, you golf less and put in a day helping with the hard household chores like vacuuming and another day mowing the lawns. I could even throw in window washing. Ever since I had two breast amputation surgeries for cancer I still have to do all those hard chores. That would really help me with those jobs and you would be staying home. That would make me very happy and it would show me that you do care." To this he replied

"So you refuse counseling. See, you're the one that can't communicate. You shut me out completely after the Tulsa trip. I knew since February that I was going. You knew where I was, I left the itinerary on the dining room table a long time ago. If you didn't read it, that is not my fault. It was even on the calendar. I did not keep any information from you. This was an opportunity of a life time. I would not pass it up for anybody. Anyways I knew you were mad about my going away so why should I call you. I knew I was going to 'get shit' so why not get 'the royal height of shit'."

When the bile comes crawling up my throat and seeping into my mouth then I know, Enough!

There were several conversation where I was just knocking my head against a brick wall. The topics of contention were alcoholism, absenteeism, withholding the truth,(I call it lying), sneaking around, hypocrisy, the constant lack of money. All had been covered several times, over several years. We were always at a total impasse. The final comment was always

"I don't have a problem. You are the problem!"

We were opposites, polar in personality and moral perceptions and values. I compare it to being in a boxing ring. Opponents coming in from separate corners meeting in the middle with the goal of beating the crap out of each other. Mind you, while all of this was going on, Dick never laid a hand on me. He must have been warned by somebody. Our yelling and screaming used to leave me trembling and exhausted. I would go up to bed, lock my bedroom door and have nightmares most nights.

My husband would go to the kitchen, pour himself another drink and crash in front of the TV. The mentioned issues would best exemplify our differences. They are, what are now referred to as, deal breakers in contemporary society. To my generation, in those days, they were things you just put up with. Remember the brides vows were 'to love, honor and obey'. The male was to be the dominant member of the family. The head of the family, no matter how inept he was. To this day, women are living heart breaking existences right here in North America, only because they need the man to keep a roof over their family's heads. The topics were discussed at intervals during the four months we were stuck living together. I would initiate the conversation and eventually give it up. Every time my efforts were met with a wisecrack. It was good, in a very sick way, because every time I got nowhere, I realized that I was doing the right thing. The only peace I could ever get in the rest of my life was to cut this freak loose.

He would summarize by saying

"You live in a Walt Disney kind of a world. He called it the Disneyfication of life".

I remembered the Jiminy Cricket song.

"When you wish upon a star makes no difference who you are, when you wish upon a star your dreams come true"

I loved that theme song. I used to sing it to my kids often at bedtime. I believed in fairies and guardian angels. I, to this day believe in the power of positive thinking. I know this to be true. Prayer, wishes, positive thinking they all play a role in making life more enjoyable and successful. That attitude, doctors have now confirmed to me, is what has kept me alive for twelve years. My oncologist once said to me

"Jo, if I could bottle your attitude and sell it outside, at the main entrance of the cancer center, you and I would be multi-millionaires."

My husband said.

"Your life has been full of distortions. All your opinions and suggestions of what we should do to make our lives together better, everything you think is 'bullshit'. You are delusional!"

I told him his older sister had called and left a message wishing us a happy 40th anniversary. That was in November, two months after the document. Maybe he should call her and tell her the truth. His younger sister called the next night. I have caller ID so I would not take a call especially in the evening. His sisters were on the west coast. Anyone who needed to contact me always called during the day when they knew my husband would not be around. I overheard him say

"Shit happens!" probably referring to the separation and

"It just petered out!"

Probably sounds like maybe his love for me. Anyways he was no more vocal to them I guess than to me. Every weekend I would ask if he had found a place to move to yet. He answered he was still looking. My lawyer had explained to his lawyer that my family physician was hoping this exercise would be completed quickly and that my husband could be convinced to leave the domicile sooner than later. The doctor felt my health was at risk. The lawyers were now moving to the almost final stretch which was the full disclosure of any and all financial holdings and the income tax declarations of the last five years from both of us. These were to be brought to their respective offices for review. I brought in our investments portfolio and my income tax declarations for those years. He had all his business and personal income tax information in his office. We always had separate bank accounts, credit cards and financial statements etc. I never could bring myself to have a joint account with him. I walked into my lawyer's office, she gave me a stack of files and invited me to sit in the conference room and insisted that I peruse all the information.

"I hope you didn't have any preconceived ideas about your husband's finances and won't be too disappointed because there is next to nothing there."

In 2002 my husband, with a gift from me of 25k, became self employed. He opened his dormant numbered company consisting of himself as a HVAC consultant. In that last year as an employee he earned 100k by 2007 he had declared an income of 28k. I actually thought he was going to work every day. How is that possible? When I broached the subject he said

"There were some years when business wasn't so good."

But this bullshit life style we had, two homes, two boats, two cars, his golf club membership. That was what I knew about! What else was there that I assure you I was not privy to? I earned as much in dividends from my inheritance than he did, so call, working. Maybe that was the game. He didn't have to work as hard soliciting new business because he could always coast on my income, that good old trusted second income. Like I said, what he showed was, declared income. So maybe Dick learned a few tricks on how to fudge the numbers and had undeclared income somewhere. Well, no point crying over spilt milk. The real question was how do I get some financial support? I sure as hell was not going to pay him off. I was adamant about this. You can break my heart, you can treat me like I'm dog crap on the soles of your shoes but you sure as hell are not going to get away with scrounging anymore money off my hide. I couldn't get a job because I was still with cancer, unemployable, unreliable to quote H R lingo. I figured a man who can spend half the day and evening in a bar and afford a golf membership can afford to keep an ex-wife. That is assuming he was not also covering the cost of a 'piece on the side'?

Enter the lady lawyer
"What do you think?".
"I'm not at all surprised. I had no idea of what the numbers were but when a guy keeps screaming he is always broke and business is slow and I have to cover the taxes on both properties and co sign lines of credit for him etc. etc. Yet the life style remains the same!! Denial again. Stay out of trouble. Don't ask questions. Write up and sign a check. That is what a good wife does. She, as a partner, if she is in a position to do so shares financial responsibilities also.
"No more! Hell! Never again!"
Now we get into the legalese. The fine lady lawyer, whom I have found myself more and more loving by the minute, says
"Well he sure as heck cannot afford to support you on this income and there is no court that can force him to. The numbers are all the judge can see and consequently rule on, by the way, yours and his".
Breathe! I said to myself. Then I remembered hearing, through an acquaintance, the story of a man who after thirty years of marriage filed for divorce because he had a new lady. The settlement consisted of his wife and he agreeing to sell the marital residence and the profits were not to be divided by two and shared by each. His wife was to receive all but there were to be no other funds expected as additional support. Bingo!!
My lawyer had verbalized that same kind of offer as a possibility to my husband's lawyer, whose job it was to present it to him. The whole purpose of all of this was actually to help stay out of the courts where court dates can take forever and judgments rendered could be dubious. Moving right along. The next night I asked my husband (remember we are still living in the same house) if his lawyer had talked to him about

the offer. He was really pissed off because he didn't get to her office until 4:45pm and the door was locked. He said

"I could see those two bitches standing there looking at me banging on the door and they knew for 'F' sake but they never came to the door to let me in Don't they know some of us really work for a living and don't just do 8 to 4. Shit stop asking me questions. I'll reschedule for tomorrow."

You know what, I was really willing to wait another day. Now his lawyer and others were actually seeing the real Dick, the 'Jekyll & Hyde', banging on a office door, frothing, fuming, and cursing.

The next evening my husband and I went over the offer together and, believe me or not, I actually had to do the math for him.

"I've actually gone back over a year of household expenses plus adding costs like a haircut or the odd movie or dinner out etc. I could manage this on 1800k a month. Now if you claim to have earned only 24k last year you would at least have to work twice as hard or cut back on half of your extravagances to be able to manage a court determined support for me. If I live, with this cancer, for maybe another ten years at best the total could reach like 300k. Worse, you would not want to be hounded by me every month for my support money or the officers of the courts showing up at the company trying to collect either for that matter."

There was total silence. It's almost like I was giving a tutorial. Numbness! Maybe it was finally sinking in for him. Then again, maybe he was finally seeing his escape route better now. I explained, very calmly

"I suggest you turn over the full ownership of the house to me as part of the separation agreement. I would agree to sell the house within a period of six months after the legal separation is final. There would be no other monetary request on my part to you for any additional support of any kind ever. Even if you became a multi millionaire, I would not be able to sue for more money. You would never have to see my face again."

There was such a long, long pause. Two strangers sitting at a dining room table both staring out the same window. I felt exhausted. In this whole process there was almost zero interaction between him and me. Except for his having to get another place, the whole thing seemed to be a seamless transaction. He answered

"OK! Have your lawyer draft it up and send it to my lawyer. We'll go over it and she'll get back to her with my answer."

THAT'S IT, THAT'S ALL END OF DISCUSSION

A few days later all was verbally agreed upon and measures were taken by the lawyers to make sure that the Is were dotted and the Ts were crossed. Now all we had left to do was get him out of my house. I wish I could say our parting was friendly. But it could not have been. I was so looking forward to not having this sickening feeling that something threatening and violent could happen any second. He was a man who always showed his discontent through hollering and screaming with rage and throwing objects across the room. His disconnect and the silence was disheartening and spooky to me. I had bought some pad locks and used them on the inside of the garage doors and the pool fence and got accustomed to locking my bedroom door. Luckily we had a large house. We each had own bathroom. We shared the use of the kitchen and the laundry room but other than opening the front door for him or trying to generate a conversation once in a while there was zero contact. That is as it should be. Considering I lived a very comfortable life, I can expect that you would wonder

"What was the big deal about? mountain out of molehills".

That's Ok! Attitudes are derived from personal perceptions. My heart goes out to anyone, with less than I had, fighting for their survival, physical, mental and emotional. But you have to do it. I, a woman, had to do what a woman has to do. If I was not going to get respect from my husband, at least I was going to get it from myself. I might appear calm and smug but honestly I was already grieving. Was it for myself? Was it for us? I know I was dying. It was just a couple of weeks before my husband moved out. In one of our short but non confrontational conversations, I asked

"Have you no pity, no sorrow, no regrets? Do you not feel anything?" to which he replied

"The only regret I have is that, in forty years, I could not be a friend to you!"

He had no tears. There was no touching. My tears streamed down my face, but as I turned and walked upstairs, my inner voice whispered to me.

"You're doing the right thing".

I don't know who this quote is from but it certainly is worth remembering

"Forgiveness is giving up the hope that the past could have been any different."

It has taken me three years to forgive myself.

CHAPTER 7

MOVING OUT

It was already end of October. The letter had been sent Sept. 11th, I was getting frustrated. It was like being stuck in limbo. Every other night I would ask

"Find a place yet? Look the paperwork is being processed. We will be signing the final documents soon. Once we do that it is presented to the court at the judge's office. We don't have to appear. You can't be here once it's final." My lawyer wanted me to find out why the delay in his moving out? He had told his lawyer,

"There was no hurry."

I would wait every day from 4:30 to 6 pm watching the cars go by, waiting for him to arrive. I hoped to God there wouldn't be any trouble. I was always scared that if I broached the subject there would be hell to pay. Physical manifestations of stress, increased heart palpitations, anxiety, anger always appeared at the end of the day. At least my good doctor had said I was not psychotic. That was reassuring. One night I asked

"What was this delay about? In 1983 at the first separation you moved in with your buddy Mike right away. He answered

"I was younger than, and I could better cope with change. It was too unsettling now to start all over again, alone at age 63." I replied

"You should have thought of that long before you started to pretend to be single. You're not alone you have all of your buddies."

"The only thing I did wrong was not call to say where we were staying. Hell I didn't even know myself until I got there."

"What about that letter with the itinerary?"

Pathological liars are disgusting people. It's kind of like watching a prisoner hanging at the gallows. The more they twist the more they choke on their untruths. This is so beyond any possible comprehension on my part

"Don't you get that this is not only about this incident but every other thoughtless, inconsiderate, self absorbed, narcissistic action of yours from the past?" His reply to my tirade was

"So I'm a selfish bastard! So what!"

I turned around weeping, imagine no remorse, no guilt, no accountability.

I should have known better because I remember an episode in our second year of marriage. He had been out all night. He showed up the next morning. A buddy had driven him back home at noon. My husband couldn't remember where he had parked his car downtown. After many tears and garbled conversation on my part he shouted

"And don't expect me to tell you I'm sorry, because I am not."

A couple of weeks later I found out the truth as to why he had not gotten his own place. He finally admitted he couldn't come up with the first and last months rent required on most of the apartments in town. So he would have to keep looking for something easier. That just blew me away. He couldn't even come up with minimum $1400. If true, that is pathetic.

Mother, meaning me, at the rescue of course. I used to say I have two daughters and a juvenile delinquent. I know we had a parent child relationship. When he was young he had a sailor's hat on which his motto "What Me Worry!!" was written. He deferred all the hard stuff to me with the wise crack

"Do you think you can handle it?"

Of course I could and damn proud of it too. Clever as a fox this guy is. He was all about good times. I found two investments funds of 100k that we had co-signed the year prior and we cashed those in. After deducting penalty and taxes he cleared 7k and I cleared 4K. That is how I got him to leave. Hey! give me a project and I can co-ordinate it. That is what I had done for a living at work for twenty five years. Dick was out before Christmas, a walk up studio apartment with a shared shower facility at the end of the hallway. He had gone from the co-owner, for twenty eight years, of an island of the 1000 Islands, mortgage free and a fine city house, mortgage free with a pool in the back yard, to a 'crash pad' as he called it in the seedier part of town, welfare alley, I used to call it. He had not wanted to move in a high rise building. He said

"He couldn't be bothered. He did not want the trouble of having to book moving elevator time and all the rules of high rise building life".

I figured, he didn't want too many people seeing him drag his drunken ass into an elevator at night. My therapist said he just couldn't accept the challenge and responsibilities of moving. I had always taken care of that in the past. He had zero experience and couldn't be bothered. He put the word out

"He was single now!"

Location, location, location, his new place's greatest asset was it was downtown, walking distance to and from all the bars. No need to drive and get pulled over for a fourth DUI.

Christmas, my youngest daughter was away to her in-laws and my oldest had invited me over to gift exchange with my grandchildren. She was going to have her father over for turkey dinner. Wow! alone at Christmas Wow! I put on my 70's and 80's tunes and danced and laughed and cheered. I even BBQ a steak for myself. The following year I bawled my eyes out. Emotionally, it has been a roller coaster ride. A lot of widows feel lost on special occasions. A lot of separated people do also. Sometimes we weep over the good and bad times. Mostly we grieve over the 'what ifs'.

I received a refund of $400 from my lawyer and the whole process took only four months. My family attorney met with me in Jan. 2008 so that we could prepare my new will. He summarized everything quite beautifully.

"I know that you love Dick and this must have been very stressful. To even have to make that kind of a decision and follow through in your condition is very brave but sad. Luckily it got handled very quickly, much faster than usual in these cases. It is for the best, you will only have one concern in the future and that is to try and take care of yourself and try to beat this breast cancer."

Here are two quotes from Martin Luther King Jr. I would like to share with you at this point.

"Our lives begin to end the day we become silent about things that matter."

YOU should always matter, if to no one else but YOURSELF. In the end it's always about survival. The second one is

"Let no man pull you low enough to hate him"

If your man can draw from you the most evil of intentions, he has won. You loose. Hate is a counter-productive emotion. It will sap you of the positive energy you need. I was never a suicidal type of a person, I was more the homicidal kind. There were two times in the last ten years we were together when I actually not only considered murdering my husband but went over a detailed plan over and over again in my mind. Can you imagine allowing myself to be driven to such a state. A bad man will work you hard and expect you to wear down and give it all up. Give yourself up. Don't do it!

Martin Luther King Jr. was referring to the 'Black and White' issues still prevalent in the USA. I think without any reservation that it could also apply to the relationships between physically and mentally battered women and their assailants. You don't have to look too far to find them. The perpetrators are either a husband or a boyfriend.

CHAPTER 8

THE BEGINNING

I've often wondered what is it that got me here. What were the events and who were the individuals who might have contributed to my making the types of choices I did along this path called my life. Is every happening interconnected?

My married life looks like a puzzle. There is a table on which rest one thousand pieces that fit with each other, yet not all the pieces can be connected. My grandmother, whom I have tried to emulate all of my life was my real care giver. My Meme was my role model for strength in adversity and positive familial love. She had a foldable card table in the downstairs family room of my parents' house, with a half finished puzzle always waiting for her to work on when she came for her next four month lay-over. She would try to teach me patience. I used to get so frustrated when the pieces did not join. Short of getting a pair of scissors and trimming them into place, how else could I make this work? I know for a fact it takes a long, long time to finish a puzzle. How long or how pretty it turns out, one cannot ascertain ahead of time. The picture on the box may be over stated compared to final real deal. On the other hand, if it's too hard we can always quit, throw all the pieces back into the box, tape the sides and stick it at the back of the top shelf of the closet.

I have created my own history. There have been places, events and people, major players and small bit players that have all over time come together connected to assemble this mosaic called my life. One thing I know for sure, in my case, a mixture of nature and nurture had a huge role in determining my attitude and choices in regards to love and loyalty. Another thing I know for sure, now at least, was that I could have reversed my ending, at any time, during those forty years. All the warning signs were there. I had free will, choices.

Or did I???

Was that what some called Destiny, Karma, Fate?

Curious! Even the greatest philosophers of all time still have not been able to answer that question. So I won't trouble my already over taxed mind. But you certainly have my blessing to draw your own conclusion at the end of this story.

CHAPTER 9

MY CHILDHOOD

I can honestly say I have very a selective memory of my childhood. I seem to remember so very little of our family life. I recently had to ask my older sister

"Did we not have Christmas or birthday parties at our house?"

I inherited all of my parents photo albums after my dad died in 2000. My father had asked me when he was quite old,

"How come all the pictures are about happy things, smiling faces. You never see pictures about hard times or sad occasions?" I answered

"Dad, I think that is because it's hard enough to try to forget, in our minds, about the sad times. Who needs them in pictures." I spent months going through the albums, touching pictures, sorting pictures. My father had to be the one person taking the photos. I know that because my mother and his girls (we three) are in mostly all of them. I haven't found any birthday or Easter or Christmas parties held at our place. Oh yes, I found one year Halloween, and of course the three First Communions. Why can't I remember anything? I am aware that all memoirs usually seem to start with a historical or chronological series of dates and names and profiles of ancestors. Sorry, even though I have all of that information I think it's irrelevant. I'm not writing a history book. I'm thinking more along the lines of events and personas that directly affected my becoming.

My mother was a very good looking woman. My dad was crazy about her. Judging from all the photos he took of her, reclining on beds or beach towels or in amazing gowns, it was evident to me that he thought she was hot.

My mother learned to speak, read and write in English within the first year of her marriage. She was a French Canadian Montreal woman, married to an Irishman. Very good catch for her. His father had already owned his own home since 1910, a five bedroom Victorian, at the base of Mount Royal. The sons were allowed to borrow the car, to impress the ladies but only when things were getting serious. His father was still working at eighty two years of age. Those were the war years and he had to provide for four daughters while their husbands were overseas fighting the Germans. His mother was very disappointed that my Dad had not married a sweet Irish girl. Apparently the only other nationality an Irish lad could marry, in Montreal in those days, was a French girl. The reason being they were also Catholic. God forbid!!! they ever got married to a Protestant, English person. The Irish hated the English no matter what country they had immigrated to.

My mother was a highly organized person. She was a perfectionist and had very little patience with her three klutzy daughters. She cooked and kept an immaculate house until my father could afford a housekeeper for her.

She sewed all our clothes and made sure we were raised with manners and couth. We were to represent, by the time we were teenagers, our father's station in society. We had become upper middle class. My father owned his house in the suburbs, a car, a cabin cruiser boat. We went on annual family vacations and his ladies were 'dressed to the nines.'

My mother was a pillar of our small community. She had never worked a day of her life outside of the home until well after the daughters were all married and then only part time retail. In those days only those married women who were not well provided for by good husbands had to go to work. Yet my mother could have been, with her skills and by today's standards, a 'right hand man' to any executive of any corporation.

My mother was a consummate volunteer. She was the president of the Catholic Women's league. She was the president of the "Center

D'Acceuil' a seniors retirement center. She was the manager of the Lachine General Hospital gift shop volunteer auxiliary.

My mother was also an amateur actress and appeared in several plays and a member of the church choir. These were all part of her responsibilities as an event planner for these organizations.

My mother was also the 'hostess with the mostest' and excelled in the art of entertaining and flattering my father's clients and bosses. In fact the suggestion was, Dad was never sure why he was invited to so many of their business functions. Was it because of his advertising expertise or my mother's charming ways. I believe it to be both. Mind you the French Canadians are a very outgoing and personable race.

My Mother did not work for pay but her contributions were priceless.

My Mother was highly respected by all of her colleagues and her gregarious personality made her very popular and sought after by anyone that needed to get things done.

That would have been what I would have written as her 'curriculum vitae'. Yet,

I WAS SCARED TO DEATH OF MY MOTHER!!!

My Mother had a vicious temper. By the time I was four or five I learned how to tread very softly and stay a very safe distance away from her. I became an expert at watching her facial expressions and body language. I now, all of a sudden, realize that from that young age, already, I was trying to stay out of trouble and keep peace. What a huge responsibility for a little kid. I became very adept at walking on egg shells.

My earliest recollection is of a fire in the kitchen of our upstairs flat. My younger sister and I slept in the bedroom adjoining the kitchen which was at the back of the house. In the 50s there were no kindergarten classes so children were at home 24/7. We always had to have a two hour nap every day. My sister and I had bunk beds. Susie had the bottom, I had the top. I had concluded, already, that my mother wanted for us to stay out of her hair or as you say today 'get out of my face'. When my mother was at the front of the apartment, my sister and I would chat and giggle and be silly, very rebellious acts. One afternoon though we were pretending to be asleep. We used to turn our bodies to face the wall and to hold our breaths so that when our mother came to inspect, we could prove we were really sleeping. Oh the innocence of children! Actually we did that because we didn't want her to start screaming her head off at us, if she found us still awake. Our bedroom door was kept just slightly ajar. Mom was in the kitchen canning peaches, a very long job, a labor of love and very economical. There was a procedure that had to do with melting wax in a pot on the stove then pouring the boiling hot liquid on the top of each jar to seal in the juices before screwing on the glass lid. Next thing I know Mom opens the bedroom door and yells:

"Wake up, get out, run outside, wait in the yard" and behind her I see the pretty, white, cotton curtains at the window over the sink engulfed in flames. We rolled out of bed and ran to the kitchen door, which she was already holding open for us. We tore down the forty stairs and stood at attention holding hands. Two little girls looking at the kitchen window in flames, crying, thinking our dear mama was going to die. Five minutes later she came out on the porch and told us it was all over. Everything was OK and we could get back in the house. Mom had saved the house from burning down. The kitchen stank of smoke but the damage was limited to the window frame. Mom was our hero. I might have been scared of my mother but I sure loved her. She was the best.

The year after, age six, was a very busy year. I started French school, grade one. It was right next door so it was not far to walk. I could never brag to my own children about those long four mile walks in snow drifts, six feet deep that so many other parents did. It was to instill courage and perseverance in their kids. The good thing also is that we did not have to get up too early in the morning. The reason we went to French school was. Firstly our small town was predominantly French. Secondly, my Dad figured that since the mother is the one in charge of the school homework duties, naturally it would be practical that the daughters study in that language. Mom being French would be better capable of helping with our school work. The English, Catholic school was in another district which meant bussing and Dad said he would be too tired after working all day in Montreal and a forty five minute train ride to come home and be stuck doing homework with us.

Thanks to that logic I have been fluent in both languages my entire life.

Oh yes! the 'Negroes', in the USA, children schools were segregated by color whereas in Quebec the school segregation was by culture, French or English and by faith Catholic or Protestant. Of course the Jews had their own privately funded schools or they were allowed to attend Protestant schools. Imagine all the taxes to be shelled out to sustain that public perception. Believe it or not the populace didn't mind funding four separate school boards' requirements. In those days you sure as heck did not want your Catholic children mixing with the Protestants. Heck!

"Some of those high school girls could get pregnant and end up with Protestant babies!"

That is what my mother told me when I was fourteen years old. That is not a word of a lie. I was not allowed to go to the YMCA dances because they were Protestant and that is the excuse she used to forbid me. Hell! I didn't even know how babies were made yet.

Yes! I was slow, a late bloomer, raised in a family with top secrets.

My first exposure to the male sex was that summer. A school chum, Jacques and I were good buds. He and I were the top students in our class and highly competitive with each other. I was a real 'tom boy'. My little sister was the only girl I had to play with. Let me try and set this up. The neighbor downstairs had a basement that you could get to from the back yard. There was an outside door that led into a narrow corridor, very private. It was a typical, "you show me yours, I'll show you mine" routine. We dropped our pants and gawked, leaned our heads from one side to the next side. We did not touch each other. We, then, shrugged our shoulders without saying a word. We pulled our pants back up and ran back out to play. I guess neither one of us was impressed. The next time I saw a penis, flaccid and erect, was in drawings in my biology book in Teachers' college. No kidding! Now don't you laugh at me. Ok! yes sure, go ahead!

Like I said, it's all about those puzzle pieces that come together to make me, ME. My mother, where her three daughters were concerned, was a prude. We were never allowed to appear at the breakfast table without being fully dressed for the day. Not even on the weekend could we appear in housecoat and slippers. I must say though, my mother and my dad did set the example. The first time I saw my Dad in his pajamas was when I was sneaking into the house at midnight after getting in from a date. He was going back into his bedroom. He didn't see me. Thank God. I was twenty one years old.

That year when I was six, something really terrible happened to me, at least in my little person's heart. It was one event that truly helped to define a crucial aspect of my personality. The outcome of which was to haunt me repeatedly in my future. I always think of children as being blank canvasses on which we parents, with brush and paints, sweep imprints, some so damaging that they cannot ever be removed from the soul. I have a lump in my throat now and tears in my eyes.

Again the event takes place in the kitchen. The back of the house seems to be the only place my little sister and I were permitted to be in. There was a hallway off the kitchen which led to a large bathroom on the left and my older sister's bedroom is to the right. The living room, to the left, and my parents' bedroom, to the right, were at the end of that hallway which was called the front of the flat. We were not allowed to play in the living room. We were invited when my father was in there on the weekend evenings. In my mind's eye I see:

It's happening so fast. My little body is running, running around the kitchen table and my mother is chasing me brandishing a three foot long, wooden yard stick. She's whipping it up over her head in wide circles like a lasso. She is screaming at the top of her lungs and her face is all contorted in rage. I can't even remember what I did wrong! All I know is I have to move faster and find a place to hide. I leap into the bathroom, slam the door shut and squeeze my little self between the bathroom wall and the pedestal sink. I squat down to the floor and hold my breath. I was safe here. This would be a good hiding spot. She'll never see me.

Oh! the innocence of children!

The door swings open and bangs against the wall, so much noise. There is always so much noise. My mother walks up to me, quiet! Now my little face is gazing up at a giant. She looks straight into my eyes. She lifts the yard stick high and brings it down crashing over my head. The side of the sink deflected the blow and the wooden stick breaks in half. One piece cuts me right across the forehead over the left eye. A lot of blood is pouring down my face. I can taste it on my lips. I am spitting and I am chocking on my own sobs. My mother pulls me out from the tight spot with both hands and lifts me up to the toilet seat. I notice my little sister sitting on the floor against the bathroom door jam, whimpering. My mother runs the water. She washes all the blood off my face and puts a bandage on the gash. My mother says

"It's not as bad as it looks. I'm going to give you a brand new haircut. You are going to look very pretty".

She proceeds to shape the front of my hair into bangs long enough to go to my eyebrows and cover the wound and any future bruising. She then says

"Now you don't tell your father any of this because YOU will only upset him for nothing".

That occurrence was to be a determining factor in what was to be my later adult response to violence and to loyalty and to silence.

I told my father when I was fifty years old, after my mother had died. We were clearing up his house after it had been sold. I had found a three foot yardstick in my mother's sewing room. I went upstairs. I broke it across my knee, right in front of him. He asked "What did you do that for?" I told him the story. He did not believe me.

I loved to construct things from shoe boxes and so on. I was eleven years old. This specific time I had busied myself with making a cardboard box television set. I had used two empty rolls of paper toweling wrapped cartoon newspaper prints on them and would roll one out across the screen which was a rectangular space I had cut up at the front. Only I could have appreciated the genius it took to spend hours and days perfecting this operation. My little sister was my captive audience and she thought it was real cool. I was so proud I called my mother out to the back porch and showed her my contraption. I manually turned the rolls so that the cartoon slipped across the screen. My mother watched my effort. The show was over in a couple of minutes and I had a smile from ear to ear when I asked

"Mom what do you think? Isn't this the greatest?" she answered

"If it were me I would not have done it that way!" She turned around and went back into the house to get dinner ready. She never even gave me an idea as to how I could have bettered my project. You see in my little kid's brain I am already assuming it wasn't any good. It had to be that, of course, because Mom didn't like it. That incident taught me another valuable lesson. I would just have to keep working harder and harder to get things done better if I was going to get anybody to value me or think I'm OK.

"I'll show you" my little heart said to itself.

I find it intriguing that I have always tried so hard to be good and loyal and productive and smart and cooperative and competent. I have done this in order to seek validation from those who truly are so self absorbed, they don't even notice. What is even more fascinating is how someone like me who has appeared for all accounts to be on top of my game 99% of the time could be so insecure. Can you imagine if the two people, I needed it the most from my mother and my husband, had given me the well deserved vote of confidence. I would have been master of my inner universe. At least everyone should get a B for effort. There are two ways these kinds of experience can go. They can be good or God awful. In my case, the great thing is I developed the skills and positive attitude that good friends and good teachers and good employers could make use of and reward me in kind. The satisfaction of achieving and pleasing someone was immeasurable for me. That attitude has been the mainstay of my existence even to this day. I used to say to myself "I aim to please".

Another time my self worth was challenged had to do with something I was thoroughly lousy in. My mother was a seamstress, an absolute perfectionist and we had beautiful 'Sunday outfits' to prove it. My home economics teacher felt so sorry for my grades in her class that she ended up finishing my crochet pot holders assignment. I was so slow and she had to get the students going on the next project, that she caved. Sister Wilfred Marie had a heart of gold. The nuns really liked me, remember teachers' pet. I was the kid that aimed to please in everything except 'home economics'. God forbid the next task is to sew a dress. Oh hell no! Sister thought since my mother was so gifted she could take this opportunity to help me learn. I cannot begin to describe the anxiety I began to feel at the very thought of failing, with my mother as witness. The stupid fabric was white with red poke dots all over the place. I was thinking to myself, because it those days kids did not think out loud. That was too dangerous. It would be suicidal.

"Even if I ever finish this darn dress I'm never going to wear it. Every teen knows what outfit is store bought or home made. Who were they trying to kid? I was going to grow up and get married to a rich guy who would give me money for clothes shopping. I would not sew my own stuff."

Back to the task at hand. The hardest part was to install the zipper. My mother had me redo it three times. By then I had ruined the bobbin or 'whatever' gadget and the fabric was shredding at the site from having tried so often. I was so scared my mother was going to hit me on the back of the head. She grabbed the material from me, shoved me off the chair and told me to get out. Luckily, the worst that happened was she called me 'stupid'. Well she did finish the dress and I got a passing grade. I have never sewn anything or knitted anything in my entire life.

In my mid teens I learned not to give a damn, which turned me into an amazing hypocrite. I played the role of doting daughter to a tee. I had to be obedient. It was a reign of terror. My mother had a saying for our happy thirteenth birthday.

"Oh Lord not another teenager in the house".

Not much celebrating with that kind of introduction. I used to be in charge of my younger sister. My mother would always say

"Take your sister with you".

I never really minded. She was a pretty quiet girl and never bugged me. She would stand around when I was with my friends and watch or we were able to combine her little friends along with mine, one big happy gang. We would walk to school and back together. I was like her protector. When my mother decided to send us girls to the YWCA camp for two weeks I was to go at the same time as my little sister so that she wouldn't be so lonely and afraid. I enjoyed camp, she hated it. Luckily her little hissy fits worked because we only had to go for two summers in a row. I was pretty good with all the little kids, cousins and neighbors. I was in charge of keeping everybody entertained. I made a lot of money babysitting. I was so reliable that one family even hired me as a mother's helper for their Cape Cod two week vacation, three years in a row.

I was very proud that folks thought I was trustworthy. It gave me a great deal of self worth. I even used to put on plays in the summer for our parents to see. I was highly organized, just like my Mom. I think that's why I knew at a very young age that I wanted to be a teacher. My mother was always busy with chores or sewing. She used to suffer from migraine headaches every month or so. She would lie on her bed in their darkened bedroom. I would tip toe in with cold compresses that I would place on her forehead. I would keep my little sister busy with coloring because everything we did had to be in muted tones. I used to feel so sad for my Mom. She was always so needy but luckily I was old enough to take care of things for her when she was not well. I so wanted her to like me.

Then before you knew it everything was back to normal! Screaming at us or indifferent to us. God she was a hard person to read. I think our teenage years were spent hiding in our bedrooms doing homework. We showed up to eat, clear the table, wash the dishes. Then back to our rooms we marched.

We were never allowed to have friends over after school or on the weekend and we were never allowed to visit any friends' houses. I still to this day have not figured out why. The date for dating was not until the age of sixteen. Phone calls were only between 4pm and 5pm and had to be for homework only, no useless chit chatter.

If my mother were a young woman from the 70s, when contraceptive pills were readily available, she would have, undoubtedly, chosen to be childless. She had had five pregnancies. There was a miscarriage before and after me. My older sister was born within the first year of the marriage. To this day she has always wondered if my parents had to get married. I did the counting with her several times and no she was born ten months after the wedding. The other thing she used to wonder about was whether she had been adopted or not. She so often had tried to figure out why she was vilified as a child. There has to be a reason why a mother would so dislike her first born. You see, my older sister took the brunt of my mother's rage.

In 1942, my father was still in the service for WW2 and was posted in another city, in another province. This was a totally English community and my mother was lost without her family and language. Lil and Harry lived in an attic flat and my father was gone a lot on military exercises. She was stuck with a colicky baby 24/7. She even moved back to Montreal with my older sister because she hated her life there. My grandmother had to call my Dad and tell him to come and get his wife and bring her back home, her new married life home. My grandmother, Meme was widowed, and was still working a full time job as the house keeper of the mayor of Montreal. She also had to convert her home, to get more income, and was running a boarding house. She still had my aunt Dora, a daughter of fifteen living with her. These were the 'Great Depression' years. Her eldest children Madeleine was a cook on the Steamship line and Roger was a pilot for Royal Canadian Air Force. They were off working and sending money home to her to help out.

"She was not going to take physical and financial responsibility" as she put it "of her spoiled middle daughter and the grandchild. That was her husband's job. She was lucky she had a husband, who even had a job and could provide for her and the baby. She should show more gratitude."

There is a saying in my clan "You make your bed, you lie in it."

It is pretty sad when I think about it. My older sister was always getting into trouble with my mother and teachers. She had the battle scars to prove it. They fought like cats and dogs. My mother used to have this saying when they argued

"I'm going to have the last word!."

My sister would make another defiant remark and the fight kept on and kept on. Until my mother beat up on my sister to shut her up. When Belle was twelve, in grade 7, she leapt up from her desk in class, ran to the window and started screaming

"The fire trucks, the fire trucks!!!".

Naturally the whole class, thirty five students ran to have a look. My parents were called in to meet the teacher that evening. Sister Pierre Claver suggested that the solution to correcting Belle's lack of control could be her being placed in a convent where the rigors of discipline are much greater and the success rate with difficult students had proven to be rather good. My mother was very relieved, finally someone understood and was going to take over and do something with this bad daughter. My sister was institutionalized for three years. That is what I call convent life in those days. She only came home on weekends. My father was glad because during the week, there was peace in the home and he didn't have to worry about our mother being so unhappy. We two sisters were content to have our 'bad' sister out of the house because Mom didn't scream anymore and we were less jumpy. Imagine growing up thinking that way because that was what you are programmed to believe by your own mother. You are the good girls because you don't give your mother any trouble. Kids that give their mother a hard time do get sent away. What kid in their right mind wouldn't try everything possible to be on the right side of their mother?

Another lesson learned—Don't rock the boat! Be passive at all cost! Confrontation will be dealt with swiftly!

I have over the last three decades tried to show my dear older sister the respect and empathy she deserves. Can you just imagine the inferiority complex she would get by being treated as a substandard person. I have a few theories. My older sister today might have been diagnosed and treated for ad /hd. Who knows? She turned out to have a great brain. Two years after she had moved back to our new house she meet a university student whom she started to date. She, because of her love for him and his guidance of her, graduated from high school with a 88%. She has battled with depression most of her adult life but has been treated properly and she and her husband will be celebrating their 50th wedding anniversary. I am so proud of them and wish my dear older sister a long, healthy life. She deserves it. She proved even though she was a battered child she had a guardian angel protecting her. She even had the largesse, a couple of years ago, to forgive our mother. She says she can't remember most of what happened. Apparently counseling might have helped to eradicate the dark side of her memories. She goes on to suggest that, if Mom had been treated properly with therapy and correct medication for her mental health, the hell would have ended sooner rather than later. What she is so grateful for in her own case. That she and her husband took every measure possible to get her stabilized so that they could both enjoy a peaceful older age. Marriage, in those days, was the only way all three girls had to run away from home.

Alcohol became a part of my immediate family's history, to my earliest recollection, around the mid fifties. My father had a great position in advertising sales with the Reader's Digest. Harry and Lil went to all the clients' and company sponsored functions. This was the 'big league'. My mother just reveled in the attention. She was beautiful and gregarious, a perfect match for an advertising executive. If any of you are familiar with the T V series 'Madmen', that is the kind of business he was in. She had the sass and sexiness to flatter the men with her attention, yet the girlfriend inclusive approach towards the wives. My mother and father could really work a room. I used to invite them to a few of our special adult gatherings because they were such great conversationalist and could really keep the right mood going. Once, the two youngest daughters got to serve cocktails to my father's clients at one of their house parties. Imagine we wore white gloves and used silver trays. I got to meet a couple of company presidents. That was really cool for me, so impressive. Mind you my sister and I were terrified of spilling anything on anyone. After the daughters debut to the brass was accomplished and well received and our duties were done we were dismissed. The more the booze flowed the louder the party got. Lord when some women get drunk their laughter can get so high pitched. My sister and I were in our room talking about how jerky most of the people were. She said that some client had tried to rub himself up against her in the hallway. She got so freaked out she ran and locked herself up in our bathroom. See! there were pedophiles even in those days.

When we got in from high school at 4:30, my mother was usually sitting at the kitchen table enjoying a beer. That was the routine every day. My mother never drank beer out of the bottle. It was unladylike. She poured it into a glass. She would also pour some of the beer into a saucer and place it on the floor for the dog to lap up. I asked her once
"Why do you give beer to the dog?" She answered
"Because I don't want to drink alone."
My mother later graduated to Bright's Sherry 54. What I refer to as 'rot gut'.
She was introduced to that drink through her neighborhood bridge club. My mother joined a foursome on the street, ladies for whom I babysat a lot. They played cards every Wednesday of every week. The alcohol tasted wicked but the ladies seem to like it. I think it gave quite a punch. The sherry was served in these very delicate, tiny, crystal glasses or stemware they used to call it. Here they were! four fine ladies in nice outfits sharing a bottle of high octane booze between them. They played bridge, a highly respectable game for the upper middle class English ladies. See! Suburban wives is not a new phenomena either. Eventually, not too long after, I realized my mother didn't need to be playing bridge to partake.
When I was nineteen I was a graduate teacher and was working at my local school. I was thrilled and loved my work. Naturally being a teacher I was whipped out often. I was diagnosed with anemia, a low iron count. I don't know where my mother got this idea but she did say that red wine or some grape based drink was good to help produce more red blood cells. Oh boy!
So she had a glass of cherry ready for me every afternoon so that I could join her in a 5 o'clock cocktail. I hated that sherry so much and partaking with her even more. I made every excuse possible to come in later. She switched to Dubonnet rouge just to make sure I, at least, liked this aperitif. It was supposed to build up my appetite. Actually I still do like that drink especially in the winter months.

When my mother was in her fifties the family doctor asked her "How much alcohol do you consume a day Lil?" She answered "One glass of sherry a day."

She forgot to mention that amber tumbler was topped with sherry all day long, every day. It was stashed in one of the kitchen cupboards. My mother grew up (I use that term because I believe that in life we are always evolving, morphing if you will, like every other being in the universe) to become a functioning alcoholic. I, an adult woman by now, asked her once

"Mom why do you drink so much. You get totally wasted at every family gathering?" she answered

"I just want to be happy!"

When she was in her late forties our family doctor started to prescribe anti-depressants, like valium. When that was not effective enough, he then ordered up Librium. In those days doctors were not well versed in the addictive properties of so many drugs. The pharmaceutical salesman would come in give up a few samples and the doctor would pass them on to their patients to try for a couple of weeks. They had zero time to research properties. Only the pharmacist knew what the real side effects were.

The favorite excuse on my mother's part was the empty nest syndrome. She was sad. She was lonely. She was depressed. She was anxious. She was jumpy. She was having a nervous breakdown. By the time my mother was in her early 60s she was consuming one bottle of sherry a day and taking anti depressants, sleeping pills and wake up pills daily. What I used to call the cornucopia of pharmaceuticals, uppers and downers plus the booze.

It breaks my heart now thinking about it. Her brain was so screwed up. I sometimes thought I would get a call from my father one morning and he would tell me she had died during the night of cardiac arrest from an accidental overdose. I had begged my Dad once to get her treated. We then spoke to the doctor. She was placed in the hospital for a couple of weeks and, without her knowledge and consent, was weaned off the drugs and the alcohol. The game plan was to tell her that she was in for observation for gastro intestinal problems. The truth was she had been diagnosed with the 'little C' sclerosis of the liver. My mother was sixty eight years old.

She understood the criteria required. Abstinence and the liver can repair itself in a few months. My parents just lived a block away from me. It was easy to drop by after work, drink non-alcoholic beer and chat with her. I was giving her the attention she always seemed to crave. I had the pleasure of a normal and pleasant Mom for six months. Then at a Christmas dinner she had so beautifully prepared, as usual, she asked my father

"Dad may I have a glass of wine so that I could join in the toast with the family please?"

"Sure why not my Dear everything must be healed by now!"

I'll never forget it. It was the beginning of the end. She resumed her daily intake of toxins and died six years later of the 'big C', liver cancer.

So now begs the question I'm sure you are all thinking

"Where was my father through all of this?"

Did Dad not know what was going on in his own house? Why not? If yes why did he not intervene and protect his girls from that physical and psychological abuse? I know for a fact that my parents did the best they could with what they knew from their backgrounds about this job called parenting. I know for a fact, from personal and learned experience that my father so loved my mother that he could and would forgive her anything. It was unconditional love.

I know because I MARRIED MY MOTHER and I role MODELED MY FATHER

My father was the arch man type of the times. He was a really good father, a provider, a protector. He fulfilled all his obligations to us. Those obligations as dictated in those times.

CHAPTER 10

"OH MY PAPA"

There was a song my mother had taught her three girls, we were eight and six and four, to sing for our Dad at one of the Hutchison house Christmas family parties. My father's clan gathered there every year at the patriarchal home. It was a really big deal. The audience consisted of my grandfather James, my grandmother Susan and their nine adult children, their spouses and their children. Naturally all the cousins were expected to put on a concert produced by the mothers. My mother wanted us to be the best and my father was really impressed. Here are the lyrics, written in the early 50s.

"Oh my Papa to me you are so wonderful,
Oh my Papa to me you are so good
No one could be so gentle and so loveable
Oh my Papa he always understood

That pretty well sums up my feelings about my father. To this day I have no bad feelings towards him. I never have. My sisters don't feel the same way. I have concluded that three children raised in the same environment by the same parents can actually have three different views on the dynamics of that very same unit. They can also have three different responses to the exact same circumstance. One's history is really about one's personal perception and interpretation of events and that will vary with each individual. The difficulty I have now, in my elder years, is that I don't have any opportunity to share family stories with my sisters because they seem to have held on to some residual bitterness. It makes for lonely times when one cannot share one's history with those who were a part of it. I have noticed, from talking with others, that this is quite common. Siblings do not necessarily have much in common, except genetics.

When I was born the world was celebrating the end of WW2. My father had had his 30th birthday august 7th and I was born august 14th. My mother was really hoping for a boy since the first child had been a girl. No such luck! Another girl was born into this world except this ones appeared quite different. Story has it that my father comes into the room at the hospital took one look at me and says

"Lord is she ever dark, her skin, her hair!" My grandmother, Meme Dufort immediately comes to my defense

"Well if she isn't good enough for you I'll keep her!"

You see, I had the very dark complexion and hair of my mother's French Canadian heritage. She adds with pride

"Belle, the first girl, looks Irish this one is French"

My father was very embarrassed and spent a few minutes reassuring my Meme that of course he could see the resemblance now. I looked a lot like my mother. There was no need for her to worry, of course he was going to keep me, he thought I was very cute. By the time I was two years old everybody on my mother's side was calling me 'la p'tite noir' translated the 'little darkie'. Originally, my mother wanted to name me Victoria in celebration of the end of the war. My dad objected. That name reminded him of a former queen of England, definitely not a good choice for an Irish girl. So he chose the name Jo. He found the name on a milliner's shop window near his office in downtown Montreal. He thought it was quite original. That is true because I did not meet anyone with my name until I got to Teachers' College. A couple of years later, after the birth of his third daughter, I was then given another name by my Dad. I was called Joseph, Joe for short. It seems that my Dad had wanted a son and my mother could no longer have children. My eldest sister was called Luigi. To this day my nephews and one brother in law and his brother, still call me Joe. Even now, I've noticed that when I talk to myself I say 'Joe'.

My father did a lot of things with us. My mother was the disciplinarian and he was kind of the fun guy. A good cop, bad cop routine would play out. The craziest scenarios took place at meal times, much to my mother's chagrin. We would all be seated, my little sister and I side by side across from my mother, the eldest daughter across from my father. Imagine the same places every day for every meal for some twenty odd years. My mother craved order. It was only in the 70s when I had four children to take care of did I realize the importance of order. Let me continue. My father would get into a conversation on current events and we were expected to contribute to the discussion by giving what he referred to as our 'two cents worth'. Eventually voices got louder and words heated, my mother would say.

"That's why I don't want anybody to talk at the dinner table. It always turns into a fight."

My little sister and I went mute but my eldest sister plowed on sticking up for her opinions against my father. Then my Dad would say

"Oh! the empty barrel rolls again" or "That's enough from the peanut gallery" or "End of discussion".

My interpretation of the first one was that her brain was probably hollow like a barrel and when she spoke all that came out was noise. Now that is my perception as a ten year old. Actually none of us girls had ever seen an empty barrel rolling or let alone heard it, at the time. Next thing you know my older sister was dismissed from the table for being too argumentative. Wonder who she got that from? By that time, I was pretty much gagging on my food because of the continuous friction.

I was always the last one to leave the table. I was a very slow eater and sometimes the food was awful. No kid should be forced to eat kidney stew or liver and onions. I would continue masticating until everything in my mouth was pureed and it could slowly drip down my gullet. My mother would keep yelling

"Avale! Avale" which means "swallow! swallow"

How could I swallow 'God awful' gunk in my mouth when I would be bawling my eyes out and had a runny nose to boot? My dear mother would then pull out her chair, take the youngest by the hand and before she left the kitchen say to my father

"Harry you make sure she finishes that supper. I spent all this time slaving over a stove, just to have her mess up the meal, blah! blah! blah!"

Thank God, I thought

"She's gone".

My father would move over to the chair beside me and coax me into slowly swallowing. Whatever I could not finish he would do so for me. He would sing this song to me about 'A slow boat to China'.

"I'm goanna get you on a slow boat to China
All to myself alone
Get you and keep you in my arms evermore
Leave all the others—waiting on a far away shore."

My father was typical of manliness to me. He was hunter, gatherer and protector, another young girl's perception. Not only was he saving me from Mom's wrath he was also showing empathy and kind of taking my side. I was truly grateful for his gestures of understanding. There were a couple of other antics he used to pull at the dinner table with his girls that really rocked my mother's world. He used to tell jokes and get us kids laughing so hard that the milk we had been trying to swallow would spay out of our nostrils. Then three daughters would leap from the table and run to the sink or the bathroom. We would all, quietly, return and apologize to Mom. I never heard my parents fighting but I'm sure she would have whispered some scathing reprimand to him while we were out of the room. Rest assured there was no conversation after such incidents and they happened often. I think our Dad just wanted to add a bit of levity and also liked to bug my mother. That's why we used to say 'oh my papa always the clown'

Another thing my father did at just about every meal was this. My mother would serve the dinner to each one of us. Dad would say grace and just as we were about to raise our first fork full to our mouths Mom would ask

"Is it good?"

All three daughters would look at dad for the cue and in unison, without having tasted the meal, would say

"It's delicious Mom. Thank You!"

That made her very happy and validated. My father then proceeded to pour salt and peeper on his supper and, let us not forget, Heinz ketchup. He would then pass these on to his daughters who did the same thing as he. My mother would freak out.

"You said it was good! Why are you putting all that stuff on it?"

No one answered. It was a rhetorical questions. The oldest sister, being the most clever, always asked for second servings so that Mom's feelings would not be hurt. Mother would be pleased with her show of appreciation. She was a good girl.

Interesting developments occurred much later, in my opinion, as a result of this. My older sister ended up with an eating disorder, obesity. She always finished every morsel on her plate. I, on the other hand, have never finished a meal. The eldest was a major cook and baker. She belonged to a club where couples got together once a month and tried international cuisine. Too bad she lived so far away. We partook in her great cuisine a few times in our lives and she never failed at creating a major gastronomical delight. She has now managed to loose all the excess weight and is much healthier. The youngest and I ended it up with major stomach problems like reflux etc. She, after major surgery, has been able to sustain a more than adequate, healthy weight. She is finally happy with her appearance and loves to shop for new things to wear. I, on the other hand was pretty slim for quite a long while. I did spend thirty years smoking cigarettes and drinking six cups of coffee. I did love eating comfort food like French fries and potato chips. I have curtailed two of those things now but still crave the 'greasy stuff'. Honestly, I do cook well but it is not my favorite thing to do. I had always wished that someone would invent a pill that we could take daily and then we wouldn't have to shop every week for food and cook 24/7. Luckily, both my daughters turned out to be great cooks and enjoy the fun and variety of the healthy food dishes they can whip up. Rest assured there is no salt, pepper or ketchup at their tables.

My father worked nine to five. He took the train into town and back every day. He got home at 6pm and we had dinner. He had all his magazines to peruse and a couple of newspapers to read after supper. We kissed him goodnight between 8 and 8:30 and at 9pm he and my mother got together to watch some television. In those days he had one coca cola and they went to bed at 11pm after the evening news. We three girls had a sip each of his coke, on the weekend evenings. My mother used to let us have one Chiclets gum to go with the coke. We thought that was a big deal. That is a very far cry from what kids expect from their parents today. My father travelled a great deal on the east and west coasts of Canada. He brought my mother along for company and to get her away from all three daughters. They really enjoyed pretending they were just a couple. I can honestly say that I never missed them. Luckily for us my Chere Meme came to live with us and took care of us in their absence. The times I was with my grandmother and at the houses of my aunts Mado and Dora, were the happiest times of my childhood. For years on August 14, my grandmother made me a date cake with chocolate icing for my birthday. My sisters and I got to eat in the dining room and I was given an envelope which my parents had left with her. It was a birthday card with a $20.00 bill. My parents were away on a three week vacation at that time to the 1000 Islands in Ontario. My dad owned a cabin cruiser. It was his get away and my parents could celebrate my father's birthday on the 7th and their wedding anniversary on the 22nd. Man that cake was good and my grandmother's love for me was greatly appreciated. I have never been able to duplicate that cake. I have always tried to emulate her ability to express affection to children. She was my true role model.

Our father did many things with us. He had a boat ever since I can remember and loved being on the lakes. He always made sure we lived near water. He started taking us across the Lac des Deux Montagnes to Oka beach from, when as far back as I can recall, probably age five or six. His first boat was a sixteen foot wood plank hull with a twenty five horse power Johnson outboard engine. I just love the exhilaration of the ride, the speed and the wind. I used to drag my arm over the side of the boat against the wash and let the water splash me. Ironically, at that time, my mother did not know how to swim, neither did my younger sister or I. Only my father and my eldest sister swam. In those days life jackets weren't even mandatory. I don't know for the life of me how my mother could stand it. She loved Harry so much that she could trust him to take his whole family on a thirty minute trip across the lake and then back in rain or shine weather to a weekend beach picnic party. Believe this, we were never in a boating or car accident when my father was in charge.

I can actually see him now. He is sitting at the back with his hands on the motor throttle and blinking so hard because of the rain pelting his face. His wife and three daughters are laying in the center bottom of the boat covered with a tarpaulin. Our mother is singing 'Cruising down the river on a Sunday afternoon' or 'when Irish eyes are smiling'. My mother is keeping a very brave front, showing no fear. I know she would have been scared. Because it was years later that we found out she suffered severe anxiety. Her man was in his element and doing 'his thing'. It would sure beat all us ladies being left behind at home, while he took off and pursued his hobby. He was happy and she obviously had a lot of confidence in him. My older sister loves boating when she can she gets on board a cruise ship. My younger sister hates it, yet she thoroughly enjoys kayaking. I continue to enjoy the soothing affect of water front living. I just don't have access to a boat anymore. Now if anyone were to invite me, I would jump at the opportunity to crew.

There was one time when we three daughters almost drowned, true story. It was not in the boat. It was at the beach, in shallow water. My younger sister and I owed our lives to our older sister that day. It was a typical crossing, a beautiful day. Everybody was in a good mood. Oka beach was a pristine area with miles and miles of beach on land that was owned by the Franciscan monks. There was no road to get to this area. Only boaters had the pleasure of enjoying the tranquil, private environment. Our parents had settled down on the blanket and we three girls headed out running through the water. We could walk so far away into the lake of Two Mountains because the water was so shallow. It was a safe place for children to play, for that very reason. We kept moving forward holding hands in the hope that eventually we would be knee deep and I and my younger sister who were not swimmers would have a chance to get totally dunked. My older sister was to watch over us.

All of a sudden the three of us fell into a deep pit and all at once we went underwater together. It happened so fast and was totally unexpected. I came up with the help of my meager dog paddle stroke. Belle came up with Susie's arms wrapped around her neck and her legs wrapped around her waist. We were yelling. We were hysterical. My little sister would not shut up. The more she screamed, the more water she swallowed. I was the only one free to move. I tried to get to the ledge of the hole but every time I crawled up the ridge the sand would keep crumbling and I would slide back under water. My older sister was very close to me but she could hardly move because Susie was facing her and had such a grip around her neck that she was actually chocking her. Finally after several attempts I was able to get my knees up on the sand and crawled to a safe, solid distance. I stood up really fast and started to call to my parents.

"DAD! MOM! we're drowning." Over and over again

"MOM! DAD! we're drowning". I heard my mother yell.

"Stop fooling around. This is dangerous" my father yelled

"Stop that! One day when it could really happen no one will believe you" but

"Dad it's really happening Susie and Belle are drowning HELP US".

I never saw my father move so fast. He ran the distance and jumped into the hole. He tried to calm Susie down by speaking gently to her but to no avail. She had totally lost it. She might have been in shock. He was helping Belle by standing behind her and holding her up by one arm. His other free hand was used to try and pry Susie's hands apart from around Belle's neck.

Nothing was working. He then told the eldest to tread water just with her legs. She was a tall girl for her age and well built. She was strong. She did exactly what he said. My dad then let go of her and gave the youngest a hard slap across the face. I could actually hear the smack from where I was standing on the safe side of the ledge. My little sister finally let go. My Dad grabbed her and swung her around to his back where she clung on for dear life. Belle was finally free to swim back to 'terra ferma'. She and I sat huddled together. My father and Susie joined us. All four of us, one father with three daughters stood up together and walked hand in hand in the shallow water towards the beach. Belle to this day is still her sisters' hero.

My mother never came out to meet us. She waited for us at the picnic site. She gave us a drink and a cookie and our towels. My Dad then decided we should go for a long walk with him. We girls were able to purge and talk and talk until our fears were finally lessened. Have you ever seen three girls all talk together at the same time. Of course you have. Well our dad let us go to it. We found a huge, dead water snake which he picked up with a stick and we brought it back to the site where Mom was napping. Luckily he decided not to wake her to show it off. He then told us it was time to go back swimming and he came with us. This time we stayed much closer to shore and ended up swimming in ankle deep water instead. There had been enough excitement for one day. My father had a few connections and was able to get in touch with a local government official. After hearing of our incident, the individual said

"Yes, there had been sand dredging authorized in that area." My father said "Signs should have been posted to that effect so as to avoid any more dangerous situations." The county clerk said

"These were privately owned lands not government parks. Ergo no signage"

There are so many little things I can remember our father would do for all of us. Every Friday, late afternoon, he would visit with his brother, uncle Charlie, who was a clerk at the smoke shop at the Central Station in Montreal. He got home and gave each of us a bag of 'Planters' peanuts and a comic book. That's actually how we girls learned how to read English. We went to French school but we read English comic books on the weekend. I read each word with the phonetic French accent and my father would correct us with the English phonetic sound. Believe it or not they are very similar. I'm am very teary eyed now. I wish I could be a kid again for just a day so that I could feel that embrace of love from my Dad. There was never a lot of hugging but my gosh his gestures of affection always seemed so sincere, to me anyways. I really, really still miss him after twelve years. Another thing he did, was he always sent each daughter a Happy Valentine's card and also a Happy St. Patrick's day card in the mail. That was the only mail we girls ever received. It was so cool. He sure seemed to know how to treat the ladies right. Once he got his company sales bonus and had the check converted to $10.00 bills. I can still see my mother laying on their bed while he threw all of these bills over her. Susie and I (Belle was still in convent) were invited to this show but honestly we didn't get it. My mother was giggling like crazy. Then he jumps on the bed with her and they're both laughing. What the hell did teenage girls know in those days anyways?

It would seem that my father could keep us all laughing. But herein lies the truth. When I was a grown woman in my early forties I was driving my father back from our having visited with my mother in the hospital and he says
"Joe I think Mom is a little bit crazy!" to which I answered
"Dad I know Mom is a lot crazy!"
Another time he had mentioned that Mom had thrown his full dinner plate across the room at him and it hit the wall behind him. He never had the wallpaper changed because he wanted to keep reminding her of her temper.
One night my mother had come back from an association dinner party and had broken the garage door. Instead of applying the brake when she came into the drive way she put her foot heavily on the

accelerator and crashed through the door. Then there was the time when they were at a company party and his wife got carried away with herself while singing on stage. She fell off and my father was very embarrassed. She was wasted. She had also gotten into a bad accident with a transport truck, early one morning. She was driving our Meme out of town. She did a left hand turn on a double lane. The commuter traffic was heavy. She didn't see the trunk coming down the ramp. She swerved to avoid it and her car got squeezed up against the underpass wall, on the passenger's side. Luckily no one was hurt because both vehicles had been travelling at very low speeds. My father took away her driving license for a month after that incident. I'm sure she was still coping with residual pharmaceutical drug effects that early in the morning. There are so many examples of her difficult behavior. However, this story is not about her. My father was in denial for fifty-two years. Perhaps he wasn't. In those days it was best to leave these skeletons in the closet.

We three girls grew up and became a little bit less than steady women, some of the time. This was probably due to the fact that my father, rather than protect his daughters' from their mother's wrath, chose to protect his wife from her own demons. Remember in our house nothing was ever said, mentioned or discussed. My younger sister explains it this way. Even though we were a family, we sisters were all totally separate from one another. We were independent of one another. Nothing was shared, no pain, no joy. Everything was kept to oneself. There was only one incident where everything went public and the family collided, never to be the same again.

The icing on the cake was kind of like this. One night my mother and older sister were discussing her wedding invitations. The argument became very heated. As usual both of them vying for control and the last word. I walked out of my bedroom to the living room to find my mother and my older sister in a physical fight. Both women were swinging at each other. I ran down to the playroom to get my father. He came up stairs broke the fight up and said.

"Both of you go to your rooms!"

The ladies disappeared to their respective corners. My father came to the kitchen and sat at the table where I was. I was so angry. I said

"This is so wrong. They were trying to punch each other out. They're just invitations. What's the big deal? Can't you give her hell for once instead of her always getting away with pushing us around. Why do you always have to take her side?"

My father looked at me than took his right hand and stuck me across the face. That was the first time my father had ever laid a hand on me. I was nineteen years old, a teacher. Then instead of crying, my pride took over. I said

"You should be ashamed." He answered with tears running down his cheeks.

"Your sister is getting married. Then it will be you. Then it will be your younger sister's turn. You will all be leaving and starting your own lives. I will be with Mom until the end of our lives. It will be easier if I stay on her side.

Unconditional love. Peace at all costs . . .

THAT'S IT! THAT'S ALL! END OF DISCUSSION

CHAPTER 11

BALANCE

For several weeks, during the summer, we girls were farmed out to some auntie or another. Belle was sent to Hutchison house to stay with Aunt Muriel and then to Aunt Annabelle in St. Eustache. They were my father's sisters. I don't remember where they sent my little sister. I was a very good student and always did very well in my final exams. I tell you just the thought of leaving home and being away for several weeks thrilled me to no end. The 24th of June was very special to me. We had a tradition. Every year my father drove me to my great aunt Laure in Montreal where my Meme was already there waiting for me. My great uncle placed my great grandmother Bergeron, who had suffered a stroke and was paralyzed, in the back seat of the car. The sweet lady was in her late 80s weighing in at ninety pounds and only 4ft. 11 inches tall. She was as light as a feather and a perfect fit. Her head was on Meme's lap and her feet were on my lap. Then off we went on a six hour trek to the ancestral cottage in Pins Rouges, north of Three Rivers. My father used to call it 'Black Fly Country'.

I was so happy. It was on those summer vacations that I developed, for myself and my future, the art form of sustaining extended family relationships. All told there were twelve of us who lived together, my Meme and I and her two sisters and their two husbands, all retired.

Sunday we averaged twelve to twenty people for a full course meal after mass. It was the weekly gathering of their clan. There were two houses on two lakes on over ninety nine acres of land. This land had been leased from the government for $1.00 an acre and worked on by my great grandfather. He and his sons were lumber jacks. This was taking place when Lincoln was president and civil war was raging in the United States of America. I am fascinated by my history. There was a sandy road that wound it's way for about two miles which connected the two properties.

I was the youngest child and the only girl. My Meme's three nephews were all teenagers. I really had to hold my own. They were expected to take care of me. I was not to return home hurt. It was OK if I was covered in dirt but bloody was unacceptable, no way. After all I was a girl. It wasn't unusual to get into a wrestling match with these guys who were twice my size. That was their way of keeping me in my place. I never really thought of myself as a girlie girl. I was a tomboy and damn proud of it. I wanted to be with them. I would never complain about their treatment of me. I know my cousins hated me hanging out with them. They tried everything to shake me off. Let's face it what do fourteen year old boys do with a six year old girl, all day long? I'll tell you what they do. They try to scare 'the living hell' out of her. The purpose being that she will hate going out with them and let Meme know that she would be happier if she could stay with her and help the ladies around the house. Not I! I was tough as nails. No guys were going to leave me behind to do boring housework stuff. I was nicknamed 'Me Too'. Whenever anyone, kid or adult, was going to be going somewhere I always screamed "ME TOO". I stuck to those guys like glue. There were a few incidents that I remember so vividly. I am so proud of those years. I guess they helped build my character. Here goes!

There was a great watering hole called 'Les Chutes' about a four mile walk from home. This was a waterfall. I honestly don't have a clue how high it was. It was so high! I'm sure if my grandmother knew, I would not have been allowed to be there. But who was going to tell right. Naturally the cousins called me chicken, told me to walk back home by myself or just 'shut up'. They were older and they were going to be there all afternoon. After watching the guys do it, I decided to try. I just wanted to show off. I wasn't even afraid. I took a running leap across the ledge and went all the way down the falls and fell through the pool. It was deeper than I could have ever imagined. I was a good swimmer but when I opened my eyes and looked up the height I would have to go to reach the surface I was terrified. I tried really hard and my lungs were starting to sting. In a flash, the oldest cousin, Yvon was by my side. He grabbed my arm and kicked harder and faster to help me. To this day I believe it was the clarity of the water in the pool that saved my life. As soon as all the foam of the jump would dissipate, we could actually see the person swimming up. The fellows saw I was in trouble and came to my rescue. Yes! you guessed right. I never did that again. I did go back with them several times but only watched and cheered.

There are two things I dislike about nature, bugs and bats. My elders believed in the children contributing to the gathering of food for the meals. For instance there was always fishing for trout and also frogs. The boys, I was excluded from this activity, used to go out at nightfall in a flat bottom boat and shoot frogs with bow and arrow. My aunties would cook the frogs' legs. Just heat up an iron skillet on a wood stove, brown lots of butter and flour the legs and toss them in a brown paper bag. You then lay them in the pan one at a time and listen to the sizzle. That is a delicacy to me. They can be found on the menus of some of the fancier restaurants in Montreal. No! they do not taste like chicken. I still cook some for myself every once in a while. Delish! We also had to gather all the berries that were in season. There were strawberries and raspberries in July and in August the blueberries were picked by the bucket full. All the fruit were abundantly available in the forest. Uncle Lennie would say.

"If you kids want your aunties to bake pies than you'd better get out there and collect buckets of berries."

There were so many bugs. There were different berries for each season and just as many different kinds of man-eating bugs. The boys used to get 'brush cuts' before coming up to the woods. I had a permanent, you know those super tight curly, frizzy hairdos. One year I had deer flies nesting in my mop of hair. Naturally I would scratch like crazy and the scalp would bleed. My Meme would have to pick the dead critters out of my hair. Finally she opted to give me a haircut. Yes of course, it was a brush cut. I have, since then, always had a short pixie, gamine hairdo. I looked pretty cute.

I also went brook fishing in the bush for speckled trout and needed special attire. I used to wear long pants with knee high socks that you folded the cuffs of the pants in. I had a long sleeved shirts whose sleeves had to be tucked into gloves. Let us not forget a scarf. It was used to cover the ears and the forehead and on top of that a hat. All of this was to minimize the number of black fly and mosquitoes bites you would get. There were times after a rain or with an early fog that you had to keep your eyes semi closed because of the swarms of bugs. My great-uncle would say that was the best time to go. The fish would be jumping after the bugs. When we got back to the house, a couple of hours later, I would remove my layers of clothing. I still had rings of bleeding bites around the bridge of my nose, in my nostrils, across my eyebrows and my writs and ankles. Oh God I hated that! But it was staying in the house or hanging outside doing important stuff. A girl's got to do what she's got to do. Also, the trout were so delicious. They were well worth the discomfort.

Oh my gosh! I'm forgetting the bat story. I, to this day so hate bats that I cannot even look at a National Geographic's picture or documentary about bats without getting totally grossed out. This is why! One afternoon, my cousins and I were walking through a field towards a dilapidated barn. The guys were always on the hunt for metal strong boxes that used to have cash or coins in them. Apparently in the good old days some farmers used to hide their stash in their barns because they didn't trust banks or their relatives either. There were always stories. I don't even know if they were true. It was something to do and the boys were never short on imagination. They arrived at the antiquated building and the guys opened the doors, just slightly. That way we could all sneak in and hopefully not be noticed by someone in the farm house several yards away. Everybody started to look behind tools and bales of hay and harnesses. I was so busy snooping in corners, trying to see through the darkness, that I had not noticed that I was alone. Then I heard this horrific banging on the outside walls of the barn and hundreds of bats started falling from their perches on the rafters. They were flying from one end of the barn to the other in a frenzy. I thought they were dive bombing me and went hysterical. I was screaming and crying and running to the barn door to get way from them and to get out of there. My cousins had locked the door from the outside. I fell to my knees, covered my head and just bawled. After what seemed to be a life time, my cousins opened the door a crack and I crawled out on my hands and knees. They ran off, of course. I followed in hot pursuit. I knew I would never catch up with them. I just wanted to make sure I kept them in my sight because I didn't even know where I was and how to find my own way home from there. I never followed them into a barn again. There was an old saying 'Boys will be boys'. I never told my elders anything.

I can honestly say those summers were just great for me. I learned to be confident, helpful, energetic, resourceful, kind and respectful. In those days it was all about team work. Everybody had a job to do to help make family life easier. I was always outside. There were no planes or loud boats or cars just uncle's beat up jeep. We were up at dawn and down at dark. I always felt loved and given attention when required. One hug can go a long way for a needy girl. I even got to stay up at night and play cards with the grown ups until the smoke in the kerosene lamps would darken the globe and our eyes would sting. I slept in the attic and got to share a bed with my Meme. What child wouldn't want that privilege? We had a chamber pot under the bed for nighttime pees. I definitely did not want to go to the outhouse at night because my uncle used to tell stories about the bears hanging out there at night and stealing the toilet paper. He always said

"There never is any toilet paper left when I go out there in the morning to do my business!". Naturally I believed him.

Since my youth in the country, I have only done camping once and I still did not like it. I don't do camping in forests or wherever. There could be a chipmunk running around the tent at 3 am and I would envision a bear. My idea of communing with nature is a two story country summer house by the water's edge, with a screened in porch. It is to be rodent and bug proofed. A German Shepherd is needed to keep the raccoons away from the apple tree and the water snakes from sunning themselves on the lawn. I did get just what I wanted in the late 70's but that's a whole other story coming up later.

The wealth of experience and human interaction of my childhood has had such an impact on me. I can hardly complain compared to some of the severe and tragic experiences of so many people. I acknowledge that my Mom and my Dad did a good job of parenting me. They did the best they could with what they knew. It was up to me to do better with the knowledge that my world was leaving for me. My chere Meme used to say "Each generation was supposed to improve on the previous one."

The immigrant background of my father's Irish side going back to Quebec City in the 1830s and the pioneer spirit of my mother's French Canadian side and their struggles taught me a great deal. I have felt, personally, duty bound to exceed every expectation and excel at whatever challenges were placed before me. I owe it to my ancestors to continue the tradition of hard work and the rewards received as a result of that effort. I have a message to leave with my children and their children. It is

"Let us always achieve that which would make our ancestors proud to know us. Never bring any shame to their good names."

I believe that their spirits are still with us guiding us and encouraging us and reassuring us. If only we stay still long enough to hear their whisperings.

Guardian Angels are real. I've seen them. That's another story coming up.

CHAPTER 12

THE 60s—CHOICES

HIGH SCHOOL years were ok. I was what was referred to as a 'teacher's pet' type which as far as I'm concerned, a good place to be at. My mother's philosophy was very simple

"If you think you are in trouble at school, wait, just you wait until you get home and I'll let you find out what real trouble is." My older sister's previous run ins with school officials and my parents was enough to deter me from any educational infractions. My grades used to run between 83% and 88% in grades 8, 9 and 10. I had also been elected class president in those classes. I was not a super intelligent student, not a brain by any means. I really had to study hard and long, usually about three to four hours a night. My studies took a nose dive in my last year. I was vice president of the class and chosen as Eaton's junior councilor. These positions entailed a lot of extra curricular activities that took quite a bite out of my study time. Thank God my mother decided that I could use the help of a tutor in my three worst subjects which were chemistry, algebra and geometry. I would ace geography, latin, French, English literature and composition, history, and religion but I was dead in the water when it came to mathematics. The summer of my graduation, I had a second chance to write those three that I had failed and finally squeaked by with a passing grade. I was totally mortified, embarrassed and felt quite guilty. Luckily though my parents were not hard on me. I had already been accepted into Teacher's College in the fall because of the other high scores which were more than adequate. Things were going to be OK.

Being chosen by the school staff and students as an Eaton's councilor was an honor. Eaton's was a major store chain that invited senior students from several schools in Montreal to attend Saturday morning training sessions in leadership, retailing and of course consumerism. It was teenager marketing of the 60's, word of mouth advertising if you will. I was even in the Santa Claus Parade. I was an elf, running up and down the street beside Santa's sleigh, handing out candies to the children lined up along the boulevard. I used to get up early Saturday, walk up to the highway and catch an inbound city bus to downtown Montreal. I didn't mind it at all because every Saturday a young fellow was doing the same thing as me. We travelled together and sat beside each other at the meetings. He attended the all boys, catholic school in our town and had been chosen to represent them. He was intelligent, an athlete and very good looking.

We actually became boyfriend and girlfriend and eventually started going steady. Mr. B became the love of my life. Looking back, my love life was really tame. We were not allowed to date until we were sixteen. I went to high school dances in my senior year and was allowed to go to the movies on the weekend. Curfew was 11: 30 pm. I remember one of my boyfriend's idea of a date was to come over every Saturday night to my house to watch the hockey game on T V. We would sit on the couch holding hands. While my dad and he shouted and shared the thrill of the game. I pretended I was interested. Oh just to be near him was enough of a thrill. The graduation dance went well. My mother had made my gown and I looked pretty classy. The after dance party was a total disaster. There were five couples invited. We were all to meet at my house after the dance for food and refreshments and more dancing. At midnight there was only me and my boyfriend and one other couple with us. My mother already had ten BBQ chicken dinners delivered to the house and warming in the oven. Nobody else showed up! Well the two guys devoured as much chicken as they could just to appease my, now very angry, mother. As you can well imagine the party was cut short. The next day my mother called all the mothers of those girlfriends of mine who did not attend the party. She had worked so hard to plan and ratted on the kids. The other guests had made their way downtown to party at one of the hotels and their mothers knew it. What they did not know was that their daughters had been invited to my house. My girlfriends were too worried to tell me they didn't want to come to my house for fear of hurting my feelings. Honestly I did not begrudge them. I would have much rather been downtown also. There was no reason why they had to submit to my family's out of date rules. That summer I worked my first full time job at my father's company. I was one of many mailroom clerks. Having a pay check every two weeks was fun. I studied for my exams and waited for my future to begin, teachers' college.

I was thrilled to be a college student. I was out of the suburbs every day into that exciting adult life style that I craved. I felt so important. I travelled by train every day, walked through the downtown core, across the university campus of McGill university and up Durocher to my academy. I felt less stress there, not only because we did not have advance math and science studies but most of the courses were geared to teaching practices. I knew very early in my childhood, that 'when I grow up' I was going to be a teacher. My father had wanted me to go into a four year bachelor of Education program at a university in the Maritimes. I chose not to because I knew for sure I would fail. I wasn't ready to kick in another four years of hard core studies. Also, I could not move to another province and leave my dear love. What would I do without him? no Saturday hockey games to watch together. This was the first, but would not be the last time I made the wrong choices for my own future. So called romantic attachments would end up being my stumbling block. I only have myself to blame. I find it quite interesting that my father and other people actually had more confidence in me than I had in myself. They were ready and willing to mentor me but I chose to inhibit my progress and accept limitations that only I created.

My college life was totally dedicated to studies. There were social and athletic clubs to join but that would have been like my senior year in high school, too time consuming. Having learned my lesson, I chose not to take part in anything. The commute back to the suburbs didn't help either. There were only two trains, one at 9pm and another at 11pm. Neither one suited me or the curfew my parents still had in place. All I wanted to do was mind my own business, stay out of trouble and graduate. The sooner I did that the sooner I could earn money in my chosen profession. Over time I had assumed I was flying well under the radar to be noticed. I was stunned when I was chosen by my class to run for Queen of the St Patrick's Day dance. I was an outspoken student and very helpful in class projects and event planning. Other students would write down their questions for me to ask the professors because they were too shy to raise their hands in class. So I guess I was higher profile than most.

I was not, in my opinion, a good looking girl. I didn't even have a figure I was skinny as a rake and had tiny boobs. I had started at seventeen to be plagued with facial acne and had quite a complex. I had circumvented that problem mentally by saying to myself

"Hey self! maybe if you flash that great smile of yours, nobody will focus on the pimples."

One of my mother's favorite songs was "If you're smiling the whole world smiles at you!"

So sure! I went along with representing my class, giving it the 'good old college try'. There were six contestants in all. Honestly I wasn't even paying attention to anything. It was supposed to be a lark, no heavy participation on my part. My buddies made posters etc. Then an appointment for an interview with four judges nominated from the senior class was set up. I died. I was so nervous. What was I supposed to say to these people, three men and one woman? These were the 'crème de la crème' Bachelor of Education program senior students. I was a measly freshman, peon of the college program. The questions had to do with my building a profile of myself and describing what assets I had that could make me, potentially, a great teacher. I would have no problem with that one. Then one guy floored me with this question

"Are you a virgin?" My face must have gone every shade of red to deep purple. I was speechless. Here it comes again.

"Have you ever had sex before?" I took a deep breath and answered

"That is a really dumb question. Of course I'm still a virgin. I'm a Catholic girl and I'm only seventeen years old and I'm not married. So of course I'm a virgin."

I have to laugh as I reread this. Now, fifty years later, a young girl would most likely answer "of course I'm not a virgin!"

Well shock! I won the contest. I invited my boyfriend to escort me to the dance. Never did that again. I got a crown and all. He didn't like the attention I was getting and pouted. He didn't feel like dancing. In order to placate his feelings, I naturally refused others invitations to dance.

What a total drag that night was. At least that experience did boost up my confidence. In my heart, deep down inside, I was pretty flattered. Somebody had actually noticed me. I had another 'worldly' opportunity while in college. I was invited by a member of the Newman Center of McGill university to a Christmas concert put on by the university choir and theater group. I thought that was so classy. It was such a privilege. I had meet this fellow at one of our several co-op theology extra curricular classes. Of course I said yes! The following evening I mentioned to my parents about this great invitation and my father asked

"Where is the young man from?" I answered

"The Islands"

"What are you talking about?" I continued

"The Caribbean Island of Barbados"

"Is he black?" Innocently, I replied

"Well yes he is!"

"You are not allowed to go. I forbid it"

THAT'S IT, THAT'S ALL, END OF DISCUSSION

I was broken hearted. I had to phone that fellow up because I was too ashamed to meet him in person. I told him

"My family had a previous engagement that we were all committed to and it was on the same night. Sorry."

No Protestant dances allowed, no black Catholic Barbadians allowed. Hell! if I was supposed to be broadening my horizon with a college education, I sure as hell was not making any head way fast. My father was probably saving me for that steady boyfriend I had with whom he got to watch all those T V hockey games with every Saturday night. That fellow at least was white and Catholic. If you can feel the resentment building up, you are absolutely 100% correct.

A major historical, global event took place in 1962. It was the stand off between the Americans and the Russians at the Bay of Pigs in Cuba.

I along with so many students heard the news over the radio. I was in the cafeteria at the time. We all stopped what we were doing. There was total silence. We turned and stared at each other.

"Is this it, nuclear war in our front yard?" Another replied

"Let's wait and see".

We went back to ordering our food or diving into our studies or chatting with a friend. There was a palpable, eerie feeling permeating the room. Were we going to be having school tomorrow? What was to be expected overnight? Were we to lean over, tuck our heads between our legs and kiss our butts goodbye. This is nuclear man! We lived many more days and years after that. Yes the 'cold war' was to be with us for most of our adult lives.

The second year was even more superb than the first. I was finding my stride and so proud of it. I had been assigned a student teacher's part-time position from September to February. The school was in the east, central part of the city of Montreal. The neighborhood was ethnic which meant, consisting of immigrant, low income, blue collar, factory worker families. St. Patrick's was an all boys' school. It was an hour and a half bus commute mornings and nights from my family residence on the lakeshore. I didn't care. I was ecstatic. Imagine real kids to teach, no more pretending. One thing can be said about student teaching.
"You either like it and shoulder on or hate it and have wasted two years of your life to find out, teaching is not for you".
My two best girlfriends who were also classmates hated it. I loved it!

I would set my alarm for 6am be on the side of the road, rain, shine, snow by 7am to get on the bus and in school by 8:30am. The first grade I was assigned was a grade three. These boys were mostly poor, key latch kids who probably had not even breakfasted or bathed by the time they arrived. I had a father come by one morning looking for his son's snow boots. The boy claimed he had lost them. The father had not believed him and while rummaging trough the kid's locker proceeded to beat the crap out of him in front of me and my class. I, of course, stepped in to intervene. I got slapped by accident, I think maybe, and he started to yell at me in a language foreign to me. I couldn't even argue with the guy. The principal arrived and told me to take the children into the class and close the door. He pried the boy away from his dad, shoved him in the class and escorted the father downstairs. At the recess break the principal spoke with me. Protocol dictates that in the future I am to send another child to the office and say there is an emergency and he is needed immediately. I doubt if an eight year old would remember all that but it could be close enough. I prayed there would never be a next time. We never did find the boots. I can just imagine the kind of reception my student got at home that night.

I really wanted to keep control over these kids. Teaching, better yet getting them to focus long enough to learn anything is enough of a challenge, let alone having thirty-two hellions on a rampage. Discipline! Wasn't that the proof of a good teacher. Had the nuns not taught me that much, after eleven years of schooling. I always liked neat rows of children, side by each, one behind the other at arm's length. Oh did we ever practice in the school yard every day, until they got it perfect. I tugged and pulled and aligned and realigned. I was not soft spoken. It's hard to believe someone so cute as me could sound so grouchy all the time. Another recess break, Mr. Principal spoke with me yet again.

"There's no need for you to be so strict. They are not in the army. You are not a sergeant major. You love them and they will love you back one hundred fold. They will follow you to the ends of the universe. These kids get yelled at enough at home. They need a gentle touch here. You can be a master at that. I know you have it in you."

I apologized for his having to rein me in again. He answered

"This is your college. I am your professor. You will find out more in the next six months than you could in four years university. I am here to help you become the best you can be. The potential is all there. I am your guide."

I for the life of me cannot remember that man's name. For that I am truly sorry. Indeed he was the most kind and benevolent educator I have ever had the pleasure of sharing part of my life with. His, were life lessons.

That November JFK was assassinated. The principal advised all the teachers at the lunch hour. We all went back to class in shock. What in the hell was the world coming to? How was this event going to affect my little people? I concluded it was not. Their fathers would still keep beating up on them. The majority in my class would grow up being high school drop outs by the time they were fourteen. They would have to get a job in a plant and work eight hours a day, six days a week to help their mother and their father put food on the table. My boys, I used to call them.

The 30th of January was my last teaching day. We had a cake in my class. Everybody was unhappy about my leaving but very happy about the cake. I filled a brown bag with whatever stuff I could claim to be mine. The rest I left for the next part time teacher. These classes must have been like guinea pigs in a social experiment. It's possible that these children always had different teachers. They had to get used to loss and get used to accommodating new so many times over. Maybe they were the true troopers. No wonder they showed such shared insecurities. It was already dark when I made my way to the bus stop, not quite two hours away from home. January is miserable in the north. It is cold, dark, wet, slippery and snowy. I pushed my way through the throng of other commuters. I was so sad. I know, now, that I was grieving, then. One thing I still cannot overcome and it seems to have been so prevalent in my life. That is LOSS. I, as a teacher took in children in my heart and soul passed them on after ten months. I pretended that was so cool, all for the best. We were moving onward and upward. I never seem to get to hold on to anything. All these slivers of my heart go missing. Pouf!! for a while I enjoyed the sweetness of kinship. Then I didn't. Stuff I can do without, people not so well. I received my teaching certificate after two years in Teacher's College. I was nineteen years old. I was the first person in both my mother and father's family who had graduated from college and I was a girl! I did feel accomplished. I remember a story about a discussion taking place at the dinner table. As usual things were tense. I made a comment and my mother said

"Oh! you think you are so smart just because you go to college." to which I replied

"Isn't that the point of my going to college so that I can be smarter."

I'll never apologize for being a little bit more educated, which was nothing compared to the university education my daughters received. They still amaze me because they are always learning more. I know having life skills from the 'school of hard knocks' is very important but a higher education will always be a compliment to those experiences and is always an extra, good ticket to have.

My first full time job was at the school I had previously attended for four year. It was all within walking distance from my parents' house. The principal was still a nun and the staff was divided in both lay teachers and religious. I was really proud to be working side by side with some of the ladies that used to mentor me. I was low woman on the totem pole but I got to eat in the teacher's room which I had been dying to check out for years. It's amazing to me now how ignorant we were, in my day, and how wide the divide had been between students and staff. I'm sure that line still exists today and the mystery lives on. I was not a smoker at the time so the room really reeked and the fridge was always growing stuff under plastic wrappings. Men and women ate together and got to share their personal vignettes about their family weekends and jokes that literally flew right over my head. I thought it was so cool to be included except that I had nothing to add, just a lot of laughing, listening and observing. I had made it man! a grown up at last. I had a responsible job earning, now brace yourself, $4,800 a year. At home I was just another daughter, still a kid. At Resurrection School I was 'a somebody'.

I had grade six boys for three years. I taught every subject. I still loathed math. In order to improve on my lessons I prepped really hard at night from the teacher's manual. I would then give a couple of memorized examples and get a couple of the brains in my room to teach the class. They loved the importance of their collaboration. I even had the students correct each others' work and coach when necessary. For example, I would match up one strong with three weaker kids and they would solve problems together. This gave everyone a feeling of equality and contributiveness. I never wanted anyone to get a complex or feel less deserving just because they were not as gifted. I grew up always fighting my feeling of inadequacy from my home environment. I was sure not to pass that on to my students. Each and everyone of us was good at something. I remember a question posed to me by a student
"What is the distance from earth to the moon?" I said.
"I don't know?" the boy continued
"But you are the teacher!" I replied
"Well it just goes to prove that teachers don't know everything. So let's pull out the encyclopedia and find out the answer."
It worked every time. For that very reason I always had a huge personal library that I would keep in my home room. All for research use. Our schools did not have the budgets to supply additional learning supplies.
Another thing that I did for which I was very proud was I had an 'apres school' program. The 'latch key' kids, those that were to go home and find no one because their parents would be still at work, were able to stay with me from 4pm to 5:30pm. They got to burn some energy in the gym for a half-hour then everyone got to do their homework with a little bit of help from me. This is something I knew they would not be

doing at home no matter how often their parents screamed at them to get it done. In fact, four other colleagues decided to do the same thing. We had contacted the parents and they gave us their approval. It was a win, win project. The parents had their kids off the streets. The kids enjoyed a little bit more tender, love and care. We the teachers got to make sure the homework was being done and the kids were getting additional help. I was very happy then.

At the end of my third year, the new principal, a lay woman teacher called me to the office to offer me a position. She wanted me to join her team and become the assistant principal. The request had been approved by the school board. I was the first candidate, the second was a man. I was so stunned, flattered but terrified.

"Sleep on it" she said.

A couple of days later I met with her and explained the reason why I chose not to accept her offer.

"I really would rather continue teaching. I really love being responsible for the kids and helping them learn interesting things. Vice-principal is very grand but administrative and political. Perhaps five years from now I would have the accumulated maturity to be able to function as a leader to the teaching staff and second in command. I appreciate your confidence in me but I think I would be too anxious to perform well in that position. Also I think my male colleague is better suited to portray the educational business image. He has ten years at the school. He's also a family man and could certainly make better use of the increase in salary than I would. He needs it more than I do. You see, I knew, the teachers would all respect directives from him including me, but not necessarily mine. It's too soon."

She must have thought it odd that here she was a career woman offering a woman a career job along with mentorship and I refused. I certainly would not do that in this day and age. My superiors have always had more confidence in me than I in myself. The unfortunate thing, in those days, I actually believed that men were to have the better paying positions because they were designated to be the main 'bread winners' and providers. On the other hand women were eventually going to marry and raise a family so it didn't really matter. Ambition, assertiveness and competitiveness, in the work place, was still frowned upon. It was not 'lady like'. Listen I was still hoping to be engaged by my 21st birthday. That was only a year away. I didn't need a career job.

Instead, I chose a transfer to the brand new high school. My home room was grade seven, enriched class. The classes were now co-ed. First time the girls and the boys would be together. Oh my Lord, talk about added challenges and distractions. That's OK but brainy kids aren't necessarily fun to work with, so serious! I was also to teach French language to grades 8 and 9, the not so brainy or better yet almost 'brain dead classes'. All I can say about that experience is best paraphrased by my conversation with the principal. "Why do I always get the failing students. The hard ass, tough guys and girls who are just doing everything in their power to get expelled?" To which he answered

"Because you and only you can keep them quiet!"

Grade 9 consisted of hard core male and female juvenile delinquents who had to be kept in the system until they reached the age of eighteen. There were several students who were from the Indian reservation across the bridge. Every kid in there had already been profiled as a trouble maker and they loved to live up to their reputations. The chemistry teacher was brought to tears one morning. I followed her with French. When I arrived she was scrunched in the door jam weeping with the whole class laughing at her. I closed the door and asked her to head down to the principal's office and file a report. I took a huge deep breath. What the hell do I do now? I walked into the class and stood leaning against the desk facing the 'mob'. We all stared at each other, finally silence. I said

"Well now that you have all proven that you are cruel and insensitive jerks and have managed to accomplish nothing worthwhile, Congratulations! You have hit the lowest of the low. I only have one goal here and that is to help you get the hell out of high school and bullying teachers isn't going to cut it. So let's get back to work."

I proceeded with my class. The chemistry teacher handed in her resignation. I cheated on the report cards by giving bonus marks to those kids who were borderline passing grade, example 48% or 49 % got a 50. Honestly these punks spoke enough street French to get by and would never in a million years ever have to write a sentence in the language. Some cried when we finished the year together. They wanted to know who would put up with them. I told them

"Nobody will! They were going into trade school to become electricians and plumbers and mechanics. Their future clients won't give a rat's ass about them. They would only expect the best from them or go someplace else. The world was going to be a lot harder than they could have imagined school could be."

I did a lot of cursing that year and was really strung out. Many of my students did get into the Academy trade school the following September. My boys were eighteen years old. I was 22 years old but they didn't know that. Those eighteen year old adults ended up with their own little shops and worked with their hands all of their lives. Most of them are probably retired now living in a mobile home village off a beach in Florida. Not everyone needs advanced education or have the level of intelligence required to pursue it. We now have a shortage of tradesmen in North America because everyone has been promoting universities rather than also promoting the trades.

In the meantime you are probably wondering what happened to my love life. Well I still didn't have one, still watching hockey games and the odd movie theater date, still a virgin at twenty. You see going steady was very common then. Playing the field was not. Most couples paired off in graduation year and got married a couple of years later and started their families. The daughters were expected to leave home and no longer be the responsibilities of their father. The husband was to provide for them instead. It was only a few decades later that my Dad had expressed the opinion

"Up to the 1970s marriage was a way of legalizing sex." It was taboo to be sexually active prior to marriage. After the 70s he would say

"Marriage! Why buy the cow? when you can get the milk for free!"

So I waited to get engaged in August, my 21st birthday.

In the year 1966, I had been dating for almost five years. In January I asked my boyfriend if we were going to get engaged in the summer. I needed time because there were so many things to organize for a wedding. It never would have occurred to me that the answer would be

"No! I'm not ready yet." I was speechless, stunned, in shock.

"We've been dating for four and a half years, exclusively, never with anyone else, why not?" he replied

"My parents dated for ten years before they married, there is no hurry" I said

"Those were World War II days. We don't have troubles like that". Silence!

THAT'S IT, THAT'S ALL, END OF DISCUSSION

It breaks my heart reliving this memory now. I never said anything. I never hit him or spat at his face or screamed until he went hard of hearing. I did nothing to show him the depth of hurt I felt. I got out of the car and went into my parents' house, crawled into my bed and wept for my poor broken heart. Acceptance of rejection, passiveness, I said to myself

"There had to be something wrong with me that I could surely fix. He was bound to be ready eventually. Oh my God I don't know anybody else. If he doesn't want me, who else would? I can't tell anybody this, not even my parents. I'll be the laughing stock of the school. Everybody thinks Mr. B and I are a 'sure done deal'."

So I did what I do best 'fake it', pretend nothing happened. That winter I shared my news with my best friend June. She was not of the same town as I. The conversation would remain confidential. We decided to celebrate my 21st birthday by going to Europe for the summer. We recruited two other girlfriends who loved to travel as much as we did. The three of them might, in those days, have been considered 'spinsters'. They were not dating anyone. In the early sixties, women in Quebec were still not allowed to go to restaurants or clubs unescorted. The taverns, which I wouldn't be seen dead in, had separate entrances. The men who were on their own used one and the couples, women escorted by men used another. Women's Liberation was still only whispered and only in the USA.

My mother was totally against my travelling to Europe. My Dad said it was OK. He knew I was going to be alright. He even used to brag to his friends that I was taking the trip. The first one in his family to graduate college and go overseas and I was paying for the trip myself. It was not the first time I was to be away from home. When I had graduated from Teachers' College, I had gone to Miami for a couple of weeks, with two college chums. It was a graduation celebration trip. Nothing happened. Mind you! I had not told my parents that the three of us were picked up on the beach one afternoon by four good looking Cubans. The young men had immigrated with their parents prior to the Castro revolution and were studying engineering or architecture at the University of Miami. Boy, we thought Canadian girls were hard done by when it came to dating rules. The Cuban girls were a lot worse off. The guys said that when they would ask a girl on a date they would have a chaperone from her family along with them, such as an auntie or a grand mother. That is why the Cuban fellows used to hang out at the beaches because they knew they could pick up women from other places who were as they put it, free! We joined them that night at a restaurant and later went to their apartment. One fellow opened a closet door to get something and low and behold there were several rifles leaning against the inside wall. I must have looked concerned because one guy said

"Don't worry we are not killers. Every male in Miami keeps guns. One day we are all going home to get Cuba back from Castro, 'a Counter-Revolution' and the American government is going to help us do it. One of the fellows drove us back to our motel in the wee hours of the morning. Interestingly, it is now fifty years since that encounter and Cuba is still Communist led.

The following summer, a colleague Wendy and I vacationed in Miami again. This time we stayed at my aunt Annabelle's house. We were just going to be a couple of weeks and she worked all day so it was not going to be a bother to her. Wendy was engaged to be married so we didn't go out much, just to the beach during the day. We used to lacquer ourselves up with baby oil and fall asleep on our towels then roll over and fry the other side. I remember a couple of guys making fun of us because to them, we looked like sizzling bacon. Whatever! Who cares? To us white northern chicks, the game plan was to come home as dark brown as an Indian and be the envy of everybody. Cancer was not even in anyone's vocabulary then. We did get into trouble on that trip, this time with my aunt. You see I had invited another friend from school to join us for a weekend. He was the physical education teacher of our school and he was taking a course at the university of Miami that summer. The problem was I omitted to ask my aunt permission to have him crash at her house overnight. Annabelle was a very, extra cool lady. She was widowed and worked as a receptionist at the Doral Golf & Country Club. She, let's say had been around the block and was not a naïve woman. I figured she would understand. It's not like we were having sex with the guy. After all he was married. YKES!! Did the fur ever fly the next morning. Apparently my dear aunt arrived at 1 a.m. from work and found this strange man sleeping on her couch. She leaned over and said

"Who are you?"

Charles gave his full name and explained he was a friend of mine and the circumstances by which he ended up sleeping in her living room. He was very sorry. She told him to go back to sleep and she poured herself a drink, went to her bedroom and then turned the light off. Of course Wendy and I were sound asleep during all of this. In the morning Charles woke up first, had the coffee made and bacon and omelets warming in the oven. We had purchased our groceries the day before. When we two girls were up he explained everything to us. I was so embarrassed and scared. Of course we couldn't eat and the wait for my aunt to wake up was the longest imaginable. She gave me a super reprimand in front of my two friends. That always works, especially, if you want to humble a young adult. Ten minutes later it was all over. We enjoyed a great meal together. Moral of the story, always notify your hostess, in advance, if there are to be any crashers. Annabelle lived to be ninety two years old. She left me with a motto I use for myself daily. I had asked her after her several bouts of cancer and heart problems, which I now have.

"How do you do it dear aunt Annabelle?" She answered

"Just keep moving!"

That Sunday Charles, Wendy and I flew out to the Bahamas to check out the Caribbean and that life style. Wendy and I were confident because we had a male escort with us. We girls were both a head taller than he was but he was a karate black belt person. We felt safe with him and he was really flattered when we walked the beach or into a resort with both ladies' arms wrapped around his shoulders. That first night we decided to check out an authentic local bar in the capital of Nassau. The desk clerk recommended the 'Yellow Canary Lounge'. It had Caribbean local food and a bar and dancing to a local band. The doorman hailed us a cab. How big can Nassau be? How big can this island be? The three of us were so busy chatting away that we never paid much attention. It just seemed to take us forever to get there. Charles asked the driver

"How much further is it? We are getting fed up driving around. Is it in the country?" with the Islands' slow slur the man replied

"Not far man, almost there man!"

Five minutes later the driver stops. 'Yellow Canary Bar and Grill'. The cab fare $76.00. US. We had to restrain Charles. There were big, black dudes at the door. It was not time to create a scene. We got screwed. Be more careful next time. Now this place was colorful. It was definitely local. I think the three of us and half a dozen more were the only whites in the joint. Naturally we three Canadians were the only ones dressed up for the Montreal Hilton Hotel lounge. I was close to broke because that damn cab fare had almost cleaned me out. Luckily I wasn't a big drinker.

None of us were. Except that night, Wendy got into the rum fruit punch and the more she danced the hotter she got and the more that 100% proof rum flowed. By 11pm she was dancing with a Caribbean native that was as big as King Kong. This guy had her over his shoulders for God sake, twirling her around. The hookers at the bar were coming up to Charles trying to solicit some business but he kept pretending that I was with him. This guy sure loved his wife. I started to really get worried about Wendy. The dude would bring her back to his table where his buddies were, instead of returning her back to our table. Wendy was beautiful, Miss Dorval 1964. She was a tall blonde and very curvaceous, real rape bait. She was also very innocent. She was just out to have fun but incapable of ascertaining the deep trouble she was getting into. Charles went over to the other table with me. We asked her to dance with us and when we were on the dance floor doing a group hug we managed to squeeze her off to the side hallway where the ladies room was. I kept splashing her face with tap water until she coughed. I explained we were checking out. Charles had hailed a taxi. This time it was to the hotel and no messing around. We got back in five minutes. Oh well another lesson learned. We poured my poor girlfriend into her bed and Charles left for his room. She was so upset and embarrassed. She had me promise her

"Don't ever mention this part of the trip to Walter, her fiancée. We have never been to Nassau. He would never understand. Please keep my secret. I'm engaged and I behaved so badly. Please keep my secret."

She vomited most of the night away. One of life's many ironies, Wendy married her fiancée the following summer. I was in Europe. Her husband managed, after twenty five years of marriage, to tell her that he wanted a divorce. He said

"She was a good Mom to their four children but he fell in love with another woman."

The woman was much younger. She was almost the same age as Wendy had been when she thought she was doing something really awful in the Bahamas.

So as you can see I thought I had enough travel experience to make it through Europe, with minimal difficulties. This was going to be an organized tour departing from London, England. All we had to do was sit back, look, listen and learn. How much trouble could I get into? Honestly! What I was proud of was that I had finally decided to give myself something worth remembering without waiting on Mr. B. He didn't show any objections to the trip either. There you go, green light! That was another benefit of being a teacher. I could have two months a year to explore the world if I was so motivated. June, Diana and I were to meet Val who was already living in England at the time. She had moved in with another girlfriend from Canada and had landed a job as a nanny. These ladies were really smart. They worked in Paris for a year as nannies for French families and taught their charges English and then vice versa. The following year they were working in London for English families teaching those kids French. They had room and board included and every other weekend off to travel. Long weekend vacations could be in Greece or Italy or where ever. Once you lived Overseas it was very easy and quick to get around from country to country via the fabulous Euro rail. There was a book written in the mid 60s called 'Europe on $10.00 a day'. So many took advantage of it's information. Travel coach, use a knapsack, eat in the market at stalls, sleep on the train or find youth hostels in major cities, walk, bus, walk, walk! It was acceptable for women to travel except those from the USSR who were never allowed to leave their countries of origin. The Spanish, Italian and Greek girls whose cultures forbade non-chaperone activities were also somewhat restricted. The most predominant travelers I met, at the campsites, were Germans and Scandinavians and Brits.

The flight Montreal to London was six hours. We landed at Heathrow airport and since we had only one bag each, got through customs quickly.

It is incredible to me how foot loose we were. We did not even have any reservation and figured

"No big deal, we'll just get a phone book and start making calls. London is big. We're bound to find something."

June and I each took a phone booth and book and looked up rooming houses offering daily rentals. In less than a half hour we found a place that had a couple of vacancies. We walked out of the station, strolled up to a lorry and gave the cabbie the address. We followed him to the back of the car. He took my suitcase and placed it in the 'boot', what they call a trunk. June trying to be helpful and independent, threw her bag into the 'boot' but accidentally hit the driver in the back of the head. Boy! was he ever ticked off. He screamed

"You stupid Yankee, you really piss me off. You almost knocked me block off." To which she replied

"For one thing were not American, we're Canadian and I'm sorry. I was just trying to help".

"Go on hurry! jump in were holding up the queue." That was our quick lesson in the British language.

Off we went, not knowing where in the hell this place was. Hoping to God we were not going to be found floating in the Tames the next day. I must say he was a really nice man and we were dropped off at the door just a short time afterwards. Our supper money was his tip. Our rooms were sparse but very clean. The only thing we had to get used to was having to share a bathroom with four other tenants. Luckily they were tidy people also. That sounds so ignorant because after all I did share a bathroom with two sisters. This was different. They were strangers. Who knows what they were carrying. Like I said, ignorant! Breakfast was served every morning at 8 a.m. not a minute later. Better show up or you go without. It was what we refer today as a B&B. Mid July was absolutely glorious. We were told we were very fortunate because London can be a rainy place, usually. We said we must have brought the good weather with us. We visited so many parks and rode the double deckers buses and ate English fish and chips wrapped in newspaper every single day. We almost got killed trying to cross the street one day. We were just chatting away totally distracted, looked to our left for on coming traffic, nothing. We stepped off the curb and immediately felt the swoosh of air. We jumped back as the tall red bus swung around the corner doing a full left turn, missing us by inches. We had forgotten that vehicles travel on the left hand side in the UK. Must say, so far, we were having a thrill a minute on this trip and loving it.

On the Thursday night we got gussied up. We hailed a cab for the Travel Club where we were to meet the tour guides and all the other travelers that were to be on this European junket. There were to be forty-eight of us. The other guests were residents of South Africa, Australia, New Zealand, the USA and Great Britain. While cocktails were being served, I kept looking for tall Bantu tribesmen. They did say Africans were on the trip and I sure was looking forward to meeting one. I asked June if she had met anyone. She said No! So of course being ignorant and uncouth I proceeded to ask one of the drivers

"Where are the Africans?"

He pointed out two white guys and one white girl. I must have had a puzzled look on my face. He proceeded to explain that they were Afrikaners who reside in Cape Town, South Africa. Boy what a way to start a trip, making friends and influencing people. The driver's name was Denis. His homeland was New Zealand. He had been doing this kind of work for five years now. He said he always found we Canadians

"Pretty naïve but utterly charming. At least he though I was".

What a line but I believed it, of course. We were to travel in two separate buses that were to run in caravan at all times. We were to set up our camp sites, sleep in the same army issue tents, shop for our food, cook and clean up with the same companions for the following sixty days. We were not to switch buses at all during the trip. Any personal, social difficulties would have to be ironed out between ourselves or discussed with the driver or guide of that specific group. My three girlfriends and I thought this was going to be fabulous. There was to be the four of us together at least and we were so used to each other and had always gotten along. It all proved to be right. We did get along well with everyone and socialized a lot but basically stuck together when we did.

I, unfortunately, do not have any pictures of that trip. I have one black and white of me and my friends celebrating my 21st birthday. It was taken at a restaurant in Barcelona, Spain. That should be the most important one at least. I took a hundred. They were all developed in slide format which I used for my geography classes when I returned home that September. After I had been married and started my family, those slides stayed with the school for everyone's use. It never occurred to me then that I would not have been returning to my beloved profession. Otherwise, I guess I would not have left them at the school. Luckily I remember all the personal incidents of my trip and over the years have been able to collect travel books and DVDs of the countries I have visited. I consider myself fortunate because we did get to see these countries and experience the authentic cultures prior to their being what I call 'polluted' with and by the 'American Way'. So many cultures all over the world have been diluted or misshapen by Americanization. Today, even in China and India some segments of their societies are copying the excesses of consumerism and superficiality so commonly practiced in the Western world.

So off we go, wearing jeans and carrying a small piece of luggage, wallowing in our new found freedom and unsupervised life style. Here we are four super straight, sheltered girls who were raised in Canadian suburbia. None of us were drinkers or smokers. We crossed the English channel by ferry and drove into Brussels, Belgium. Such idiots we were. Imagine how silly we were. Four girls in their twentieth year ended up giggling at the sight of the 'Mannequin Pis'. The first try at setting up camp was unsuccessful. It took us several efforts but we did get to put up our tent before nightfall. There were six of us. The campsite was very well maintained. There was a canteen where we could order food such as sausage and pommes frites, cheese and fruit. Coca Cola was expensive, $1.00. Back home, in 1966, a coke was only a quarter. The use of the lavatories was another matter all together. We four Canadian prudes stood in shock and embarrassment at the sight of all the open stalls that were not showers but rather toilets. You squatted to do your business. There were four sinks to which women, carrying their toiletry bags and towels, were lined up. One behind the other they stood patiently waiting their turn. Some women were short, some were tall, some large, some tiny. One thing they all had in common they were stark naked and they didn't seem to give a damn.

I got over my ultra conservative complexes and prudishness rather quickly I must say. When I was young I had to flush the toilet when I was urinating so that no one would hear my pee. When I was fourteen I had been invited to spend a ski weekend at a friend's family chalet. On the Saturday night after dinner the four teens and I went out. We built forts and rolled around in seven foot snow drifts. It was totally dark. We had a blast. At bedtime everyone used the bathroom, brushed their teeth, whatever. I woke up at four in the morning with a bladder full. I was so shy to get up and go down the hall to the bathroom. I held it in for what seemed an eternity. Then Bingo, you guessed it. I totally wet the bed. My friend who was in the top bunk woke at dawn. I started to cry. I was so embarrassed. Gail got up and got her mother. She came in and changed the bed linen. She wrapped me in her arms and explained to me that everybody knows everybody pees and everybody makes the same noise. Everyone makes grunting sounds when they poop and we all smell awful. This is perfectly natural. What a relief! I am forever grateful to that dear mom's kindness. Believe it or not, in grade nine, the nuns even had us convinced that we were not to wash our genital area because it was wrong, like as in sinful. Now I know why! God forbid we should get a twinge in that private area. We could end up being the cleanest teenage girls in town. It's really interesting to me to note the evolution of the modesty that I acquired. When I was five, I used a bed pan and an outhouse on my summer vacations with Meme, yet when I became pre pubescent I started to feel shame. I hold my mother and the nuns responsible. Children from the onset are extremely natural. Whatever unease and discomforts a child develops are usually instilled by adults.

The nudity of Europeans was highly exaggerated in those days by what one might call the Puritan influences of North Americans. In my case it was Catholic upbringing. Which in fact was total hypocrisy. It did not take me long to get really comfy in my skin. What was the old saying
"When in Rome (Europe) do as the Europeans".
What I appreciated the most was that the multi-nations travelers were at ease with their bodies and unabashed. They seemed to be unaware of all their different sizes. There did not seem to be much emphasis on the shape. There were no 'stick women' as there are today. In their mind set they were all OK, or seemed to be. I started to relax more and enjoyed ridding myself of old taboos. Now the open stall with the hole in the middle was something I never got used to. Over time I did perfect the squat so that everything landed directly in the hole and was able to twist slightly around to grab the chain behind me and pull. The key was to be able to leap out of the stall fast enough in order to avoid getting your feet soaked by the water flushing into the drain. There was no toilet paper, as we know it, in the campsite bathrooms. You wiped with newspaper or fine wrapping tissue paper which was hanging on a hook. Totally useless! So the girls and I made finding a store that sold 'real' toilet paper our priority. No problem! After that, we never left home without it. Be it in St. Peter's Basilica or at the Eifel Tower, my buddies and I were always seen with a wad of rolled toilet paper sticking out of our jeans' back pocket.

Another interesting adjustment that had to be made was our shopping for foods in the local town markets. The guides divided us in groups of four. We were all put on cooking duty on a rotating basis for a period of seven consecutive days. So we really didn't have to cook but every third week or so. We had zero experience shopping and cooking for twenty four people, our bus group. I hadn't experienced cooking for even one person. My mother was the cook. The kitchen was her domain. You'd think a mother would want to share that craft with her daughters. Not mine, she probably didn't want to relinquish any control. This was the routine on the trip. After arriving at a camp site the driver would take that week's cooks back to town and drop us off at the market. In '66 there were no large grocery chains. There were small grocery, butchers, pastry shops (my favorites) and pharmacies. It was a wonderful outing. The trip alone was an education. It was a social event. Everyone chatting, very little shoving, it seemed like a slow, graceful ballet. Each shop was side by side so you went from one to the other at a leisurely pace. Everyone carried a cloth bag in which to put all the provisions. Europeans only bought enough for a couple of days. The market stalls were for the local farmers and were set up in the town square. My girlfriends and I kind of devised a method to facilitate the task. We thought if we estimated the food intake of a woman and then that of a man and multiplied by the numbers of each gender on our bus we should have the right amount required to buy and then prepare. Easy right, one carrot each, one potato etc, except when we were asked

"How many grams? How many kilos? How many liters?"

Canadians did not use the metric system then, so we were clueless. Assuming a kilo was probably the equivalent of a pound we ordered everything that way. Boy we could have fed two bus loads of tourists with our first escapade as food shoppers. The leftovers were eventually finished in a couple of meals. Everyone got a big laugh and our driver wrote the conversion metric/linear numbers down for us to use in the future. These are experiences we never would have had if we had been booked in hotels. In sixty days we visited Belgium, Holland, Austria, Germany, Switzerland, Italy, Spain and France. In most cases we were able to take a week in each one. Here are some of my recollections.

Holland is very flat but the farm land is rich and goes on as far as the eye can see. Their coastal dike and damming system is, indeed, pure engineering genius. The houses in Amsterdam were very narrow and so close together they seemed to touch one another. I always wondered how the city would handle fire emergencies. The larger pieces of furniture that were not able to get through the front door were hoisted up on pulleys four flights up and through a large attic window. I loved the canals where barges were moored and they became floating homes. Each house though was unique. To maintain their individuality in an urban setting, each owner chose to paint the exteriors in a different color and not one home was without dozens of miniature, lush flower gardens incased in flower boxes. There were so many little bridges and everyone travelled via bicycle. The streets had designated bicycle lanes. Everything was so clean and well organized. Then, to we Canadians, there was the seedier part of town known as the 'Red Light District'. Our group checked it out, accompanied by our drivers and tour guides. It was nighttime. There really wasn't anything offensive that I could see. We and all the other tourists were gawking at very sparsely clad women in different suggestive poses in what would be best described as store front windows. I guess I was a bit disappointed. I thought I would get to see something pornographic. Maybe if a person went through the door. We chose not to. I think I was exposed to more nudity in the camping washrooms. I guess guys would appreciate it more because of the implied eroticism. In 2012 my grandchildren see the same thing on 'Much Music' videos on the television.

Austria and Germany and Switzerland scenery wise were very similar. The only way to describe it is, spectacular. What I loved was travelling those two lane highways high in the Alps. The roads were narrow and winding and steep. The tunnels were fascinating. I used to think of all the manpower needed to get that work done and the danger. Not like our very wide Canadian highways through the Alberta and British Columbia Rockies. Mind you I was in the Alps in '66 and in the Rockies in 2009. Perhaps the Alpine roads are now autobahns. The cities of these three countries differed greatly. Each one had citizens with quite different personalities. Vienna was my favorite. The elegant architecture, the magnificent boulevards and again the spotlessness. My friend June figured she had put on five pounds in the one week we were in Austria. Every other store is a café—pastry shop. Montrealers used to rave about French pastries. Based on the varied and wide experience in the consumption of European pastries that I had on my vacation, it is my opinion that the best was definitely those of Austria. I enjoyed all the tours scheduled for us. Everything was a learning experience. Some were more impactful than others, of course. One was the salt mines in Saltsburg. WOW! that was creepy but I am so glad I psyched myself out of my claustrophobia to experience this. At the entrance, we had to lie down on our backs, one behind the other on a polished wooden curved sled. All of a sudden we were pushed and gravity took care of the rest. We were, literally sliding through these shafts which were no more than four feet wide and two feet high. You could not lift your head for fear of hitting the ceilings which seemed of polished stone. I can best describe it to bobsledding. Then the sled would stop at certain levels and we would have to get out, get into another sled and off we went again. The terminology 'light at the end of the tunnel' applied well here because long before each landing we could indeed see the glimmer of a distant light. Apparently this was the method of transportation the miners used back in the day. Except it was not as tidy as when we tourists used it. Not bad for a woman who to this day has trouble riding elevators and won't use the metro or attend concerts unless accompanied. I think it's the thrill of a new possible learning experience that used to drive me to try things out in those days. I was invincible. What is really interesting is that a year after I was in Saltsburg I met a guy in a bar in Montreal who just happened to have been born in Hallien, Austria which believe it or not was just a few kilometers from Saltsburg. Isn't that a strange coincidence. That man became my husband.

Every other day, there were no planned tours. We travelers were on our own. We were in Heidelberg, Germany. My buddies and I had done a lot of walking getting to know the town, visiting museum and such. We were having a late lunch in a restaurant before we were to meet the bus to return to our camp site. Behind our booth were three local fellows in uniform. They looked like police constables. Nothing we couldn't handle. There was a lot of flirting. They spoke English and we all switched to a longer table. As is customary each fellow sat beside the girl he thought he could get to know better. That is a polite way of saying 'get lucky' or today 'hook up with'. I just thought of something funny, to me anyways. When the guys found out we were from Montreal they wanted to know if we were French? At least I must say they were more educated than most. So of course we said Yes. Then they started singing a pretty popular song at that time called "Voulez-vous couchez avec moi ce soir?". Too much! Well they bought a round or two. Then when it was time to go the guy beside me asked if I were still back in town tomorrow maybe we could meet for a late dinner.

"Why not? I could stay behind, get to write up some postcards and catch up with him after his work, same place, same station, say 7pm.

That night the girls spent quite a while trying to convince me that meeting a total stranger especially away from home could be dangerous. The next day rolled around, my girlfriends came with me to the 'rendez-vous' restaurant. The girls were getting nervous leaving me alone there. They would have to leave with the bus in a half hour or so. They started to feel jittery.

"You don't know this guy. He is a total stranger." On the defensive I answered

"Hey! he is the first date so far for any of us. I'm on vacation in Europe. If he doesn't show up a half hour after chosen time, I'll check out and take a taxi back to the camp. Ease up, will you. You would do the same thing as me."

In unison they replied "NO WE WOULDN'T!!!!!" and then they were gone.

I remember this happening as if it were last weekend. I don't really know how to vocalize it. I guess the truth is the only way. I can only thank God I left physically unharmed. I recount this story not in a bragging way but more as a cautionary tale. The old saying 'safety in numbers' is definitely correct. I will proceed.

Well look a here! Doesn't the handsome, dark eyed, dark haired German show up out of uniform, only ten minutes late. That was pretty good. We had a delicious, Bavarian style meal and some wine. The conversation was easy. When we finished we headed out the door and on the sidewalk he asked

"What hotel are you staying at?" I answered

"I'm not in a hotel. We are all camping through Europe and I am at the camp site outside of town."

The scowl on his face said it all. I think he thought I was a rich, spoiled Canadian tourist doing my thing and that he had been misled. I got a little bit spooked so I said

"Do you have a car, you can take me back to the site?"

"I live close by and the police department gives me a car for my work only. I don't want to go to my place. Let's walk awhile."

Heidelberg has many bridges along the river that connect both sides of the town. It was very cute with all the lights bordering the walkway along the water. We ended up under a bridge and started to make out. It was getting out of control. All I knew was that I had to stay upright, vertical. In no way was I going to let myself lie down. I spoke softly, calmly, (inwardly terrified) saying things like

"It looks really wet and dirty and full of bugs".

It did not take long. After a few gyrations, he finally ejaculated between my thighs. Just goes to show, I advertised myself as 'hot' and ended up, in the man's mind set, as a 'cock tease'. Oh well he kind of got what he wanted.

We straightened our clothes and walked back up the stairs to the road above. He took a ring out of his pocket and put it on. He told me if I kept walking that way, pointing to my right, I should get back to the camp site in about fifteen minutes.

I am not being flippant about this. I was really scared especially walking alone on the road. I knew he was not following me. I checked but I was terrified a car would drive by and stop. Better yet that I would get lost. I have a terrible sense of direction. I did get back without danger. It was still early, probably around 10:30 or so. A lot of the folks were still around the camp fire. My girlfriends followed me back into our tent.

"How was it? Did you have a nice evening?" I sheepishly replied.

"You were right it was not a good idea to meet a stranger alone but I'm safe now. I'm not ready to talk about it yet."

That is the true story of my being almost raped under a bridge in Heidelberg by an obviously married man. Moral of the story is

"If you're not selling. Don't advertize".

I used to say that to my teenage daughters. It took a few more weeks before my chasteness was challenged again.

Italy was my favorite country. We were there for well over two weeks. The winding roads through the Alps and then the sundrenched Italian Riviera peppered with small fishing villages really appealed to me. There was sunshine and greenery and unimaginable flower gardens up and down both sides of the boot. We visited Naples, Pompeii, Florence, Piza, Portofino, Venice, Capri and Rome. Oh my gosh everything was spectacular. I can't travel outside of Canada anymore because I am uninsurable due to health problems such as cancer and a heart aneurism. Yet if I could, I would spend another two months just in Italy. The art, the history and the architecture in the cities of Florence and Venice and Rome were, honestly, just like I had seen and read in my history and geography books. I was never disappointed. I was mesmerized, stunned, drugged, like stepping back in time. I understand why the adjective romantic is attributed to Italy. The people, the food, the wine, the music, the climate, and the scenery all exude sensuality. It is irresistible! Everywhere I went especially on the coasts I felt I was floating, soaring.

The thought of it gives me shivers. See that must be part of the master plan also. That I got to view such naturally beautiful places and enjoy the sensory stimulation they provided for me while I was young. What a blessing that was because I obviously wouldn't be able to do it in my older age. The amazing gift I still have and so appreciate, is that I remember!

Pompeii has the ruins from the eruption of Vesuvius. There is nothing there except crumbling walls and ash and a catacomb like building that we women on the tour, in 1966, were not allowed to enter. When the men came back we asked

"So what was that all about?"

"Oh just a whole lot of pornographic drawings and carvings on the walls and the ceilings."

I wonder if women are allowed to view those pictures in the year 2012? So if you're interested in my opinion, you can skip dirty Naples and Pompeii. Venice is really interesting. It's still sinking but don't worry you don't feel it. We couldn't afford a gondola ride and it looked pretty scary to me. They seemed to be forever dodging large power driven taxi boats that can hold about forty passengers. The wake from these taxi boats is powerful and the fumes from the diesel would make you nauseous. I really can't see the romance in that kind of a boat ride. My buddies and I were in Plaza San Marco and decided to make our way down a lane to a local restaurant for lunch. Everything was so cute, the checkered red and white tablecloths, the basket bottled wine. The ambiance was perfect. Since we couldn't read the menu we all thought we could enjoy Italian spaghetti. I ordered but the waiter didn't seem to understand what I was saying. I don't know if it was a language issue. So I tried to describe to him with signs what we wanted. Charades anyone? It didn't seem like he had ever played that game either. So I proceeded to take the menu and show him how we eat spaghetti and meat sauce at home. I pointed out to pasta, to meat, to tomato etc. He nodded in agreement then turned and headed out to the kitchen. It was a very small place maybe eight patrons and us. It seemed to take forever. By now we had become accustomed to having wine so we indulged. Finally the meal arrives. We each received a bowl of pasta, a plate of sizzling steaks (horse) and a tomato salad on the side. Well we ate everything which was delicious and drank the bottle of wine and had so much fun, three hours for lunch. That is still my favorite kind of meal, the easy, relaxed, slow kind. It is only when we came back home and Diana told her dad about our adventure in Italian culinary art that he explained.

"Italians don't eat spaghetti and a meat sauce. That is an American dish". The horse meat is called 'chevaline' and is common in Italy and France. It is sliced very thinly and pan fried quickly on each side, 'Blue' or very rare as we would call it. It is tender and scrumptious. I just loved travelling because I could be exposed to so many things that were not common at home.

I'm quite sure I lost my virginity somewhere between the Italian Riviera and our arrival in Rome. The reason why I think that, is that instead of going into the tour of the coliseum in Rome, I chose to sit on the curb beside our twenty six year old bus driver Richard, from New Zealand and wait it out.

He distinctly said

"Don't waste your time sitting here. Go in and see everything." I answered totally smitten

"I'd rather be with you!"

The story of my life, self restrictions due to romantic notions. Yes of course you are right. I'm being extremely facetious. So let me back up. Loosing one's virginity, I think I put it down on the beach in Capri and forgot to pick it back up! Virgin in the dictionary (esp. women) does not apply to males. Definition is a female who has not yet had sexual intercourse. So I never really lost anything. I should say I acquired something, sexual experiences.

If memory serves me right. Richard and I had become buddies. June had become buddies with the driver from Australia. Then one night Richard invited me to his 'bachelor pad' by night, the back seat of the bus. I went several times. We were into some heavy making out on the long back seat where he usually slept. Then he says

"I had a girlfriend in London for three years and I'm used to more than just foreplay. (Bear with me here! I'm trying to clean it up). To which I replied "OH!".

Denis was no taller than I and very slim and not especially handsome. Certainly not like Mr. B back home in Canada. Mr. B who? you ask.

I am such a comic! You got to love me though. I look back on my life, like my virginity or my cancer or my marriage or even last night's heart palpitations, as just fodder for humor. If you let go of it all, a little

bit at a time, just for a couple of seconds you realize in the larger scheme
of things it's all such nonsense. They are all just acts in a great play that I
have been the director and producer of. One thing I have learned over so
much time, is not to be so hard on myself anymore.

Enough philosophy, back to sex.

That night all thoughts of a steady boyfriend along with my virginity
flew out the proverbial window. Richard slowly climbed over me and
became a part of me. It was all slow motion and gentle. Nothing was
forced or uncomfortable. It was the first time, and unfortunately the
last that I have ever reached climax during penetration. Beginners
luck I guess! Our romance was not torrid and bold. It was discreet, no
smooching during the day. What I liked the most was sleeping on the
bus' back bench with a man's arms wrapped around me. That was so cozy.
I think of it as primal comfort. Sure beats being alone on a tent cot. I
didn't stay every night. There were a lot of fun things going on that were
really worth taking part in. When we got back to London, in late August,
I stayed at Richard's place only once. We talked about my going back.
He wanted me to stay in Europe. He could get me a job with the tour
company especially since I spoke both French and English. I couldn't. I
was already signed up for a 1966-67 teaching contract. Anyways I did not
feel any great, amorous, passionate attachment to Richard. Rest assured I
did not tell him that. It was the same for him, I'm sure. You see I know
that because he used to speak about his former girlfriend quite a lot. He
still loved her. I must say, we were very respectful of each other's feelings.
He gave me the company number where I could leave a message with
someone who would find him no matter where he was and he would call
me in Canada. In case anything ever happened and I needed his help.
It never occurred to me, so innocent, the help could be regarding a
pregnancy. I was not with child. There is that Master Plan again.

Meanwhile back to the trip. There was an American guy that kept
driving in to all the same camp sites as us. He drove a station wagon that
he had bought in Holland. He also came along on all the tours as well.
I think he was pretty clever. He didn't have to figure out what direction
to take the next day or what wonderful sites to see. He just had to follow
us. He tried to hit up on all the girls. He was a huge guy, at least 6'5",
built like a bear and good looking. He was really charming and so funny.
I feel so bad now, I can't remember his name. He got me in his station
wagon once but I felt too uncomfortable. I drew the line at making out,

or getting down, or screwing around, whatever you want to call it, with two guys on the same trip. A young woman has to have some principles, even in Europe, after all. What I did notice though is that I was appealing to men and that in turn made me feel confident.

The first time I ever got wasted was on the Costa Brava near Barcelona, Spain. The lunch was in a huge, open air restaurant on the beach. The place was packed. We were at least ten at our table. It took forever to be served lunch, which I have come to realize and appreciate is really a European custom. After all, what is the hurry? In the mean time the guys kept ordering pitchers of Sangria and we kept on drinking and drinking. It was so hot out and the drink was so cold. It actually tasted like fruity Kool Aid. It did not taste like booze to me. Finally we ate. The bus was not leaving for another couple of hours. What to do now? Well hit the beach and jump in the ocean, of course. When the bus was ready to leave my friends found me and 'Big Bear' passed out on the beach. I was face down covered from my toes to the tips of my hair in sand. I'm surprised I didn't suffocate. Something did stick in my mind. It was a smell. 'Big Bear' was a hairy guy and it was a tangle of salt and sweat and sand. The scent was like that of a dog when it comes out of the water. It amazes me how acute my senses are. That night I was the butt of everybody's jokes. But I didn't care I was having so much fun. The next day we went to the bullfights in Barcelona. Can you imagine eight in a row? Just spectacular! The pomp and pageantry is remarkable. I was surprised by one thing though. In Spain the spectators do not yell OLE. No! Every time the matador swishes his red cape along the head of the bull as he rushes by, just inches away, the whole crowd hundreds of spectators HISS in unison. It is the eeriest sound. If the matador shows weakness and stands too far away from the bull the crowd would BOO. Such excitement! My 21st birthday was celebrated in Barcelona. I could not have imagined this type of celebration in a million years. The 'three musketeers' and I and our two drivers went to a restaurant for a seafood dinner and a Flamenco dancing show. It was a once in a lifetime, unique experience.

It was that night I wrote what is known as a 'Dear John" letter to Mr. B
A 'Dear John' letter was known, in the old days, to be a letter written by women during WW II to their boyfriends. It usually was a goodbye letter. No one would be waiting for them when they come back home.

My letter wasn't that dramatic. It pretty well said all the fun I was having and all the people I had met. That looking at him and my father watching a hockey game on Saturday nights was not going to cut it. That I did not want to go steady anymore when I got back home. The last city we visited was Paris. The drivers thought it was pretty cool that I could speak French. It was less of a struggle being understood. Nevertheless, I found that the Parisians did not appreciate my efforts at all. They never switched to English to convenience the tourists. Instead they would watch the person struggle with their language and pretend to not understand. There was one incident. I had finished explaining our order, all in Canadian French. We purchased quite a bit of supplies. As we were leaving the store I overheard the clerk say

"That one, she is a colonial. I can always make them out because their French is so inferior."

That left a very sour taste in my mouth. I have known a few people from Montreal who have visited that city even in the last couple of years who have said that that urban attitude towards foreigners, in general, has not improved. Many Parisians are pompous and rude. Luckily the rural folks are so hospitable that it does make a huge difference. The camaraderie of the village residents left me with a much better impression of the French.

There was a very sad and probably historical event that took place the last night we were there. My girlfriends, 'Big Bear' and I were enjoying the fabulous lights of the Eifel Tower. He made an announcement that literally jarred me. His father had sent a telegram to him stating that there was a letter, received at home, from the government of the United States which was a draft notice. He was to report to the hometown draft office for a physical exam. At that time the war in Vietnam was at it's highest. The USA had a method for inducting or conscripting young men into military service. It was called the draft lottery. It was a lottery by birthday drawing. There were 366 blue plastic balls containing every possible date affecting young men between the ages of eighteen and twenty six years old. There were close to 850,000 people whose lives were in the balance. 'Big Bear' put his head on his raised knees and started to weep. At first it was very quiet sobs. Then he rose and stated to yell and curse at the top of his lungs. Our two drivers came over to help him. They too, being Australian and New Zealanders, would have been up for the draft. They beat it way in advance by coming over to Europe and getting fulltime jobs instead of staying in their respective homelands. We spent the night, up until dawn trying to console him. We came up with every scheme available even coming to Canada. I must admire him. He had failed his first year at university, "goofing off" he said. He never took the draft scare seriously. He had planned the trip to Europe to get away from the mess in the States, a form of distraction. Now he was ready to accept service. He wouldn't try and cheat the system because he knew there were so many guys, like him, stuck and they were going to war in Vietnam. He sold his wagon to the other younger American who had decided to stay behind after the tour ended. During that week, 'Big Bear' let us take him to the Charles De Gaulle airport. He gave me his family telephone number in case I wanted to call. Even if he was in Vietnam, I could talk to his Dad and he would gladly give me of his news. I never called, a cowardly act on my part. I still wonder about several people who impacted my life. Are they still here on earth or have they crossed over? I know with 'face book' you can find people who want to be found. I'm too scared to get the answer. I, even though I know it's not right, feel better with by blinders kept on. Like what they used to put on horses in the olden days so that they wouldn't get spooked by passing motorcars. I also think it would be very presumptuous of me to think that my being with them would have proven to be that memorable an event.

So back on British soil we were. Seven more days left and we fly back to Montreal. June and I found a studio flat for the week and froze our behinds. We ended up sharing the same single bed because it was so damp. We would each take turns during the night putting coins in the gas heater seven feet away from the bed. Whoever's turn it was to get up had the honor of facing the heater and getting a little bit more heat. We were good pals. One of the musketeers stayed on in the UK and travelled to the then area known as "behind the Iron curtain" to Moscow. I envied her. The travel queen came back to Canada in the early 70s. It was then, after having lived in Vancouver for several years that she returned to Montreal and had to be treated for acute depression. She had been the most calm and cool and collected of all of us crazy young women. I'll never forget her visiting me and my daughters at our duplex. She was as calm as a cucumber. What she explained was
"Yes! I was tested and treated for depression and take a couple of pills a day to stabilize my moods." The doctor told me.

"Now you know the problem, you know the origins of the problem both mental and personal and you have been given the solutions. You can harp on all of this and all of your past or you can move on with your life. Only you are in charge of your life."

My dear friend's words have been such a lesson to me.

The eagles have landed. Watch out Montreal, brace yourself. We're back so much more different than the way we were when we left two months ago.

Boy! How quickly did we settle in our usual routine. It's kind of sad. Maybe that's why they're called holidays and vacations. Nothing lasts very long. You have fun then you have to buckle down to the real life. Oh well! I didn't care. There were other trips to plan for next year. Might as well earn some money to save up for the next plan. You notice I say save. There were no credit cards in those days. If you didn't have the money to buy, you went without until you did. I got my groove teaching again. I didn't see Mr. B. I was not going out to dance clubs downtown. The only difference between before and now was that I did not have to watch Saturday night hockey games. Isn't that what I wanted? Freedom! no going steady. Yes but this is boring too. Everybody else I knew was married or engaged. Since I wasn't paired off, I was not even invited to previous friends' social outings and parties. The girls were very paranoid in those days. They thought a single woman could ensnare their boyfriends. Who knows maybe the same applies in this day and age?

Home life was becoming more and more stressful. The feeling of self sufficiency and independence that I had had in Europe was completely thwarted in my parents' house. My mother would need to pick a fight. I can't even remember some of the topics. When she would rage I would turn around and walk into my bedroom and lock the door. The fighting and shrieking used to make me feel sick to my stomach. At one point she was so frustrated with my indifference she kept banging on the door screaming.

"At least, when your older sister Belle was still here she would stand up and fight."

I was twenty one years old, locked up in my room and my younger sister was nineteen years old locked up in her room. My older sister was twenty three married living in the USA. The only difference between then and our childhood was that the two remaining daughters could lock themselves up. My father just kept on reading his newspaper downstairs in the family room. A couple of days later I spoke to my father and mother together and told them

"I have decided to get my own place. I am able to afford a small apartment near the school. I would be much happier and I would have peace and quiet."

My mother said

"You will probably turn out to be a spinster since you have given up your prospect for marriage."

Mr. B had, apparently, contacted my younger sister at the end of the summer to tell her I had broken off with him. My father said

"I cannot accept that and hope that we could all make an effort to get along. I can't let you move out. What would everyone think? People from my family and the neighbors would say that I could not take care of my own daughters."

My father was always very concerned about appearances. For instance, always hold your wife around the waist, when at a party. It looks like affection. It means, in reality, you're trying to hold your wife up so that people don't realize she is a stumbling drunk. I do understand that now. I had to use the art of camouflage when I was married, in fact several times with my husband. My father was a good mentor. So again because I loved my Dad so much and didn't want to give him anymore hardship than he already had, I chose to stay. Instead of moving out, notice I always seem to have a plan B, I went shopping for a car. Yes! I was going to check out every weekend. I could take my Meme to visit aunt Mado or aunt Dora. You name it, I was game. Have car will travel.

My father discussed the benefits of a car like the Rambler, fuel economy etc. He wanted to get involved and help me make the right choices. I ignored him. I went to the GM dealer and the salesman helped me pick out a brand new sky blue Corvair. It was so cute and very cool. It actually had the engine in the back like a Volkswagen and the trunk was in the front. The car was very sporty looking, just like I felt at he time. I went to my bank and applied for my first loan $4000. Everything was in order. The bank manager said I had a good job with no prospect of unemployment and could easily meet the monthly payments on my present salary except

"You need someone, a man, to co-sign on this loan." I asked

"What does that mean?"

"Someone, who in the event of extenuating circumstances such as an inability on your part to meet the monthly payments, would do so on your behalf."

I almost died of humiliation, right then and there. Back in that day women were not given a loan for anything unless it was co-signed by a man. Men were considered a good risk and had usually guaranteed long term incomes. Women were not. There was a high likelihood they would marry, have children, stop working and have no means of income to continue loan payments. The Feminist movement was no where in the near future. So I tucked my tail between my legs, like a chastised dog, and went home to approach my Dad. He was very disappointed with my choice of car. Since I had not yet signed a contract, he drove me to other dealers to see his recommendations. I held my ground and he, after two weeks, acquiesced. We went to the bank, I signed, he cosigned. We then went to the dealer to sign for the Corvair. YIPEE!!! I did not yet have a drivers license so my father drove the car home and my mother later drove him back to get his vehicle from the dealership.

The car stayed parked in the driveway for two weeks. I walked or took the bus to work. I was getting super annoyed. My father said I can't drive the car without a learner's permit and he did not have the time to teach me how to drive. He was only available on the weekends and he was certainly not going to let me learn on his car. So what is a girl to do? I convinced my mother that I had a lot of confidence in her driving skills (not true) and begged her to take me out when I would get back from school. I was so excited. If I had to deal with the devil I would. I just had to start using my car. My mom loved the little Corvair. She started to use it during the day for her errands and so on. We went for lessons several days in a row. But she scared the life out of me. When I would turn around a corner she would grab the wheel from me and pull hard which caused me to hit the curb often. I think she was very nervous but at least she never quit or forced me to stop. We were just in the sub division. Of course the neighbor ladies thought this was so much fun to watch and would cheer whenever we got into the driveway in one piece. Apparently my mother had been bragging during the weekly bridge games and this, after all, was a shared 'Chicks' secret. Three weeks later my mother felt confident enough in me. She drove to the license bureau and I got my learner's permit. I drove back home in what I called my 'Bijou' (jewel). I was so proud. The only rule was that on a learner's permit a driver must be accompanied by a licensed driver. I cheated. In the morning, after my father had left the house to walk up to the train station, I jumped into my car and drove to school and got back before he arrived from work. He never came for a ride with me. He was probably still annoyed that I had not followed his advice. Oh well it certainly would not be the last time I disappointed my dear dad.

I was twenty one, of legal age. The always existing concern about my moving out helped my poor dad realize, he didn't have much choice but to cut me some slack. I started to smoke cigarettes, only in the teachers' lounge. I was embarrassed to always be bumming fags so I decided to buy my own. That was the end of it. The more you smoke the greater the addiction sets in. I smoked for thirty eight years. I quit, cold turkey, after I was diagnosed with breast cancer for the second time. I just loved driving. By the time I went to apply for my permanent driver's license the instructor was stunned that I had accumulated so much mileage on my car. I told him I had taken my boyfriend everywhere, Quebec City, skiing in the Laurentians, in the Eastern township and in Stowe, Vermont. It was slightly embellished but all true. I was proud to brag. I drove my mother and grandmother to the States several times. My driving skills were fine, no reproach but my eye test proved that I had poor vision of the left eye. I would have to get glasses and pass the test again which I did two days later. Then off I drove into the sunset from Verdun to Lachine during afternoon rush hour. I was ecstatic!

I did see Mr. B a few times that winter. We had gone to a club downtown. There was a brawl and I remember our hiding behind an overturned table, my getting soaking wet with spilled beer. That was the beginning and end of the club dates. I drove us up to do some skiing a couple of times. He didn't think his car would make the trip because it was older. I didn't care as long as he shared the trip expenses. We went to Quebec city once with my sister and her boyfriend. We had sex a couple of times but nothing remarkable. I remember asking him

"Is this all there is? Couldn't we do it again?" he answered

"A guy just can't do it all night long you know!"

He was probably just being super cautious. I was never impregnated then either. We never discussed engagement or marriage. In fact on both of our parts it seemed more like a 'ho hum' kind of a relationship. We can take it or leave it kind of a feeling. Birth control was not even considered.

I find it very interesting but puzzling about how discreet the women I knew were about our so called indiscretions, sexual escapades. My sister was on the 'birth control pill' when she was sixteen. She to this day claims she was never told that was what it was. Dr. Gordon had prescribed it to her, with my mother's knowledge, to help regulate her menstruations and make them less painful. Here was my sister three years younger than me having sex with protection but I without. You go figure? The master plan again! So far I had learned three things about sex. Size does matter and penises come in all widths and lengths. Most importantly, is that foreplay for a woman is a great deal more sexy than actual penetration.

My girlfriend Sally was five years older than me. We taught at the same school. She had been dating a Danish fellow for a few years and was engaged to be married in the summer. We used to hang out together. She drove a red Mustang convertible. She was an only child and spoiled rotten. Her daddy bought her set of wheels. She was called 'Mustang Sally', like the late 60s song. Victoria Day 1967 was a three day holiday. Sally's fiancée had already left for Barbados where he had begun his internship in oceanography. She and I decided to drive to the country and check in on Mr. B at his family cottage. The late afternoon, surprise visit was not well received. So we hung out with his sweet mother and chatted a while. We asked Mr. B if he wanted to go out with us. There was a club with a great band in the local village we were thinking of going to see. He said no he couldn't, he had already made plans. OK! so we checked out and got back to the club in time for dinner.

It was really noisy but not yet packed. It was only 9pm. There was a gang of about ten guys who were hooting and hollering enough to tick me off. We couldn't even hear ourselves speak or the music for that matter. Just as we were ready to head out two guys come over and asked us to dance. They kept coming back every once in a while. The guy with me was named Dan. He was not very tall and worked with the CP railroad and was here visiting his tall friend, Dick, who was chatting up Sally. The tall guy said they had all been racing their cars at the local drag strip. He was wearing tight white jeans and had great thighs. What I used to refer to as hockey skaters' thighs. Then after a couple of hours the guys had decided to switch partners. That's OK! I preferred tall. The four of us stayed at our table and the rest of the guys stayed at the longer table, still making a lot of noise but not coming to bother us. By 1 a.m. I was getting tired and decided to leave. Sally came with me. Dick saw me to my car and mentioned he would like to have my telephone number. I said

"That won't be necessary."

He leaned in to kiss me and I rolled the car window up his face. He started to laugh and kissed the window. I headed out and on the 2/20 highway I kept seeing a car tail gating me. I would accelerate and so would he. Finally he passed and cut me off. Dick and I spent the last thirty-five miles passing each other until I exited off the highway to drive my girlfriend to her house.

That Monday Sally must have been bored because she called and asked me if I remembered the tall guy's name. I said it and she looked it up in the phone book. She said there is only one family in Montreal and this is the address. Let's go and see if he's home. Well he wasn't. She insisted that I leave my name and telephone number and slip into the mailbox at the door. I said

"Why me?" she says, "because I'm engaged, remember!"

Mr. K calls during the week and invites me for a dinner date in the Laurentians.

"Would my girlfriend like to double date with his buddy Dan, the fellow that she met at the club?"

I called Sally who said sure and I confirmed back to Mr. K. I could leave my car parked on his street and we would all travel together. He drove a Chevrolet Impala two door, steel grey. It was a company car. He used it all day for work in HVAC contracting. He didn't have to pay for it or gas or insurance. It was a sweet deal. He was studying engineering at night school. I was very impressed! We had dinner in a lovely auberge by a lake. He knew all about European foods and wine. I was getting smitten really quickly. This guy was acting like a real man. I didn't believe him when he told me he was twenty two. That was the same age as I. I thought he was twenty six or more. Maybe it was the receding hairline or perhaps that he seemed so knowledgeable. He showed me his driver's license to prove it. It's funny because we were two couples there but we barely spoke to each other. It's as if each couple were in their own space in time. A cabin had been rented in advance and then I got really spooked. Sally and Dan went into the bedroom. I went out on the screened in porch. We started to neck and he groped but I just wasn't ready. I told my date that I wanted to go home. He said he wouldn't bother me anymore. We could just sleep together and be off early in the morning. That was not my plan. I wanted to go home now. I'm sure by now he was probably disappointed because he was not going to score. He probably thought he should have chosen to stay with Sally when we had met at the club. I held my breath while he spoke to his friend. They agreed we would go back. Neither one wanted to go back to the city. He would come back for noon the next day to pick them up. So Mr. K and I left for Montreal. I did kiss him goodnight as I got into my car, still parked in front of his parents' place. I thanked him for his understanding. I told him in all sincerity

"When I'm ready you will be the first to know. I won't hesitate to show you either. I just like to be the one to start things and not get pressured."

He called me the next night and every night after that we were on a date.

So I was really excited. I was starting the summer dating an intelligent fellow who seemed worldly and interesting and respectful. Even though he was not super handsome he was a very sexy guy with a lot of energy and a huge repertoire of interesting dates to take me on. I must say being with Mr. K was never boring. For a guy to want my company was the most rewarding feeling in the world to me.

A world wind romance best describes my new relationship. The 'Master Plan' is now definitely in full play. My mother was hospitalized for a few weeks. My father was, to say the least, very distracted. He was not paying attention to me at all. That is just the way I like it. My little sister was doing her thing romancing her beau. I got away with murder. Just about every night Sally and I met up with Dick and a couple of his buddies at the Montreal World's Fair, Expo "67. Wow! What a fabulous place to party. There were pavilions from around the world with restaurants showcasing their gastronomical delights and bars with the music of each country for us to dance to. We had a total blast. Sally hooked up with a new guy. She kept busy circulating while her fiancée was away in Barbados and didn't seem concerned at all. I got to meet two new younger girls who were seventeen at the time, Stella who was hooked up with Murray and Carol who then hooked up with Wayne for a while. Stella and Carol and I have been friends for forty five years. We still call or email weekly. That is loyalty and friendship. I was really happy to have ladies to be with because often the guys' escapades proved to be totally extreme. I liked to pretend I didn't know this crowd of hellions and Carol and I and Stella would stay out of sight. I was really glad I had always had my own car so I could get out as soon as things were getting out of hand. In fact I usually ended up driving the girls home, which I didn't mind at all. It was much safer that way for all concerned.

The five other guys, played the field and what a field it was. They all had a rented duplex that they were evicted from after a year because
"The residence was being used for reasons other than domestic". Let see the guys had converted a regular coke dispensing machine into a beer machine. Different girls came through the place as through a revolving door, in and out most nights. One was called Cecile but the guys called her 'Cecil the slimy serpent'. She could be found laying stark naked on the coach smoking a joint. She would regale anyone, who would listen, with her story about how she and her girlfriend went across Canada hitchhiking without a penny. She was bragging that they came back with sixty bucks. Then one Saturday night after the 'Quarter Mile Drag' races, two of the drivers drove their semi rigs to Lacombe street, a very fine residential area in NDG and parked them. They then got the dragsters off the rigs and proceeded to race their loud, shrieking machines at full speed until the police showed up. I guess that was the straw that broke the camels back for all of the neighbors. I could not have convinced my Dick to get out of there if my life depended on it. That was where the action was, with the gang. Dick was even described by his own buddies as a 'wild and crazy guy'.

There were always tales shared by all. Each guy trying to upstage the other with their prowess at being totally insane but not yet arrested. Trash and Dick used to hang out after work at the local pool hall/tavern. One Saturday the two of them head up to the Laurentians to his parent's cottage. Several bars later they are totally wasted and drive back to Montreal. A police car tries to pull Trash over but no way. So he takes off accelerating to a hundred miles an hour going down ditches, cutting people off, driving on the wrong side of the road. Then Dick hears a weird, zinging sound and it's bullets hitting the trunk of the car. The police are shooting at them. Trash speeds through an intersection and gets into a subdivision leaving the police car far behind. They stop and hide behind a factory figuring the cops have the license plate number and Trash will be picked up tonight for sure.

The two madmen get out, go to the back of the car and check out the back plate. The license plate is so encrusted in mud, the numbers could not be deciphered. Dick was known for what Bill used to call his 'horror shows'. Dick never discriminated. Being offensive to girls especially and guys was his specialty. Four guys and their women were making out in the upstairs living room of the ski shack. The fireplace was roaring and very romantic. Dick shows up at 3 a m, alone as usual, but thoroughly drunk, as usual. He had to go to the bathroom but instead of going downstairs he decides to unzip and proceeded to urinate into the fire place. Even the guys didn't think that was funny. The stench stayed in the house for at least a couple of days. That really broke the party mood. Then he passed out on the floor.

Another couple of incidents took place before he even came to Montreal. One day his father was driving back home after work. He was passed by a fire truck at the intersection and proceeded to follow the truck wondering where, on his street, it was going. It stopped at his house. The garage was totally engulfed in flames. The fire was put out and a report was filed. It was arson. Dick and his buddy had dowsed an area with gasoline and had inserted matches in a couple of pellet guns and started firing. Some of the matches would hit the wood side of the garage and ignite. Unfortunately things got out of control. Then there was the time he and some buds decided to go to the States to party at a beach. They ran out of beer rather quickly so they decided to break into a liquor store. They ran off with a lot of hard booze and drank the night away. They came back home the following morning. Dick always bragged about his genius on this occasion. The next weekend the same guys went back to the same beach. Dick was the only one whose stolen booze had not floated back out to sea at high tide. He had dug a fairly deep hole in the sand in the trunk of a fallen tree. The walls of the trunk protected the stash from drifting away. I could keep on with more exploits of the juvenile delinquency of Dick but I won't. To me at the time when I used to hear all the recounting I figured it was just bravado, bragging, and showing off between males. Who could be the worst of the 'bad boys'? Anyways it didn't matter. It was way before my time. Boys do grow into men and give up their foolish ways. People do change. Right?

I will have other horror shows to share with you, the ones he did when we were married. After hearing this you are bound to be asking yourself

"Why is she still dating this guy for? He sounds like he was trouble with a capital T."

You are right but I was of the mind set that all 'bad boys eventually settle down'. This coming from a young woman who had next to zero experience with guys, a good Dad, home at six, coca cola at nine, bed at eleven. I had no brothers to learn the ropes from and a boyfriend who watched hockey on Saturday night. Europe was a yawn compared to this kind of action. Let us not forget that I was falling in love and he was a really nice guy and wasn't doing anything bad with me. YET! The school year was coming to an end. On the flip side of the coin was Mr. B. He had asked to meet me to talk. My sister had kept him informed of what was happening. He said

"I want you to stop seeing this other guy. Your sister says he's trouble and you're getting a little bit wild" I replied

"Who are you to tell me what to do? You offer me nothing." I had talked to my dad that night and he said

"It's not right to date two guys at the same time. You have to choose between one or the other, Mr. B or Mr. K."

My dad used to refer to Mr. B as no1 and Mr. K as no2. It was the code he used when one or the other would call me on the phone. Mr. K had phoned the next evening and I told him

"I could not see him anymore. That Mr. B wanted me to only date him exclusively. Mr. K said he would be at my house tomorrow afternoon around 4:30 p.m. to bring me back the money he had borrowed from me last week. I was nervous all day. I really didn't want a confrontation. I was really too shaken by all of this. All I wanted was to have fun. Why was everything so complicated? I was alone at home, thank God. Dick was right on time. I opened the front door. He gave me the money. He said

"I would like for you to tell me straight to my face that you do not want to go out with me anymore." I froze then replied

"Mr. B told me to tell you I couldn't date you anymore" I started to cry. I was so embarrassed. He said

"I ask you what do you want, not him, you?" I crawled into his arms and said

"I want to stay with you".

He kissed the tears off of my face and that was the end of that story.

He left and called that evening. I was too tired to go out, too drained. When my father called me to the phone and said it was no2, Mr. K said

"Correction Sir! I am now no1."

See that was why I wanted to be with that wild and crazy guy. Can't you see it. He was a fantastic human being to me and he wanted me. I could not resist him. That was part of the 'Master Plan'.

July was already with us. Di, a colleague and I decided to drive to Florida for a vacation. Both she and I had boyfriends but not sure what the future had to offer. I really liked to get away. I had the travelling bug. I really didn't want to get into that wait for the boyfriend mode anymore. We were only going to be away for a few weeks. Wendy had moved to Vancouver and Sally was getting married in Barbados. I had called Mr. B and told him I would not see him again and wished him the best. I was loading up the trunk of my car the morning I was leaving and Dick shows up with a rose. I was barefoot and he told me to get some sandals on because it was illegal and dangerous not to. It had something to do with electrocution. Bossing me around already but at least it showed he cared. I just loved it all. The road trip was very interesting. I did most of the driving. Di was an ok driver. The time I did let her drive was on the interstate and she would break going down a hill in the Pennsylvania mountains. That drove me batty. It was best anyways. She didn't have to be nervous about driving my car nor I about her. Some of the roads were only two lanes. One day, it took us six hours to go two hundred and fifty miles. It was in the deep south. We drove through Georgia, North Carolina and South Carolina. It was our first experience with the Black culture. We were able to see all the country side and the shanty shacks used for the cotton pickers. This was 1967. We pulled into a town for some gas. There was only one gas station with a manual pump. Sitting outside were a few black folk. There wasn't a white person to be seen anywhere. Nobody was moving off of their stoop so Di and I get out of the car and started walking over to them. Then I felt the short hairs go up at the back of my neck. I told Di to go and sit in the car. One of us would be enough. Finally an old man gets up and meets me. I tell him what we need and he goes to the pump. He wouldn't talk and I couldn't talk. Those good old boys were probably wondering what the devil are those two crazy white girls doing on these back woods roads. I paid the man and stepped in my car and sped away. Di and I compared our frights. Ignorant still! I think back at how dangerous those times were. Imagine 'the Civil Rights Act' did not take place in the USA, until 1968. It probably would have been worse had it been the other way around. A black person, let alone black women, being served by a few white men.

That would never have happened. It was the first and last time in my life I have ever experienced reverse discrimination. I mean the fear of being in the minority. Gosh! those people were so really black. Back then my small suburbia town did not have any residents of color. We, in Canada had a very sheltered life. Profiling done by the news media to keep us scared had worked.

Di and I were having an easy vacation. We got a lot of rest. We only drove seven hours a day and stopped at ocean side motels with a pool and a restaurant so that we could relax. I wrote Dick over a dozen letters which I still keep. It's nice to read how passionate I was in those days. The letters also indicate that he called me long distance half a dozen times. He even sent me a letter that I have reread five times today while I write this. He addresses me as dear lover, that he misses me and loves me. That is really nice to have as a souvenir. Helps me get over my feeling that he never loved me. I'm so much wiser now and should know the difference in that love probably being more like lust. Surprise! one afternoon, we get a phone call from Sally

"My fiancée and I are not getting married. I have a flight tomorrow from Barbados arriving Miami airport at 2 p.m can you pick me up? I'll stay with you until I figure out what to do."

"OK! we'll be there."

Di and I looked at each other and thought

"Hell two is company, three is a crowd, especially if she is depressed and all. Wonder what happened?"

I didn't have any trouble finding my way to the airport. We got back in time to walk the beach and laze around the pool.

Story has it, she and her fiancée had had a couple of days together on the weekend but once the workweek came, he was back on the boats doing dives or in the science labs doing research. She became bored and they decided he should continue with his studies, of course, and she would see him back in Montreal in September. The engagement wasn't over. The wedding had just been postponed. That night, when we were getting ready to go out to the piano bar and restaurant of our resort, she removed her engagement ring.

The set up was really great. The pool was in the middle and the rooms were around it. We had a great neighbor, in his forties, who was kind enough to oblige us. One night he had a hot date. If all went according to plan, he was not coming back that night. He gave us the keys to his room. He had a suite with a utility kitchen. Di and I could use it to have dinner or watch TV or fall asleep. Sally, the night before, had hooked up with a guy and invited him to our place. Except they got in our suite at 3pm and never came out and she had locked the door. I was so ticked off. Di and I decided not to create a scene. When our neighbor returned, around 1 a.m, he called our room and let the phone ring and ring until she finally picked up. Thank God for someone with experience in these matters. We got into the room, threw the guy out and had a long talk with Sally. We would very much appreciate that, in the future, she made out with guys in their own place. Di and I were paying for this unit and did not appreciate being locked out of it. Di and I had decided to head back home on Saturday. She was welcome to stay on the third week of our holiday and fly back or we could get a refund with small charge for cancellation and she could drive back with us and share in the costs. Di and I were missing our boyfriends and looking forward to the rest of the summer with them. Sally then said to me

"You shouldn't get your hopes up too much." I asked

"What the hell are you talking about?" to which she replied

"Dick and I went up north to a party together. He called me for a date. Don't worry! We didn't do anything. He was so drunk I had to drive home while he napped with his head on my lap." I didn't know what to say.

"How often did you go out?"

"Just that once, but he seems to have trouble deciding between you and me. I just don't want you to be surprised when you get back."

I just stood there stunned, staring until Di said

"Come on let's go to bed".

We headed to our bedroom and closed the door. 'Bitch' wasn't even a word in my vocabulary then.

Two more days to go and we were finally off. I've never wanted to get out of a place so fast in my entire life. It's really a shame how I was able to allow someone whom I presumed was a friend be so hurtful to me. Peace at all cost. It's only now as I reread that I realize I was a chump for anybody to target. The smart move would have been to have driven her back to the Miami airport. In those days I didn't know the moves. Life is just one huge game of chess. I drove back, all the way. Di was the navigator. We three were broke. Just enough money for gas. There was one incident that is worth mention. Just goes to prove what a screw-up Sally was at that time. Anyways I wasn't a shrink. I was not the type to pry. One evening, at dusk, we had pulled into a turnpike service center to buy some snacks for the road and fill up. When we got out of the store Sally who had stayed behind was chatting up a guy in the Lincoln parked beside me. He said he was a travelling salesman on his way to Charlotte, North Carolina. I can see it as vividly now as it was then. He said if we wanted I could follow him up there and we could stay at a very inexpensive motel he stayed at where he would get two rooms with his company discount. Sounded pretty harmless to us three ladies. We had fun on the highway. He would pass us. I would pass him. It can get really boring driving those roads. It was late evening when we arrived. He invited us to his room. Di and I declined, Sally did not. I couldn't care less anymore. Di and I went to bed turned on the TV and fell asleep. I was dead beat. By 7 a.m I woke up. No Sally? I really got spooked. I woke Di up. We got dressed. We ran to the guys motel room. We noticed the Lincoln was till parked there. Hopefully that was good news.

We knocked on the door, Sally and her new beau for the night come out and he invites us to breakfast. We load up the trunk of my car. Sally gets into the Lincoln and we follow them to the restaurant. Like no sweat! this happens all the time! No words were ever spoken. Who was I to judge? I remembered Heidelberg the year before. Oh well Sally had gotten us the last night accommodations and breakfast meal for free. I sure as hell wouldn't do it? Mind you she was six years older than us, obviously more experienced. This is what I refer to when I say how we girls were all so discreet. Most of the time we never knew what each other was really doing. Thinking back now I wonder why I didn't ask her about birth control? That would have been either too intimate a question or accusatory. It was a taboo subject!

I drove straight through from Charlotte to Montreal, seventeen hours in all. We would have gotten home sooner. We got waylaid, lost on the New Jersey turnpike and ended up on the waterfront. After trying desperately to find our way out, without any success, we used Sally's talents to help us. We were waiting at a stoplight and there were two guys in a convertible sports car beside us. She leaned out the window explained our plight. They agreed to help us. They cut me off when the light turned green and escorted us out and up to the Upper New York State Parkway. I dropped my girlfriends off at their respective houses. I knew Dick was going to be at the gang's place. We had spoken on the phone the night before. You have to realize there were no cell phones in those days. I drove there directly instead of going to my parents' house. I was so pumped, high on adrenalin. The door was always unlocked. It was 3 a.m. He was asleep on the living room couch. I leaned over and kissed him. He opened his eyes and enfolded me in his arms. I had started to speak to him and he was listening when all of a sudden I was sound asleep. He woke me at nine and he left for work and I left for home. We were to see each other on the weekend. He took me to a fantastic seafood restaurant called 'le Pavillion Atlantique' which was at Expo. It was just the two of us so we were able to talk a lot and get to know each other better. This guy was such a connoisseur of foods and wine. He was such a great conversationalist. We would get into some debates but he seemed to respect my opinions and intelligence. Like many superb restaurants, still to this day, dinner took a few hours.

Let me tell you a little bit of my new boyfriend's background. I am assuming everything he told me is true. I have lived with him for forty years and have been deceived so many times by him. I have also accepted the fact that he could be a pathological liar. Yet I have always given him the benefit of the doubt to this day out of respect for him and of course for his family. His family was originally from Berlin. His mother had been an overseas telephone operator, daughter of a teacher. His father was an architect, son of a high ranking officer in the German Navy, until all of Germany became employed by Hitler. Then his father became a soldier. They had declared war with the rest of the free world. In order to protect his family from the wages of war his father, an officer in the Nazi army, sent his wife, two children, his mother and sister to live in Austria which was then occupied by the Germans. They lived in the Austrian Alps, "the hills are alive with the sound of music" neighborhood. Yes the exact ones as the movie 'The Sound of Music'. No kidding! After the war was lost all Germans were transported in railway cars back to Germany. In the early 50s, the father decided to emigrate and the family started a new life in Canada. His father had worked in many towns in British Columbia as a project supervisor in construction work. He had chosen not to pursue his Canadian certification as an architect because there were now six in the family and money was scarce. By the early 60s the eldest daughter graduated as a lab tech. She worked for over thirty years and retired with a pension. She said she never wanted to be like her mother dependent on a husband. She later married and they have been together for fifty years. My husband's older brother joined the American Navy as soon as he had graduated high school. They both affirmed that they had to get out. Their father was away most of the time on jobs. When he returned he was unemployed, prone to depression and took his frustration out on his children through violent behavior. He would act like that until the next contract came and he was off again. I can relate to what a relief his absence would have meant to his family. My husband never said anything derogatory about his father to me. Once he said

"I thank him for this much, at least he got us to Canada."

In the mid sixties his father got a very good job that would provide several years of stability. He was to be project supervisor for the construction of 'Place des Arts' in Montreal. Dick was in charge of taking care of his mother and youngest sister. He drove his mother across Canada and the family settled in. After the project was completed his father opened a company with two associates. The company failed and his father was held financially libel. His father declared bankruptcy. He continued to look for any job across Canada. His mother who had experience as a tailor started to take in students and taught sewing lessons.

When I met Dick he was the sole provider for his family. I had such respect for that man. He had a truly troublesome, love hate relationship with his father. At times it proved to be violent. There was an incident that again confirmed to me that he was a really nice guy, a kind and helpful son. I got a phone call around 5:30pm and Dick apologized but could not make our date that evening. His mother said his father had been admitted into a hospital in Ontario, a six hour drive from Montreal. His dad had had a heart attack and was now stabilized. The doctors suggested that he be transported back to Montreal and be in a hospital there where he could be treated until recovery. The family could certainly not afford the ambulance service for such a distance. Dick was to go and pick up his father and bring him back home. Of course I wished him a safe drive and would see him another day. He appeared very upset at breaking our date. I assured him that was not important. I understood the gravity of the situation. He registered his father in hospital and brought his mother there to spend the day with him. It was 8 a. m in the following morning. He had to go to work. He had not slept for forty eight hours. That evening we drove to the lakeshore and Dick got to talk it out. He had wanted to see me but was obviously exhausted. He started to weep. I had him rest his head on my lap and he slept for a while. It was then that I vowed that I would, no matter what, make sure that my Dick wouldn't have to feel pain ever again like he did then. I was going to 'have his back'. It was later in our life together, several times actually, where I got to do just that. In those same circumstances, nowadays, it is called 'enabling'. Who knew? Sometimes I think the old saying 'no good deed goes unpunished' describes my life quite well.

Not everyone felt the same way as I did and these people did not mind making not so subtle derogatory comments about my new boyfriend. One Saturday afternoon my family and I were on our usual cruise. Dad had a thirty eight foot cabin cruiser with fly bridge, called 'the Whistler'. He was just turning in to the dock at the club, when two guys in a motor boat jumped his wake at full throttle. They were screaming my name and waving frantically. It was Bill and Dick. Oh boy! how to win friends and influence people! Oh wow! I thought his was so cool. I didn't even know they had a boat. It belonged to Bill's father. The guys knew we were going to be out on the lake that day and decided to come out and find me. That's what those guys did. They just thought of something and went ahead and did it. My father turned to me and asked

"Which one of those bums are you going out with?" I was so excited with such an unusual, surprise visit that I answered without getting upset.

"The tall one, anyways he isn't a bum. He has a full time job as a project supervisor for an HVAC contracting company. He also has his own company car and is studying engineering at night at Sir George Williams University."

I'm surprised I didn't add 'so there!' My dad did not invite the guys to dock. That meant he didn't want to meet Mr. K who was no2, now no1' guy. So I yelled at him that I would see him at a later date and they turned around and took off. My parents and I didn't speak for the rest of the afternoon or evening. That was OK we hardly ever spoke anymore. Except for "pass the salt, pass the pepper" all conversations were too toxic.

His so called 'comrade in arms' Bill took an opportunity to warn me once about my dating Dick. He had rented a motel room along the beach of the lake. There was a dance club and restaurant where we used to hang out. On weekends people wanted to get away and party and our parents' homes sure were not conducive. Rod did this often. He organized it so that the gang would get in at 1pm and often stay until 3 a.m when the bar closed. Having a room was a good idea. A place to crash if they couldn't drive. I don't remember the exact circumstances that created this scenario. It was late afternoon and I guess the party was getting a little bit too rough for my taste. I certainly had had enough 'White Russians' to last me a very long while and I wanted to go home. So it was Bill who drove me home in Dick's car. Dick was stretched out on the back seat. Next thing I know as I am getting my stuff out of the trunk he takes off into the yard an hides under the kitchen porch. I think I had had it by then. That was probably why Bill drove because Dick might have refused to take me back. I went into the house and when I came back out Bill was trying to convince him to

"Come out from under there."

I tried also but still no response from this fetal like man in the corner, scrunched against the cement wall. Bill and I went into the kitchen. I offered him a coke. I asked

"What is wrong with that guy? He just like lost it" To which Bill replied

"He does that a lot. He's an alcoholic. He drinks to get drunk, every time, all the time."

"Well you are a fine one to talk!" I said. To which he answered

"I got you home didn't I!"

So back out we went. I didn't even know if Dick was asleep. It was impossible to tell. By now I figured our neighbors were hiding between the sheer curtains in the playroom wondering what drama was unfolding. I'm glad they never called the police. Bill told Dick he was going to take off with his car with or without him and he could take a cab back to his house. A second later out crawls Dick. Not a single word was exchanged. Then they were gone. I should have known then, there was going to be trouble. I just put it off as an isolated incident. I always gave my boyfriend the benefit of the doubt. I even thought at the time that Bill's comments were very disloyal of him.

Most of the time our dates were with the gang. We would go to the drag strip or a club. The girls did most of the dancing together. Then the guys would get up for the very slow songs and do some grinding. I heard this expression yesterday on TV. Now it means when a guy leans his groin into a girl's behind and they start gyrating. In my day it was crotch to crotch gyration. The longest slow song on record then was 'Hey

Jude' by the Beatles. Dick never got up to dance until after 11 p.m. By then he was well oiled and loose. Anyways he and Murray were too busy 'bullshitting' each other. Murray was fourteen years older than us and had quite a repertoire of stories, real or imagined. Dick and he used to fuel each other up like a brush fire. His girlfriend Stella became my best girlfriend. She and I had so much fun. We would really get a work out on the dance floor. To this day her way to unwind is to put on the tunes and do 'her thing'. I've even seen her holding a broomstick up to her mouth pretending it was a microphone. The amazing thing is she still remembers the lyrics of most songs. One night Dick had excused himself to go to the men's room and Murray announces to Stella and me that Dick told him, he was going to get engaged to me.

"Maybe he should ask me first before he makes any pronouncements!"

Dick came back. Murray leaned in and whispered something to him then Dick shouts

"Hey do you want to get married?" I said

"OK!" That was how I got proposed to. Well at least there were several witnesses. We had dated for three months.

One evening I was to meet Dick's at his parent's home. I rang the doorbell. He yelled

"It's open."

He is at the top of the stairs and there are very few lights on. He says

"Welcome! My parents are away in Quebec City for the weekend. I thought we could stay in for a change."

I thought then as I looked up at him that 'tonight is going to be the night'. He had a bedroom to which the outdoor gallery was connected. We sat out there for hours sipping wine and then a liqueur under the branches of a very tall oak tree. It was kind of like being in the tree itself. The conversation came around to love making.

"I told him I was not a virgin". He said he was.

"I asked if it mattered to him about me?" he said

"Definitely not".

Several years later, after one of our sweaty love making sessions I said to him and I wasn't kidding

"I still don't believe you were a virgin when we met. You must have had a lot of experience. How is it possible that you know so much sexy stuff?" he answered

"I read a lot."

You have to believe it. When he moved his humble belongings into our first apartment he must have brought at least fifty playboy magazines with him. Oh yes back to the gallery! We went into the house through his bedroom and landed on the bed, naturally. Our first love making was a disaster for me. It was instantaneous for him. He was very apologetic. Luckily he was a young man with great stamina. I still have that ringing in my ears of Mr. B saying in Quebec City

"Well guys just can't do it all night long"

This guy could. Finally we did get serious and planned our wedding for December 23rd which was his parent's anniversary. How sentimental! He was going to plan to meet with my father that week and ask for my hand in marriage. Another important issue came up. He asked me if I was on the pill.

I replied

"No I wasn't. Sex wasn't something that I planned happening on a regular basis and anyways Catholic girls didn't use birth control except for the rhythm method. Was he going to use condoms?" He said

"No it didn't feel the same or that is what he was told". I added

"Well, I guess we'd better make a promise to each other now that we will take full responsibility for the consequences in case a pregnancy does occur."

He agreed and I did trust him to keep his end of the bargain. What a fantastic memory! I think I can, with certainty, say that was the night I learned how to achieve my womanhood sexually. It had nothing to do with my so called virginity or lack of same. A man's ability to draw out a woman's sensuousness is paramount.

The following week I had a teachers' union meeting. When I returned home, Dick's car was in the driveway. Designated parking now if he thought he was going to be the son in law, right. Apparently my boyfriend and my father were having a very good conversation about all the construction in Montreal. Dick had purchased a bottle of champagne which was chilling in the fridge. He opened it and poured for my parents and us. We had a toast to us. Dad welcomed a new member to the family. BLAH! BLAH! BLAH! I do respect Dick for having gone through the required protocol. This was in early August so as you can see things were already moving at an alarmingly quick rate. I do have confidence, now, that he must have felt something for me. He got all of these things in motion without our even knowing I was pregnant. My older sister dated her beau for five years while he attended McGill. Here I was engaged after three months. Most of our life together has always been what some might think impetuous but to us it was more like

"Strike while the iron is hot". For Dick it has always been

"Live now for tomorrow you may die."

His family's German history would have certainly contributed to that philosophy. I always thought we were tough enough to deal with anything life threw at us. It was thirty-five years later that I found out, we were not. The engagement ring(s) story is hilarious. I had told my fiancée that I was not into all the engagement, wedding hype. All I wanted was a wedding band. Let's keep things simple. He came by the house one night and showed me two tiny velour boxes in which there was a small diamond ring in each. I asked

"What are these?"

"They are rings my brother gave to two different girls he was dating. The engagements were broken off and the rings returned to him"

"So what does that have to do with me?"

"Well you try them on, see if they fit and if you like one of them, my brother said you could have it as my engagement ring for you and I'd just have to pay him". I did not know what to say. I was really ticked off. I closed the boxes and said as sweetly as I possibly could

"That is really thoughtful but if you are so sure you want me to have a ring then let's go out and pick one. I don't want your brother's hand me downs."

Well his family must have conferred. His father's best friend was a jeweler. If we wanted to design the engagement ring and our wedding bands he would make them for us. We could get them at cost from his shop. Dick then proceeded to draw the rings which I still have today and hope to pass on to our grandchildren. The design was ingenious. The bands were yellow gold circles on the outside running along a white gold engineer's circle on the inside. His was very wide and masculine. Mine was narrower. His greatest ambition was to become an engineer. That is why, that symbol was incorporated in the band. The engagement ring consisted of the two small diamonds from his brother's ring flanking a larger diamond in the center. Dick had purchased the new stone from Hans, the jeweler family friend. Everything turned out so beautiful. Over and above the beauty of the jewelry, everything had become so significant because the gesture was so personal and sincere. That's why I'm sure if a man would go though all of those motions, he surely must have had very strong feelings for me then. Nobody can fake that. My husband rarely wore his wedding band. Over time he stopped wearing it all together. Either it was too heavy or created dry, scaly skin on the ring finger or best yet

"The construction association regulations does not allow for any jewelry to be worn on job sites, no bracelets, no chains, no rings. They were a work hazard."

By the way my husband never did become an engineer. Oh well

"Shit happens", no degree, no marriage after forty years.

"Ain't life a bitch."

The summer was coming to a close. I used to really like to spend the last two weeks before school getting psyched up for the coming year. This one was going to be different. It is what we call 'middle school' today. I would definitely have to dig deeper in my bag of tricks. Most of the kids knew me already by reputation. I wasn't too concerned but the subject matter was also going to be different, albeit more interesting. I know I needed time to brush up and ready myself. Before getting serious I had one more celebration and that was my birthday. Dick managed to get Bill to lend us his parent's cottage for a couple of days. You had to take the boat over to an island and climb up fifty stairs to get to the cabin. It was just going to be the two of us. What fun! I was so looking forward to that experience. I, unfortunately, knew very little about cooking. I was to do breakfast. My fiancée was to do BBQ dinner. I did a lot of sunbathing and swimming and reading. We made love a lot. Ten times in three days is bound to get a lady pregnant. For anyone who should hear this but does not want to, hear this anyways. A man pulling out before climax is NOT a form of birth control. There is always some ejaculation prior to 'coitus interruptus'. There may not be one hundred million little sperm entering the female body at that time but there could be, oh let's say! for argument sake forty million. I always thought our first born was conceived with post coital remains. A little bit of research has taught me that those microscopic suckers can stay alive for a couple of days. Enough dirty talk! I'm blushing. After two days Dick got pretty antsy.

"I want to get back and see what's going on in town."

He was bored. He was obviously a guy that could not sit still for long. So we agreed we were to head back a day early, tomorrow morning would be good. The phone rang during supper. Bill's mother and sister were at the dock.

"Could Dick please come and get them."

By the time they got in, the cottage was nice and tidy. I had met Bill's sister before but not his mother. She and her mom really liked Dick. They knew he was going to be at the cottage but Rod had omitted to mention that he would have company. That night Mrs. A and her daughter used the guest room because we had already bunked out in the master bedroom. Mrs. A said not to worry. She would move back into her bedroom after we left in the morning. I thought I was going to die. I slunk into the bedroom and slept with my clothes on. Dick whispered

"What are you doing? Why don't you but your nightgown on? It's too late now. I'm sure she knows we've been having sex all weekend. She wasn't born yesterday especially with Bill as a son."

Things started to get back to normal. I wasn't going out during the week. I was much too busy with school work. Dick's parents invited me for dinner. It was my first time meeting them. I found his mother very intelligent and well versed on world affairs. His father, on the other hand, unnerved me. He seemed very pompous, superior somehow. We sat down to dinner and I was surprised not to be served roast beef or a meal of that nature. In it's stead the dinner consisted of German sausage and kale and red cabbage and very hard, dark bread. This just showed my ignorance in general. I did not eat very much. The taste definitely took getting used to. The men had retired to the living room for a cigar. I was helping Dick's mother with the clearing of the tables and doing the dishes. It was definitely a patriarchal environment, much like my parent's home. The lady of the house stopped what she was doing and looked me right in the eyes and asked

"Do you really know what you are doing?" I hesitated for a moment. Then it occurred to me what she meant. I answered very firmly

"YES, of course I do!"

To this day I still don't know what she meant to say. Maybe I should have asked her. Her opinion, then, would not have mattered to me anyways. Another person now, his mother no less, had obvious doubts.

It was in late September that I realized I had not yet menstruated. I wasn't too concerned. I had always been irregular, sometimes skipping three months at a time. This is so absurd but still a good reflection of the attitudes of those times. I took an earring that looked like a wedding band and put it on my left finger. I headed out to the drugstore. The pharmacist gave me a cup in which I was to deposit the first urine of the day. Here was one time when I was very happy that we were upper middle class and had three bathrooms in our house. My mother never got up with us in the morning since I was about ten so I didn't have to sneak around the house. I did bring the sample back to the pharmacy early morning, the following day. The pregnancy test results would be available in three days. It's crazy that I did not go to our family physician. I, at the time, feared the good doctor would tell my mother. The usual sentiments of the time, ignorance, fear, shame, secrecy, sinfulness, and punishment were all interwoven in my psyche. I was not even cognoscente of the fact that I was a twenty two year old adult with full rights to privacy. The stress was exhausting. My colleague Sally accompanied me to the drugstore

"Yes, the results are positive. The rabbit died. You are definitely pregnant. Congratulations!" The clerk seemed very pleased. Sally and I jumped around hugging each other. We left the store, got into the car and I thought I was going to throw up. Then I started to whimper. It took me a couple of minutes to compose myself. Oh Shit! I'd better give Dick a call. I was very brief and straight to the point

"I had a pregnancy test done. It came out positive. I'm sorry. We'll have to get together." He sounded calm when he replied

"Oh don't be sorry. I'm as proud as a peacock. At least I now know I can make a kid. My mother was always worried because I have such tight pants and apparently the lack of air circulation might damage the sperm count. Well I proved her wrong. Anyways I always figured the girl I married would probably be pregnant."

He appeared to be very cool with it. We met the Friday night and talked. He had seen Bill who gave him the name of an abortionist we could make an appointment with. It was at a medical clinic downtown and we should get there a s a p. I was stunned. Abortion had never occurred to me, never. I was literally on auto pilot. I didn't object, I didn't fight. I just remember being so worried about loosing not only face with my community but being fired by the school board. I was totally silent as Dick led me into the clinic that Saturday morning. He had already made the appointment. The clinic was immaculate and the doctor's demeanor professional. First there was to be the examination and then he would explain the procedure at which time we could make our final decision. This was the first time I had an internal examination. I was very embarrassed. Absurd when you think about it. I thought I was old enough to have sex but prudish when it came to another man using utensils in my vagina! I got dressed and returned to the office where, by then, the doctor was chatting with Dick. The physician said the fetus was in good condition but he could not perform the abortion because the pregnancy was just completing the first trimester and the fetus was actually a fully developed baby. I was so relieved. Now that was what I refer to as 'Divine Intervention'.

I am still a Pro Choice person but also Pro life. I believe that a woman regardless of age has a right to choose the outcome of the life of her baby.

Notice I say the life. Meaning there are choices that do not include abortion such as single parenting with the help of parents or the community. There is also adoption. So many couples are agonizing to love and provide for a child. That decision is the most humane. I had a girlfriend who had an abortion. Two other friends had chosen adoption. These ladies used to look at little babies and wonder where theirs were. Yet the lady who chose abortion grieved for many years over that death. Did she ever recover from the loss? She would sometimes say to me

"My baby would be the same age as your eldest now."

It's a really hard call. I, having been through it, do not wish it on anyone and I will not judge. Obviously birth control for males and females would be much more practical. Dick and I saw my family physician that week. Another examination took place. That undoubtedly humbled me, yet again. Doc Gordon was very direct. He summarized by saying

"Jo do you love him?" To which I replied

"Yes!" next question

"Dick do you love her?" To which he replied

"Yes!"

"Well you better change your wedding date because you will look really pregnant going down the aisle at Christmas time."

Dick's buddies threw him a stag party. There was a problem though. No one had a projector with which to show the 'stag' movies. Apparently you cannot throw a party for a guy without porn. So guess who provided the projector. I did! My parents rarely used theirs. I figured I could sneak it out of the house and let Bill borrow it for the evening. It's not like I could go up and ask my dad

"Oh can I borrow your projector the guys want to watch pornography."

Well the day after the party, I went up to the bachelor pad to pick up the projector. Bill and another guy took great pleasure in telling me everything that happened. They watched the movies then two 'working' girls came down the stairs to the basement. They were hired to service Dick and for the guys' entertainment. Dick got so mad when he saw the women, he threw a bottle of beer which broke against the wall just over their heads. The 'ladies' went running back up and got out of the house. The buds poured Dick into a cold water bath to calm him down and he ended up retching all over himself. It's a wonder he didn't drown in the state he was in. Lucky! I wonder now! Then the men called the women to come back and they got what they paid for. Now was I to surmise, assuming the story is true, that my fiancée loved me enough to refuse the paid for favors of two prostitutes. Naturally that's what I concluded and was so grateful. You have to wonder what would have gone through my head to even get involved with that crew and worse to listen to the recounting. I so wanted to be a 'cool chick'. You know ultra liberal 'boys will be boys' attitude.

We took old Dr. Gordon's advice and told my parents about the date change. Christmas was too busy a season especially at school and to also have to plan a wedding would be too much for all of us. So we'll do it Nov. 4th. That seemed easy enough. My parents knew that I did not like all the fanfare they had gone through with my older sister. The tension was something I did not relish. I told them I wanted an intimate, families only, reception. My father wanted to make up for the difference in the costs between my sister's affair and mine. He offered us a honeymoon trip that he would get his secretary to arrange. My life became so much less complicated. Both my fiancée and I were adults with good paying jobs. We could provide for a new child. We were going to get married before anyways. The fact of my pregnancy did not have to become public. It was our business. What story telling, there was so much cloak and dagger stuff in those days. I shopped for my own wedding trousseau. I didn't want anyone to join me, not even a girlfriend. This was going to be all about my day. No one was going to have any input. I was not going to justify my choices to anyone. I walked into a bridal boutique in Place Ville Marie and picked "a perfect size 7" the sale's clerk said.

It was a beautiful white suit, knee length sleeveless dress, with matching coat and pill box hat. It was, totally, the 'Jacqueline Kennedy' look. I think back now and that was probably the last time I made my own decision about my life for at least a couple of decades. Dick had asked me what my choice of flowers would be and I said "a single orchid". My fiancée, being a non-catholic, had to take a course in the principles of my faith. He would meet with the young priest one evening a week until the wedding. That time was spent mostly at the rectory sipping scotch and debating precepts. They did get along. I had confession, in the privacy of the confessional and mentioned my pre marital sexual exploits. After all, I had to have a clean soul before receiving a sacrament. That was a Church doctrine. The night before my wedding my father yelled at me through my bedroom door

"Get off the phone. You've been talking for forty minutes. It's ten o'clock." I replied

"For God sake Dad I'm taking to the man I am going to marry tomorrow. You think you could give me a break."

I could hear Dick laughing in the background. My father replied.

"You will be talking to him for the rest of your life. Now get off the phone."

The next day could not come a moment too soon. The hairdresser was scheduled for the morning and by the time my father went and picked up my Godmother, his sister and my dear Meme I had already changed into my wedding attire. The orchid had already been delivered by the florist and was in our fridge. I just had to get out of the house. I was so looking forward to not having to live there anymore. Tonight I was going to sleep in our own apartment. It was pouring rain and much too early to go into the church. My father and I parked at the docks across the street. We did not say a word. We just both stared out the windshield watching the pouring rain. That didn't even bother me. My father was the first to speak

"I'm sorry I yelled at you last night. It wasn't really about the telephone. It's just that (long pause) I want you to know I'm really going to miss not having you around."

I couldn't reply so I just squeezed his hand and moved over and leaned on his shoulder. I couldn't for the life of me admit to him that I just didn't feel the same way. My mother used to have a saying

"If you do not have anything nice to say you shouldn't say anything at all." That is why I chose to remain silent. We could see people starting to arrive at the church. There were no written invitations sent to anyone. There was not to be a reception. Everyone knew what the day and time of the wedding was to be and all my friends and colleagues wanted to come and see me get married. Some even brought their mothers, all of whom I knew really well, to meet me and my groom and congratulate us. I was a very blessed young woman. My father and I went into the church at 2:55 p.m. Every one was seated. The usher came to us in the vestibule and mentioned to me that the usual priest could not officiate because he had urgent business to attend to out of town. There was going to be a new priest that I had never met. The good news was that some boys from my class were to be the altar servers. I could not have been happier. So everything would turn out just lovely. It's now 3 p.m, no groom! Where can he be? There better not have been an accident. 3:05 p.m Dick shows up with his four buddies in tow. The guys stepped into a pew and Dick went to stand beside his father who was the best man. The organist started the wedding march and down the aisle, towards the altar, I strolled on my father's arm. At that very moment I never had a single doubt or reservation. I knew I was exactly where I was supposed to be, doing exactly what I was supposed to be doing. It was the 'Master Plan'.

In retrospect I have to say that I was going to prove everybody wrong, my father, Dick's mother, his friend. I have reread my letters to my husband from the time I was in Florida including several written many years later. In summary, the words seems to indicate my gratitude to him for wanting me. How appreciative I was that he loved me. How his love for me was an immeasurable gift that kept me whole. It would seem to me now, that I was so needy. My greatest fear throughout my marriage, was that he would die in a car wreck or one night never come back home or he would regret having had to get married to me because I was pregnant. It's almost as if I was expressing that he was doing me such a great favor. I have concluded, after many years of soul searching, that once I had been rejected by my first love of five years Mr. B my being wanted by another man was desperate, even to me. Surely the bubble would burst. I could not have been that lucky this soon. I had to make sure to insure that I never disappointed him and that I made his life with me so worthwhile that he would never have any reservations about us and our future.

The wedding reception was dinner for ten in a very fine Montreal restaurant. All went very well. My husband and I went back to our place. We were able to have the apartment the week before to set everything up. Our furnishings were meager hand me downs from my parents. A TV and hide a bed for the living room and a collapsible bridge table and four chairs for the dining room. The den had Dick's desk and his single bed. The bed was the one souvenir of our first love making. The master bedroom had my bedroom furniture from home. We had bought a new double bed and linens. I don't remember the wedding night. Someone who has been making love a lot prior to the wedding doesn't have much to add, if you get my drift. The following morning we were awakened early by the buzzer. Dick's parents were in the lobby. They had brought breakfast for us. I jumped in the shower and Dick let them in. My in-laws rummaged through the kitchen cupboards and got everything required to serve. They stayed for a few hours. I wasn't sure if that was a European custom or not, In-law invasion so soon after nuptials. I was too scared to ask. My husband and I went back to work that Monday. Naturally, the wedding ceremony was the talk of the school. I was very proud and super excited. It was a good idea to go right back. The kids were able to get it out of their system. I had so many things to prepare for the substitute teacher. It was my first time ever leaving a class behind.

The following Saturday we boarded a plane to Bermuda, one week's vacation as my Dad had promised. The honeymoon was to be spent at a lodge at the end of the Island. It was called Sugar Cane Point. There was nothing to do there. Mopeds were available for rental and we could get to see the rest of the sights on the island that way. The inn looked like an old English cottage. We were led to our room. When the host opened the door we noticed there was no double bed only twins. I found that very odd. Dick never said a word to the inn keeper so naturally I didn't. Wasn't that the husband's job. He proceeded to push the twins together. Maybe, that was my father's idea of a cruel joke. Dinner was served at 6 p.m and breakfast at 8 a.m. It reminded me a great deal of my stay in London. Luckily we did have our own full bathroom. We travelled all over the Island. We tried a restaurant for dinner one night but were refused because Dick did not have a tie and jacket. The first night I wore a frilly, short baby doll pajama. My husband hated it. He thought it was cute but way too itchy.

"What do you need clothes on for when I'm just going to take them off you anyways?"

Dick was a very logical man. There were a couple of things I disliked and decided I should express my opinion. The sleeping arrangements were very uncomfortable. We were the only visitors in the place. I mentioned to Dick that surely they could change us to a more comfortable room. We could always pay the difference if there was one. He never even inquired with the inn keeper. He told me

"Everything was fine with him. We weren't going to be long enough to warrant a change. There was no need to make a fuss."

I think what bothered me the most about that attitude was that I was the most travelled person between the two of us and from experience I knew anything is possible. One just needs to ask. The other incident was the setting of a scenario that was to replicate itself all through my married life. I couldn't keep up with our every day escapades. Riding the bike was very tiring. I was after all, though we always forgot, four months pregnant. One afternoon I told Dick I would like to have a nap. I curled up in bed and asked him to join me. He said

"I don't do naps ever. You rest up. I'll find something to do. I'll be back later."

He got back around 5:30. I had awakened and had been waiting on the gallery for two hours. He had found a pub down the road with a fun bartender. He got caught up on all the Island tales. We had dinner and he regaled me with all of the stories. Every day after, until we left, when afternoon rolled around he suggested I have a nap and he headed down to the pub. I was never invited to join him. I did not even know what was happening. It made sense to me. I'm tired, I needed to rest. He heads out to drink and chat it up with somebody, anybody. Who was I to argue? I fit in beautifully as a wife. I now realize that, then, I was already deferring to the decisions for better or worse of the husband.

You know that 'hot shot' twenty two year old teacher, the young woman who was a world traveler and drove that cute little car? She was already disappearing. I didn't know that. Hey! I got what I wanted I was married. Wasn't that supposed to be the greatest thing in the world.

CHAPTER 13

THE 70s—MARRIAGE,
THE ROLLER COASTER RIDE

I wonder if that first year was the beginning of the end. Certainly all the signs were there. Since I did not see the writing on the wall, I will continue on my merry, blind way feeding you information about my deluded, middle class, marital bliss.

All was going pretty well or as I expected. We headed to work every morning. Dick had a couple of nights of school. Sometimes he came home right after work. We would make love then eat a quick dinner I had warming in the oven and he would be off to university. There were two other times a week though that he would not get back home until 2:30 in the morning. I lost my temper one night as he was coming in and told him this could not go on.

"You have to realize that I sit here or nod off and wake up again wondering if you are in a car wreck or in the hospital or something awful has happened. You never even call to say you're going to be late."

Naturally I was bawling my eyes out. Raging hormones from pregnancy that we did not know anything about in those days. We moved from living room to the hallway to the bedroom and I still would not stop my blubbering tirade. He grabbed both my arms and shook me. I got really scared. He said

"Get the hell out of here. You go and sleep in the living room. Do whatever you want. Just get out. Next time you want to talk to me, you can just bloody well make sure you are not crying your eyes out and are ready to explain yourself clearly and rationally. Only then will I be able to hear you properly and pay any attention."

I did not answer. I froze, then turned around and went back to the living room. He slammed the bedroom door and went to sleep. Nothing was said the following day. There was no apology for being so late. In due course the many commandments of Dick would become carved in my heart and on my soul. One being

"And don't expect me to tell you I'm sorry because I'm not."

Another of his rules of engagement was

"Ask me no questions, I tell you no lies."

It was then that I learned to develop a seemingly calm disposition when faced with any argument. If there was a plan or a project I would like us to undertake I would explain carefully from A to Z and hopefully I could get the 'patriarchal' approval. The build up of stress and angst trying to keep up that front was to prove itself, over time, very damaging to my overall physical well being.

So long as Dick was keeping happy and busy doing his 'Shtick' everything should work out just fine. Saturday and Sunday were to be designated for visiting the families. Friday night we went out with the gang. Luckily my new girlfriend Stella was usually around. Here is a perfect example of Dick's mania of always wanting to go out or should I say never wanting to be home. Once I asked

"Could we please stay home this Friday and just relax and be quiet?" He answered

"Are you crazy nobody stays in on a Friday night."

I remember once I was so tired after teaching all day. I fell soundly asleep in my chair which was right beside the stage where the band was playing that night at the club. Stella kept an eye out on me and Dick woke me up when it was time to go home. I just didn't see the need to try and change anything. It was going to be too much of a hassle. I didn't like fights. I had enough of my mother's screaming when I was a kid. I had promised myself I would not have that in my own family. We had also paid our share for a bedroom at the ski chalet buddy Bill and the guys had leased for the winter season. Luckily I had only kicked in money for two months. We would drive up Friday evening and get back to the city Sunday night. One weekend I walked into our room which was on the first floor and as I went to turn down the bed spread I noticed it was covered in dried blood. Apparently one of the guys had, earlier in the week, come up to ski and had gotten into a bar fight late at night. He had lost obviously and was too loaded to find his own room so he crashed in ours. After that I made every excuse possible not to go there and I told Dick

"The hell with the money. That crowd was way out of my league."

There was always a party to go to in town or a club to go to. The couples were paired off and a lot more tame.

The New Year 1968 get together was spent with both our families at Dick's parents' place. We made the announcement of my pregnancy. My in-laws came out with a beautiful gold brooch to show me. It was a family heirloom and it was to be given to the first daughter in law who gave birth to a male heir, one to carry on the family name. 'No pressure right'. Actually I didn't get the point at all. I was not into gender bias. I thought girl or boy I didn't need a brooch. I shared that with my husband that very night. There better not be any expectations because I had no preferences. Neither did he. We were on the same page about ignoring parental input. As soon as I thought I had things figured out, then something else happened to throw me off balance. Early in the new year my husband announced that his sixteen year old sister was coming to live with us. His father had gotten a job in Ontario and his parents were moving out of Montreal in a couple of weeks. There were only six months left in the school year and it was the graduation year for his sister. She might as well stay with us, commute with Dick in the morning at least and take the train to visit with their parents on the weekends.

"But we are going to have a baby in May!" he answered

"It's OK my sister and the baby can share the den. We would even be able to have free babysitting when we go out."

I tell you the decision had already been made by his family. I really didn't have a say in the matter. I wondered if that was a 'German' way also. I did find out much later, through a European acquaintance, that the father is the dominant one as long as he is living. The daughter in law is usually relegated to the fringes within the family circle. If she is compliant, things will go well. If not, a cold reserve will exist. So I had left my family's large house of four to my new apartment of two and now to three and soon to be four. I just hadn't quite bargained for surprises. I thought I had heard someplace that married life was supposed to be stabilizing.

I worked until the Easter break, two weeks before due date. I was pretty proud because I was the first female teacher to be allowed to work in a state of 'pregnancy'. In the past, Catholic school teachers who were pregnant were expected to retire in the fourth month when the pregnancy was starting to be apparent. The regulation obviously had something to do with contributing to the delinquency of minors by suggesting sex had taken place! Who knows? Our baby was to be born in the first week of May. I went by the house and picked up my younger sister one afternoon and we drove to visit my Meme who was staying at my aunt's house. They were the first three with whom I shared that our baby was scheduled to be born the first week of May. She was not going to be premature. I didn't want anyone to worry about that kind of thing. Well my Meme stood up and gave me a big hug then we all stood up and snuggled. I was so happy to rid myself of the cloak of secrecy and share. Now all we women could get ready for the blessed event, in our special French Canadian way. On the way to my parents' house my sister and I dropped in to the store to buy some diapers. I was so excited to be buying something for my baby. My teaching colleagues had given me a shower before I left school. I needed very little.

I walked into my parents living room and sat them down and proceeded, beaming from ear to ear, to tell them my good news. I had no qualms at having postponed the announcement because after all Dick and I were both in our twenties and we both had full time jobs. We weren't kids and could do what we decided and not be subject to parental judgment. My mother was happy for me but my father didn't say anything. I excused myself to go to the bathroom and I heard him say

"Well once you fall of the Empire State building you can never pick yourself up again."

I, to this day, don't know what that meant. I can only surmise that he might have held me in high esteem and now that he found out I was pregnant when I got married he no longer felt the same way and never will. When I was looking at my reflection in the mirror I thought

"Frankly my dear I don't give a damn."

That isn't completely true. I had always been very dependent on my father's good opinion of me. But it was not to be, not this time anyways. I must say before he died he released me of any guilt or misgivings. As I was kissing him goodnight, he hugged my face and said

"You are a good girl, my Joe!"

Just like I was a little kid. But that's OK. Who knows he might not even have been lucid. What matters is my perception. I had finally been absolved of any wrongdoing, my confidence was restored. I was fifty five years old, my father was eighty five. He died five hours later.

On April 30th at 11 p.m, I was on my hands and knees washing the kitchen floor. My sister in law was watching the Jonny Carson show. My husband was not yet home. Where in the hell is he? I went to bed around midnight. I was really uncomfortable in bed. Every turn I took brought me just another ache. I started to feel really weird then realized I was having contractions. I tell you, the first time no one can actually describe to you that sensation. There were no pre-natal classes then or whatever. You just have to live it. Dick still had not come home. You'd think I would have gotten used to that by now. But this was really important. I shouldn't do this alone. At 2 a.m the door opens. I'm all cramped up and in a fetal position on the bed. I told him what was happening. He said we should wait a while. I said

"Well if you can stay up this late and stay awake, another couple of hours won't make that much difference. You are going to have to time these contractions and the time in between each and write them down. That's the man's job."

At 6 a.m my husband called Dr. Gordon who recommended we head out to the hospital. I got dressed and walked into the den. I woke up my sister in law and said

"The baby is coming now. You're on your own."

It was a beautiful morning. May is a fine month to deliver a child to this world. The daffodils and tulips, the lilies of the valley and the bleeding hearts are out and some of the lilacs are starting to blossom. The color green is becoming stronger and brighter every day. A city such as Montreal has winter for a minimum of five months. Spring is when everyone gets frisky. People hum when they walk. The short sleeve shirt is the dress code of the day. The mini skirt was in vogue and the ladies got to show off a lot of leg. I still remember both my daughters births as if it were last week. Imagine good family planning. Both girls were born three years and eight days apart from each other. Evidently in both cases the month of August proved to be a very fertile, productive month. I used to blame those hot August nights.

When we arrived at the hospital, a nurse escorted me to a ward. My husband was busy registering me at the front desk. It must have been overwhelming. He had not slept for twenty four hours and now a nun was giving him the third degree about health insurance coverage. Oh life can be so tough on some guys. Bite me! Dr. Gordon came by while doing rounds. He said I had a while to go. This was not going to happen soon but best that I be in the hospital. I know for sure with the hospital confines of today they probably would have sent me back home. I sent Dick to work. No point both of us waiting around. I was comfortable in a bed near a window, at the end of the ward. I was just going to have cat naps in between contractions. By noon my mother and my younger sister came by to visit. Mom was worried that I would be hungry since my last meal was supper the previous night. She brought a cup of coffee and a cookie for me. I appreciated the thought. My mother was glad Dick had called them regardless of my father's mood. She wanted to be here to help. OK! everybody is touchy, feely. Next thing you know I upchuck. The nurse comes in and reminds us that I am to have nothing to eat. This is hilarious, I see my sister and Mom sitting side by side in the corner. As I breathe in and out during the contractions they are doing the exact same thing as I. Inhale pause, exhale pause. What a riot! Dick came by twice during the afternoon to check. I had stopped contractions completely by 4 p.m. Oh God was I ever discouraged. The nurse said that if I don't begin again by evening Dr. Gordon was going to give me a shot to induce and that would kick start me up again hopefully. Well my child must have heard the news and decided to give it a renewed effort. In those days the gender of the children was not known to parents. The science had not gotten there as yet.

It was supper time and nothing was happening. Then all of a sudden this hurts like hell and of course I was alone. Luckily I didn't feel so frightened because I knew the nurses were coming in and out. Meals were being served to the rest of the ladies in the ward. By eight o'clock Dick was back to visit. The ward was filling up with visitors for the other young mothers. I could feel the excitement in the room. I could hear the voices and conversations of everyone. I felt totally out of it. I was not on any epidural. This was natural childbirth. I and my body had disconnected ourselves from the rest of the world. My child was doing her thing. I was merely the conduit. I did not make any noise. I remained quiet. I did not want to upset all the people in the room. I just know the sun was setting. Thank God Dr. Gordon is kneeling beside me and says

"We are going to take you out of here. Give you a bit of privacy. OK!" I said

"Oh please! What time is it?"

It was 8:45 pm. They wheeled me into an operating theater. Dr. Gordon put a mask on my face and said

"Start breathing."

I woke up later and felt pain in my bottom and opened my eyes. I looked down and there I could see the good doctor's head I yelled

"What are you doing down there?" he replied

"Just a couple of stitches to repair a little tearing. By the way you have a daughter."

We named her Marie. I was then switched to another bed and wheeled to a private room where Dick was waiting. I asked the nurse

"Where is my baby?" the nurse replied

"She is in the nursery at the end of this floor. You can go and see her anytime you want." I asked confused

"Shouldn't she be with me. She was just born." The nurse explained

"Since you have chosen not to nurse your baby, she will not be brought to you every three hours for feeding. We will take care of all bottle feeding in the nursery."

I guess I was so exhausted I stated to cry and then fell asleep for several hours. So I am proud I did experience natural childbirth but one thing I am ashamed of is that I did not breast feed my child or at least try for a few weeks. Why you wonder? Well this is the reason. This is why I'm embarrassed. In the last month or so of the pregnancy I had told my husband that

"I would really like to try to breast feed our baby. It's supposed to be very healthy and convenient." to which he replied without hesitation

"No! I do not want you breast feeding. THEY are mine!"

I cannot believe I obeyed. Yes! oh yes! in my marriage vows there was "love, honor and obey".

I visited my daughter at least ten times a day. My parents had come by one evening after having stopped by the nursery to take a peek at their first granddaughter and the first grandchild born in their vicinity. I did see them at the entrance of my room but they did not come in. There were many of our friends visiting at that time also. Can you imagine people were allowed to smoke cigarettes, in those days, even in hospitals. I overheard my father say loud enough for my benefit

"No point going in there now. They're throwing one of their usual parties."

I felt bad because I sure could have used a hug from my Dad at that time. The ice would have finally been broken. Instead the disappointment on his and my part just became greater. He was right, there was a celebration taking place. Dick and Jo were the first to have a baby (legitimate) in the gang. Five days later I was finally able to leave the hospital. In those days, as you can see, Medicare was very generous with hospital stays. My husband drove me home with our daughter in my arms. No infant car seat required in the back seat to transport babies. My biggest worry when I came home was

"Is this really our child? I never held her in the hospital! What if this was the wrong baby girl?"

There was only the plastic wrist tag with her official name on it that said that this girl child was ours to love and take care of.

Bear with me here. It is unfathomable to me, even now, to realize how inept I was at the family game. I hadn't even ordered a crib for the baby. Changing table? What's that? I wasn't materialistic but come on now. My girl needed a bed. So the moment we got into the apartment I put her down on our bed and got out the laundry clothes basket and layered it with a pillow and baby bed linen. She was swaddled so she didn't take up a lot of room. Her nineteen inches of burning love fit in beautifully. At night the basket was placed on top of the dresser. Her new place of repose was turquoise and had white handles. (I'm looking at the picture right now as I write. I'm smiling). That was very convenient actually because I was able to carry her to and from each room in the apartment. If I was in the kitchen she was sleeping on the dining room table. If I was in the living room ironing she was sleeping on the coffee table. My sister in law moved to Ontario, where her parents were, in late June. My mother ordered a crib, a small dresser and a changing table for the den as a gift to her new granddaughter and Sears delivered the next day. Regardless of whatever animosity I might have felt towards my mother I can honestly say she was a tremendous help to me. She came everyday for the first week Marie and I were home. I was clueless!

Marie was a very good baby. She slept for four hours at a time, then had a bottle of formula in about twenty five minutes and two good burps. The first night she was home I stayed awake most of the night waiting for her to wake up needing me. I hadn't quite learned that when a baby really wants something they yell loud enough that they whole neighborhood can hear them. Dick was in charge of making six bottles of formula every morning. He was very diligent in that job. Mornings he could be counted on. It was useless to have any expectations for night help. He wasn't home. The changing of the diapers was a 'woman's job'. When I would first ask he would always answer
"What's in it?"
My mom arrived at 9:45 proceeded to undress the baby and give her a bath in the bathroom sink. She would suggest that I try but I declined. I was too frightened that, in her slippery state, I might drop her. The second week my mother said I was in charge. The first bath I gave my daughter was sheer terror. She screamed through the whole thing. She probably felt my hopelessness. When it came to her face I couldn't remember if my mom had washed her eyes or not. Do babies' eyes need to be washed? I never cut her nails. I used to, carefully, bite them off. In a previous life I must have been from a tribe in New Guinea. My daughter and I became good companions. Those evenings that Dick was home were often not to his liking. I always used to brag to him about how great the baby was. I don't know why she chose 7pm to 8:30 pm to be her fussy time? It was always during the 'Jeopardy' show that she would screech. He would say every time.
"Why do you always tell me she is such a good baby? You call this good. All she does is scream for an hour and you jump up and down like a Yo Yo."
I preferred the days. My daughter and I would go for long walks along the lakeshore. I had great company. Talking to a baby is different than talking to yourself. Although they cannot answer back at least they seem to be listening. My daughter helped me fill a huge void. I was becoming lonely. Out of boredom, while she was napping, I even took up ironing all the cloth diapers and bed linen. I had never developed those hand craft hobbies women acquire. I was the only one with a child now. It seemed I was out of the loop.

My mother brought my Meme to meet her great granddaughter. What a memorable moment in my life. I have the picture of the four generations of females on my mother's side. Marie was my mom's little doll. Luckily for us mom was always buying clothes for her and getting her all prettied up. When she was five she even had her in a fashion show. What a real cutie pie! Everyone that could got to meet our daughter. Dick's brother and wife drove up from Pennsylvania in the summer. His older sister and family flew in from British Columbia that Christmas. We would all meet at my in-laws house which was only an hour and a half drive. Even Dick's buddy Bill came to check her out. He took a look in the crib then as he was leaving the room he left a dime on the dresser and said

"This is for your girl. Save it for her and when she's eighteen have her give me a call."

He was such a jerk. Always had to make a disrespectful wise crack about everything. I answered back

"Over my dead body!!"

The only person who had not yet met my girl was her grandfather, my father. I can just imagine the conversations between my parents. Then again I just realized that probably nothing was discussed. That was the way everything was dealt with. Remember the wall of silence. My father set out the edict, my mother followed through. She was allowed to do what was needed to help but keep him out of it. It had to be early August. It was a beautiful Saturday but it was hot and muggy. I don't know where my husband was, maybe golfing? I knew my parents would be at the yacht club which was just a twenty minute walk from where we lived. They always came back from an afternoon cruise up the lake in time to join friends for cocktails and BBQ dinner. I pushed the stroller on the gravel road passing several moored boats and gave, those that I knew, a wave.

I got to my father's boat slip. He and my mother and four others were on the dock sipping something. I yelled

"Hey Dad! hey Mom! Thought I'd join you for a cocktail"

Not a word was said. Then Auntie Minn, a family friend and fellow boat owner said

"What's that in the carriage?" I proudly answered

"It's my new daughter!"

Well that woman shot out of her chair along with her husband and my mother and came to see my beautiful child who was already three months old. They were all so excited. My mom was having fun telling Minn all about her stories with her granddaughter. Then my father got up and came to the carriage. I picked up my girl and gave him his granddaughter to hold in his arms. We all walked down to the dock and the ladies got to pass the baby around. They hadn't seen someone that small in decades. Dad poured me a coke and we all got along just fine, all comfy, cozy like bugs in a rug. Boy! were we ever well trained in sustaining and maintaining family image. I left at dusk and my girl fell asleep on the way back home. I got to put her to bed without waking her. Thank you Lord that was all behind me. My child was finally 'out of the closet'. No more stepping on eggshells for me, well about this anyways. My husband was not home yet, not back from his golf day.

"It's dark out now! Well it's not like I'm alone on a Saturday night, after all my daughter is here. Right!"

Dick was great with all of my relatives on both sides. He always took us to visit my aunts and my Meme and my dad's sisters. He drove us to Pins Rouges so that Meme and I could show off our new girl to her sisters, which would make them the child's great-great aunts. We French Canadians were always very proud of our lineage. It's amazing that all of them were, though in their mid 80's, still very spry. Dick always helped fix little things around their houses. Everyone loved to play cards and the men drank a lot of beer. My aunt Mado loved him because her first serious love was Canadian but from German parentage. You see I say that because Canadians then as now have always had some relatives from someplace else. Her man was an aviator in the RCAF (Royal Canadian Air Force)who unfortunately was shot down in the second world war by Germans, no less. My Meme, half way through the evening, would look at me and say about my husband,

"Celui la! c'est un vraie chanteur de pommes" which means a charmer who passes out a lot of compliments but is not sincere. You know the saying 'from the mouths of babes' well there should be a saying for the elders and their sage advice. At the time I thought it was so cool that he got along with everybody. It was a couple of years after we were legally separated that my husband told me he thought of himself as a 'chameleon'.

"I am whatever I have to be, given the people I'm with, or the circumstance I'm in." When I was a young woman I used to say

"Will the real Dick please stand up."

To this day, even after having lived with him for forty years, I really never knew him. That is obviously just the way he wanted it.

Just about every weekend there was a party. I was one of eight young mothers in our building. We got together at the park or in our apartments or at the swimming pool. We would commiserate about the joys and pitfalls of parenthood and marriage. We all took turns having a party. Sometimes some different wife with a different husband or visa versa would sneak out and come back later. Everybody minded their own business. At least those nights I didn't have to worry about drunken driving. There were parties at our place but I only invited those tamer members of the gang. When my best buddy Stella married Murray and moved to the USA I was totally lost. We were the only ones with our own apartment so that meant we all didn't have to go out and spend as much money in a club. Dick and I would take the baby to his parents in Cornwall for an overnight visit. They were the official baby sitters. We would throw a party Saturday and go pick our daughter up Sunday morning and get back in time for cocktails at my parents house. There were two instances that really made me so angry. Dick was supposed to be picking up his sister on a Friday afternoon and we were all supposed to go to his parents' the next day. He got in at 1 a.m without his sister. I was sleepy and confused. I asked

"Where is your sister?"

"She's still at the party. I had to come home so I left her there with my friend Trash. She was having a good time and said it was OK!"

"Are you crazy? She's sixteen years old. She is in our care. How could you leave her alone? Surely you could have made her come home" he said

"What for? She is safe with Trash. It's not like she's going to tell my parents she stayed at a party and didn't come home. You sure as hell are not going to tell them either. Anyways you and I can now be alone."

"Now I know you are crazy!"

I went in the den and crawled into my sister in law's bed beside my baby's crib and waited for her to wake for a feeding at 2 a.m. It was so irresponsible. It was the next incident that really opened my eyes for the first time to that major and so controversial flaw. You see in my day we didn't have what is referred to today as 'deal breakers'. The philosophy then was, in my family at least

"You made your bed, you lie in it".

I was on my own now, baby and me makes two, not three. Dick's life had hardly skipped a beat. The going out on Friday night was still in full swing. The only difference was that I could not participate most of the time because I was not told or that it was the kind of action I would have probably frowned upon. This incident happened probably in July of the following year. Dick's sister was definitely no longer with us. My daughter and I are sound asleep and I am startled awake by the phone ringing. That has to be the most frightening noise on earth. It was Dick. The time was 2:30 a.m. His words were slurred

"Come and get me. I'm downtown in a phone booth and I can't find my car."

He was so drunk I could hardly make out what he was saying. A cab drive from downtown Montreal to LaSalle would be about $30.00. The guy was so loaded he didn't even realize that I did not have a vehicle to go and get him in anyways. He had the only car and now he had misplaced his company car. I told him all of this and added

"Call whoever you were with and tell them to go and get you and do not come here tonight."

I hung up and ran to the bathroom and puked. The next morning at 11 a.m. Bill calls and says Dick was found sitting on the floor of the phone booth. He had spent the night at their place. Could he bring him home now? They arrived at 1pm. I answered the door and told Bill he needn't stick around. I closed the door.

Luckily our girl was napping. I told Dick

"Sit down, take off your glasses"

He did so. Then I took my fist and with all the power I prayed God could give me I hit the man in the face and gave him a bloody nose. Yes by God you can cheer for me now! I said

"Do not ever do this to me again".

He never said a word. I went to sit on the couch to read my book. He got up and went to the bathroom. When Marie awoke, we took her for a walk down the lakeshore road. He never apologized ever. He never did that again but rest assured Dick tried many firsts with me, several times over. It's very sad that I had no recourse even in those days. I was so ashamed. I couldn't confide in anyone. Was I going to admit after only eighteen months of marriage that everyone had been right and I had been wrong? Oh gosh, NO! NO! NO! It was much too early yet. Surely this could be fixed. It was after all still an adjustment period and I so loved him. Everything would be OK!

On another occasion, Dick had come home very late claiming he had been at a car show and announced
"It was time to have another child."
I was, in all honesty, not ready for that prospect. I was just getting used to the rhythm of one child. My daughter was toilet trained and easy to travel with. Other than her still being dependent on the 'blanky' and the pacifier having to be placed in her mouth every two hours during the night, things were going very well. By the way while we are on the subject. I ruined my first and now that I think about it my second daughter's teeth (another chapter)by the time she was three. Our dentist said she had just about as many cavities as she had teeth. Slight exaggeration but he was always very theatrical. You see, and don't do this ever, I used to put jam on her pacifier so she wouldn't wake me at night. This was a very expensive mistake I was accountable for. I feel so rotten because here I was terrified of the dentist yet putting my girl through all of this. I have to tell you though. She was a real trooper, a lot stronger than I was. That's for sure.
Back to planning for a second baby. I was, subconsciously, frightened to bring another child into our family. My rationale was as follows
"If I am the only one to take care of one child then how can I be able to take care of two? Dick is hardly ever home. What if I decide I need to go back to work again? Let's be frank! That total confidence I had the day I got married was definitely waning." I asked him
"Why do you want another child? You're hardly involved with our daughter's care." He answered
"Marie's care is your fulltime job. You are the mother. Anyways a child needs a brother or a sister to play with. We don't have to have the new baby immediately. Just go off the pill and we'll see what happens and when."
Two months later I was pregnant. I was really OK with it and very proud we could make another human being. I can only explain my feeling in this manner.
"The beauty and the power of the body to actually be able to create this miracle has always been magical to me."

Perhaps the fact that I never had 'morning sickness' and had an easy first pregnancy and birthing made it easier on me to be accepting. The fun of having this second child was getting ready in full view of a receptive and hopeful family. There was no way we could continue to live in a two bedroom apartment. That is we could have but I wouldn't. Dick the 'provider' just had to dig into his deep pockets because I the mother was not going to put up with anything less than a bedroom for each of my children. If I was going to stay home and raise my family then by God we were going to have space. My mother got involved from the ground up. She was very familiar with the goings on of her community. She was able to find us an upper duplex flat that was at least 1100 sq. ft. It had 3 bedrooms, dining area and even a large den which we could convert into a children's playroom. The building was right behind hers. We were able to talk to each other from our upper balconies in the back yard. Was it too close for comfort? No not really. My dad was working every day and my mother had her volunteer activities and they travelled a great deal. The chances of their just popping over were non existing. They were pretty formal in that regard.

Dick was home the night that our second child was arriving. So it had to be a Saturday or a Sunday night. We were laying on the coach fooling around and I said

"Oh Lord this is definitely not an orgasm!"

Within the hour we had called the babysitter and the doctor. I was in the hospital in seven minutes. Since I can remember, we were always fortunate to live within even walking distance to a hospital. This was a different hospital. The first was born in a French Catholic hospital run by a religious order and the second was a secular hospital. Imagine all in the same town with a population of 100,000. That would be unheard of today. In fact the two facilities in my home town have now been converted to retirement residences for the elderly. Interesting the demographic changes in one's life. Quebec had become an aging population where each family had five to six siblings and on the opposite side of the spectrum a less than 1.5 family birth rate in the last forty years. I was on the bed on my side and Dick was in the corner of the room reading his sci-fi novel. The nurse had come in and was washing my face with a cold compress. After she left I grabbed the cold wet cloth and threw it at Dick's head. I yelled

"Do you think you could tear yourself away from the book and be of some help?" He stood up and walked over and said

"What do you want me to do?"

"How about rubbing my back which is killing me and holding my hand and talking to me. Bring over a chair. Connect!"

Everything, relating to togetherness, seemed to be such a chore. An epidural was administered an hour before the baby was born. I was wheeled into the delivery room. There was a mirror suspended to the ceiling and I was able to see my baby's head crowning. I was totally grossed out. The nurse seemed to be pinching the sides of my vulva. I asked

"What are you doing?" to which she replied

"The doctor has not arrived yet and the baby is ready so we have to slow it down, by tightening up the opening."

Well, now, I really feel bad for that little Philippine nurse who was standing on my right side wiping my forehead. I had my arm around her waist and in the next contraction, slid my right hand down to her buttock and squeezed so hard she had tears in her eyes. I looked up at her and asked

"Have you ever given birth?" She said "NO!"

"This hurts like hell. The epidural has stopped working. Now let my baby be born!"

The doctor arrived just in time. He scolded me for having interrupted his breakfast and being so hard on the nurses. OOPS! there is my new baby girl. It took only six hours. We called her Trudie. This time I was able to bottle feed my girl. One nurse really pissed me off. She said the baby kept upchucking her night feedings and that I would have to bring in our own baby clothes because my daughter had used up all her quota for the stay. So we did. I was thoroughly insulted that the nurse deemed it correct to complain about my child.

"Who does she think she is?"

We did get home after four days. I was really happy because my father had come over to the duplex to visit with Kelly the afternoon she arrived. I can honestly say I was such an amateur even with a second child. She would wake every three hours and I would let her cry for an hour and then feed her. My first child only needed to be fed every four hours and I had been told, by my German in-laws, that I had spoiled the first daughter by picking her up too often when she whimpered. Crying was good for the baby. Naturally by the time Trudie completed her bottle she had been so ravenous and had drunk so quickly that she would, when burped, do a volatile vomit routine that could scare even the most seasoned parent. I mentioned this problem to old Dr. Gordon at the first check up. He said well by golly

"She is starving. Each and every baby is different. So if she wakes just feed her, never mind the time. Do not let her get into a frenzy."

She never woke up at night for a pacifier, what a relief! Instead she would have a way of flipping onto her belly and got her knees tucked under and rocked herself to the sound of her own mantra. I could hear the crib movement. There were times we couldn't get her bedroom door open in the morning. She had managed to rock hard enough to move the crib partially up against the door.

There was an accident that I, to this day, have not forgiven myself for. The TV was on, an afternoon soap was playing. I had Trudie who, at the time, was about eighteen moths old at the bottom of the inside stairway. I was teaching her how to climb up. I turned around, went into the family room to turn off the set. I heard the most horrific howl in my life. My daughter was sprawled at the bottom of the stairs covered in blood. The stairs were made of ceramic tile, a very hard surface. She must have tried to practice on her own and lost her balance. That took place in less than three minutes. I picked her up, ran to the phone to get my babysitter over, ripped the curlers out of my hair and called a taxi. My baby's main injuries were across the face, cheeks, forehead and in the mouth. As a result of the impact, her upper teeth had been shoved right back into her gums. I have a pain in my heart just reliving the scene now. The doctors in emergency confirmed there were no broken facial bones. She would be black and blue for weeks and it would appear like she had been beaten. The dentist was seen the following day. What torture to see the damage done to my girl because of my momentary neglect. The huge ache in my heart and conscience were definitely my punishment to bear. He confirmed that it was best to do nothing and the teeth would grow back out in due course. I was married and had the luxury of being able to stay home and take care of our children and we were being provided for more than adequately. My heart felt sentiments and encouragement go out to all the parents out there. I know how hard it is to rear children. I remember clearly as if it were yesterday. The girls had awakened from their naps. Both were in surly moods. I was obviously in one also. I know I wasn't doing anything important. Trudie was bawling. Marie was whining and complaining about God knows what? I just lost it. I felt my fist clench and walked to the children's rooms. I looked in and yelled at each one. I then turned around went to the fridge. I got a cup of juice for one and a bottle for the other. I put one in the crib and one on the night table and told the eldest

"Do not come out of your room."

I slammed their doors then walked right to my bedroom. I opened the closet door and crawled into the closet and settled in the back behind our clothes. That is where my husband found me three hours later. Luckily, he had come home early this day. He walked in, called for me, no answer. Marie opened her bedroom door and they looked for me until I called back to them. I was totally out of it. I wish I could say things were calming down. I guess you could say they were. Either that or I was getting used to the set up. Resignation can be a pretty potent sedative.

My faith as a Catholic, I should correct that and say my loyalty to the Catholic Church was tested, not my Christian faith. I wanted to have our second child baptized. She was just over one year old. I got in touch with our local parish and was interviewed by a priest. We got into a formal debate about my beliefs on let's say for argument sake 'the Immaculate Conception', the 'Papacy' oh let's not forget 'Celibacy'. Topics that were for ages highly contentious. They are decreed and not open to debate. I did not pass the screening. I was deemed, in the opinion of that priest, not eligible to have my child baptized because I would not be able to provide her with the mentoring she would need to grow up as a good Catholic. I would have to become actively involved. That is receive the sacrament of penance and attend Mass every Sunday. I said, politely

"I don't think Jesus Christ would have withheld grace from an innocent child created in the image of God because of the sins of the mother."

To which the 'holy' man replied. Call us when you are ready to comply. I went to my father's house to visit to explain everything to him. I was so indignant. He said if that was the least I had to do to get her baptized, than so be it. It took me a month to get over the snub and finally comply. My father even came to the church with me to ensure I did go ahead with the priestly directives. Together, we called on the priest the following afternoon and my father was witness. We then scheduled Trudie's baptism for the spring. I only went to Mass with them when they started French, Catholic school until when they graduated high school. In university they could make their own decisions.

There were other times when I truly found myself inadequate as a mother. Late one afternoon, the oldest had a fever and I decided to check how much. I slipped the thermometer in her mouth and a couple of minutes later went to check. The thermometer had broken in her mouth and she was bleeding. I had used a rectal one and now there was mercury in her body. I freaked out. I called the Poison Control Center. A person explained that the amount was negligible but to watch for specific symptoms and if found, proceed to the hospital. I remember now why I was distracted. I was having my Aunt Muriel and my parents over for dinner. Oh my Lord! I called them up and said I had to cancel and why. My father said not to worry they would take my auntie out. Luckily there was no damage, no glass in her mouth. Everything probably came out the 'dirt shoot' the next day, anyways. As usual I felt super guilty. Another instance was when the same daughter had pin worms. Yuck! She would wake up several nights in a row and complained about pain in her bum. Finally I did check and here were miniscule white worms wiggling out. I was so disgusted. I gave her a bath that night and changed the bed linen. We did not have internet at that time so out came the huge, heavy Readers' Digest medical dictionary. I stayed with her the rest of the night. She fell asleep calmly. The following morning I got an appointment with the pediatrician who after examination explained that these are quite common in small children and are usually as a result of playing in sandboxes or dirt that cats might have used in the past as litter boxes. The condition can easily be cleared with antibiotics. The biggest problem is that these worms when out of the rectum can travel by air and lay eggs everywhere in the house such as in clothing, lamp shades, curtains. The clothing of every family member and the linens were to be sterilized. The whole house washed down with a strong disinfectant. The medicine got rid of the problem and my daughter never had worms again. I told my husband the bad news that night and he proceeded to rave and rant about
"What a bad housekeeper I was, that I could leave a place so dirty that worms could infect our daughters!"
He must have missed the part about kids being in places where cats were using sand boxes as litter boxes. I took it all in. I felt guilty enough, why not accept more flogging. I was left with the daunting task of getting

this place cleaned up to the best of my ability alone of course without the help of my spouse.

I think back now and it makes me sad because I know I was far from the best Mom. Taking care of children is the most demanding, physically and emotionally, job in the world. There is no trial run for family life. There was a famous pediatrician, by the name of Dr. Spock, in the 60s and 70s who sold millions of books. His writings were our guide lines. Prior to committing suicide, much later in his life, he left a letter apologizing to the world for having misguided a whole generation of people. I know for sure that I am the kind of person that prefers toddlers to infants. I don't deny that. I find infants so needy and although I take really good care of them on all levels I feel disconnected from them. I love kids when they become little humans. My oldest sister is the opposite. She used to say

"As soon as they can talk I develop a dislike for kids. They always have to argue."

I know so many women, just like my two beautiful daughters now, working so hard at both home and outside jobs and trying to meet all the needs of their children and trying to sustain a marriage and say to myself

"Boy am I ever glad I'm all done."

I know from serious past experience that we women

"Cannot have it all".

Something has got to give. Are we loosing a bit of ourselves or a bit of our children? Some might suggest that our generation of woman had to sacrifice so much. I disagree. Firstly, taking care of our kids and postponing our outside of the home contributions was not a sacrifice. It was a job that we did most of the time willingly and at times begrudgingly. So what else is new about any job! I just know for sure that even the outcome, our children now adults, isn't sometimes at all what we expected. There in lies the mystery. The elastic band called womanhood can only be stretched so far. The willingness to try and seek out the positive in all aspects of our lives is critical. This can be passed on to the children. It's a form of osmosis. I have always maintained that I can look myself in the mirror and tell myself.

"I did do my very best as a mother." I'm OK with that.

Life was indeed changing. Maybe someone had talked to Dick and suggested that with two children more active participation was required by the father. He even got home every Tuesday at 6 p.m so that I could use the car and get downtown to my pro bono tutoring sessions at a Montreal juvenile detention center. My buddy Carol had gotten me to sign up to tutor for the French lesson. Carol was a really active single person. She might have been thought by some as being somewhat totally guy crazy and she was but she more than compensated by being very generous in a volunteer capacity. Now working in an institution lock down facility with a hundred adolescent males can be pretty scary. This was the home of male delinquents who had committed crimes of some kind or another. They had become family, biological or foster, rejects. They were signed off by the parents into the custody of social services. They lived in a building where they were provided the basic staples of life, food and a roof over their heads. They all left in the morning to schools within walking distance. If they didn't show up the police went after them. They each had their own room but it was locked from the outside after 10 p.m. The reason was that personal belongings were always being stolen by each other from one another. Carol and I always went in together. We were let in at the front door, after identifying ourselves. We were only allowed in a couple of classrooms or in the public rooms. We would walk in the room where some boys were shooting pool and be given a look that would make the short hairs on the back of my neck stand up. The sneer could best be defined as predatory. The young man I was tutoring was almost eighteen years old. He would be out soon but in the meantime he still had to pass a high school French exam. I had experience with tough guys in my grade nine class but this was different. This fellow was six feet tall and big. He had a chip on his shoulder the size of an oak tree. He didn't give a damn either way and let me know without any reservation that "I was wasting my time". I went there every week for nine months. I went over his school lessons every time, just enough for him to be able to get by. I was even able to get copies from a former colleague of the type of provincial exam that had been given in the past. I met him the final night and I thought he was ready enough. The following night I called the facility and asked permission to speak to him. It was granted. I was pretty excited and asked

"How did you do?"

"I didn't" he answered

"What do you mean?"

Yes you guessed it. He never showed up for the exam. I hung up the receiver slowly. There was no point trying to prove anything.

He had warned me. He was going to be thrown out of school in three weeks anyways and off assisted services two months after that. He was going to be eighteen and nobody could touch him. I wonder if he is in a penitentiary, maybe here in my home town. At least he had been polite enough not to tell me to

"go F . . . myself".

That was the end of my tutoring career. I don't regret the experience. I did get out of the house once a week and tried to do a good deed. You know some people like to win. I was always of the philosophy that at least trying to the best of my ability was just as good as winning. That way, I never felt that I was a looser. At least in my mind, I did get that satisfaction of having contributed something.

"Because at the end, all that really matters is, how you perceive yourself!"

The fifth wedding anniversary was a memorable event. It sets another layer to this relationship of ours that I could best describe as a 'Rubics' cube.

There were a lot less parties to go to, anymore. The apartment building crowd had phased out. People were buying houses in the new subdivisions in suburbia. Most families were getting larger and let's face it a lot of them were also maturing. In retrospect, I think we could have been considered by many as undesirables. I can definitely see why. One Saturday, Dick and three other men had a golf date. The wives had met late in the afternoon at our place. All the children were in their respective homes with babysitters. It was supposed to be a couples only get together to help everyone catch up. The men got back and I served a buffet. The evening seemed to be going OK. The conversation began to get serious. Politics and the war in Vietnam were the topics. Dick mentioned a rally downtown on the following weekend and asked if anyone was going to go and join the protest. One fellow said

"What the USA does is none of our business. Who cares anyway?"

Well that set Dick off and a loud argument ensued between the two of them. We all tried to distract the guys but to no avail. Dick called the guy an 'A hole' and told him to leave. Then another couple left also. There was only Maureen and Perry left. So we all poured ourselves another drink and the rest of the night went off without incident. I didn't care either way. Those kinds of people were just acquaintances, no great loss. I certainly was not going to call on Monday and apologize. Easy come, easy go! Maureen and Perry became our best couple friends. We did alternating Saturday visit at each others' homes. The men played golf. The moms took the kids to the mall or the petting zoo or a local farm or carnival. The men got back in time for the BBQ. Then it was cards and eventually the sleeping kids were packed back into the station wagon and deposited into their own beds. I never missed my husband those times because Maureen and I could keep each other company. I know, for sure, my husband preferred the company of his new buddy. Everyone got along really well.

It was much later in my life that I noticed that so many couples always hung out with another couple. For instance even in a car, the men sat together in the front and the ladies sat together in the back. In a restaurant the same gender sat side by each and carried on conversations with each other. It appeared to me that the men and the women were, willingly, excluded from each other even though they occupied the same physical space. The husbands and the wives were together but not really together. Maybe I would still be married today if I complied with that kind of arrangement. I doubt it because much later I couldn't find any couples that I would consider myself compatible with. If there had been any functions where couples were invited, my husband never extended that invitation to me. When my husband and I went out for dinner I used to watch older couples and I always said

"Look at that couple over there, they haven't said a word to each other since they got here. The only conversation they have is with the waiter. The day we are ever silent to each other is when we can call it quits."

My husband would say

"Mind your own business. Why do you have to snoop on everybody?"

The last ten years of our marriage we rarely went out for dinner, maybe twice a year. We, undoubtedly, would have been silent because we were that way at home.

The plan for the celebration of our fifth anniversary was to go to dinner and dancing at the Montreal Playboy club. The men each had their companies' membership card. That was a big deal in those days. The men would take clients to the Club for a liquid lunch and to check out the Playboy bunnies' boobs and butts. The five children were to be babysat by our very competent, neighbor's daughter, at our duplex. We had a blast! The dinner was delicious and the show hilarious. We danced until two in the morning. I was totally wiped out. The four of us left the club, arm in arm, in a super good mood. We crossed the street to the parking lot. Perry paid his bill and he and his wife walked to their car. When my husband came to pay his parking ticket he had a fit. He started to scream at the attendant who was sitting in the booth.

"I've only been here for five hours man. I'm not buying the 'G.D'. parking lot. Go F . . . yourself I'm not paying this!"

I tried to calm him down. I got my wallet out to pay and my husband tore it out of my hand and threw it across the lot. I ran to get it while he was unlocking our car. I got into the passenger's side. Dick put the car into drive and plowed right into the booth. I jumped out of the car and ran to the attendant to check on him. The guy said

"Don't worry I just called the police. They're on their way."

"OH SHIT!"

Here comes Dick again. He hit the booth again, this time knocking it over. He then backed up and sped out of the parking lot. Perry and Maureen pulled in beside me and picked me up. We drove for ten minutes through downtown trying to find my husband. I was so disgusted I said

"The hell with this. Let's go home. We have kids to take care of!"

We got back to our place. All was quiet. We paid the babysitter and our friends took their kids home. Perry, before leaving, asked

"Are you going to be OK? Do you want one of us to stay with you? Call us as soon as you get any news."

I went to bed and started to cry. I finally fell asleep exhausted and the girls were up chipper as ever at 7:30 a.m. I never did get a call. I honestly did not know whether my husband was alive or dead. What is really sad about this scenario is that I was really worried and I really cared.

"Why doesn't he call?"

What a terrible anniversary! I truly felt lost.

Dick got home at 1 p.m. The first thing he wanted to do was have a shower because he had been stuck in a cell with four stinking thugs all night long. He would tell me all about it when he got out. We never did get to talk because my aunts were arriving, that afternoon, to visit with the children. I opened the bathroom door and handed my husband a towel. He walked out, down the hallway, and apologized to the ladies for running a bit behind. I was so happy to have company. I loved my aunties so much. We all got together in the kitchen and they both had a daughter on their laps and were having grand conversations while I prepared sandwiches and tea. Dick came in being his charming self, as usual. He opened the fridge and got himself a beer. Good Lord my heart is actually hurting, no kidding, right now as I relive this. I just know for sure that some kinds of love can be so overwhelming that one's soul can indeed suffocate. Having to conceal everything hurtful for the sake of appearances is so detrimental to the psyche. People should be held accountable for their wrongdoings. I just didn't know how that was to happen. I was not earning any money. I was totally dependent. I was ashamed. What is a woman to do? I can just hear his voice now

"Just put up and shut up!"

You have to remember that I only had one example of marriage and that was of my parents. I know my mother had pulled a lot of 'bone head' stunts and yet my father always seemed to be very forgiving. Those matters were not to be discussed. Even when we were adult women if my sisters or I brought up any subject what was less than favorable about our mother, my father would say

"That was a long time ago."

I never pried into the final outcome of my anniversary night. Dick did tell me that the cops pulled him over after getting the license plate number from the attendant and brought him to a police station. He called his boss who then called the company lawyer who was going to represent him at a hearing to be held during the week. The charge was drunk and disorderly and property damage. Back in 1972, in the province of Quebec, there still were no DUI laws put into effect. No big deal! He didn't seem to feel any regret or guilt. Life continued as per usual.

The trip from hell can be best described as a Winnebago road trip in the dead of winter. That is a huge recreation vehicle, in case anyone is interested. As previously mentioned my dad, every other year, liked to take his family on a trip such as New York city or Washington D.C. and the Maine sea shore. Thinking back I guess he never understood that we women and my mother did not get along. This togetherness bull was really hard on us. He wanted all of us to go to Illinois to spend Christmas at my older sister's house. The whole family along with all the grandchildren were going to be assembled. He was going to make all the arrangements. He was to pick up the RV in the east end of Montreal in the late afternoon on the Friday. We would leave right after supper and drive to Toronto where we would pick up my younger sister, my brother in law and their baby son. From there it should only take another twelve hours and we will have arrived in time for brunch. Well I guess that would be feasible in spring, fall or summer. The morning we were to leave a blizzard was raging. My father had to maneuver this monster machine in about six inches of snow from the east end of Montreal to the west end. What would normally take an hour and forty minutes took three hours. He was undaunted. Our departure was delayed. The kids and I had supper but Dick still hadn't arrived and as usual no phone call. All I kept thinking was

"Oh! for the love of God, not tonight of all nights."

He got in at 8 p.m. He was so excited because he had gotten a $50.00 a week raise and had stopped into the liquor store to pick up a bottle of champagne to celebrate. All I kept saying was

"Hurry up we are so late. My parents are waiting for us."

Needless to say he was really ticked off because I was not showing the required appreciation for his good news. Off we went to Toronto, my husband pissed off with me instead of the other way around, my father angry because of the delay we caused and a powerful northern storm already dumping close to a foot of snow. We were at the front of my younger sister's house by 2 a.m. The Montrealers stopped in for a quick whiz. The Torontonians climbed aboard. My sister and I and our children settled on the large back bunk. Her son was six months old, my daughters were a year and a half and four years old. The two sons in law sat on the passengers front bench and kept my father company. More likely to keep him awake, that is. My mother was sitting at the fold out table sipping her sherry. Their Schnauzer dog was stretched out beside her. That dog was probably the most comfortable of all of us. The snow just never abated. As we arrived at Customs USA, my father side swiped the column that separated the lanes. He tore off the driver's side view mirror. My husband had brought his trusted tool box, just in case. With some duct tape and a twisted hanger he managed to secure the driver's side mirror. Dick was the best 'Mr. Fix It' that ever was. Now the brothers in law were getting a little bit nervous about the 'old man'. So a conference call with the daughters was called at the back of the vehicle.

"He's been driving for six hours and won't give up the wheel. It's pitch black out here in no man's land and we think his eyesight can't be all that good. He did hit that column and that place was flooded with lights."

My sister and I whispered

"Hell we can't talk to him. He wouldn't listened to us. We're girls to him. You guys convince him you are bored and want to take turns driving."

The next pit stop my father obliged. At least he got a bit of rest before taking over again as we were entering my older sister's home town. He wanted to be the one pulling up the drive way.

My dear sister was thrilled. It wasn't long before the tension started to build. You could hear the hissing of that pressure cooker valve. My older sister's husband was a gracious host but you could tell the invasion was wearing on him. He scolded me one morning at breakfast by saying

"Why don't you make your kids eat the crust on their toast? Don't you know how wasteful that is?" to which I replied

"Because I save their crust for me. That is my breakfast!"

Then there was our mother who continued to get inebriated. That is one way to get through a family reunion. My older sister's three year old son bit my father in the leg enough to draw blood. To which my dad exclaimed

"What's wrong with that boy?"

The six year old son cried on Christmas morning because he no longer believed in Santa Claus. He said he was sorry for all those years before when he never said thank you to anyone for all those great presents he got. What a sensitive child! Then my older daughter asked

"What? There is no Santa Claus? That's a lie!"

My family got all dressed up for dinner. The men even had jacket and tie. A neighbor came by to take a picture of the whole family. Oh what a party! My older sister outdid herself with a fantastic meal. She is still a gourmet cook. The children were finally put to bed. All should have been quiet. No such luck! We were having a liqueur in the atrium and my mother decided it was time to pack up the van. She didn't want to be stuck doing it in the morning. My younger sister ignored her. I stood up to head down the hallway. My husband barked

"SIT DOWN!"

So back and forth my mother who was loaded and my husband who was loaded decided to go at it by yelling at me to

"Get all the stuff ready to pack the van" or

"Sit down, you're not her slave. We'll do it when we are good and ready."

Here I am torn between the two people, both alcoholics, who could wound me the most. This scene is still a puzzle to me even to this day. What power did my mother and my husband have that made me try to comply? Was I so afraid of public confrontation or it's aftermath that I willingly dwarfed myself. I deferred to a higher power. I assumed my dad would take control of this ridiculous scenario. After all wasn't he the head of the family? My father never said a word. I had tears in my eyes. My younger sister's husband got up and said to all of us.

"Party is over. Let's get packing."

No one spoke until the following morning at 6:30 a.m. The adults had a coffee. The kids had cereal. We said goodbye and thank you and everyone got a hug. Then the Canadians, three children under the age of four, one dog, three women and three men boarded the Winnebago for the sixteen hour trip home. My younger sister and I never, as long as our dad was alive, had the nerve to tell him that trip had been sheer torture. Oh well! he did have the best of intentions and was very proud of his present to us all.

The duplex was a fine home for our indoor living. As the girls were getting more and more active, the outdoor space proved to be awkward. We shared a backyard with the downstairs neighbors and had converted the side yard into a private patio site for meals and so on. The folks downstairs were good people. The family consisted of an older couple with a daughter who had a child of about four years old. The man and the daughter went to work every day and the grandmother took care of the house and the little girl. Already the social norms were changing and unwed mothers were no longer prejudiced against. You note I use the term 'unwed mother' that was to remind the young woman that she had sex outside of marriage, as if she needed reminders. HA! At least today we let the poor woman have some dignity by referring to them as 'single parent'. Being upstairs proved tedious. I was dragging a stroller and a plastic pool and lunch trays and toys down to the yard then back up to get the girls. I had to be super careful in order to avoid another accident. Marie was to begin school in the fall. I was able to convince my husband that it was time to get a house with a yard of our own. I could hardly contain my excitement. The year was 1973. The budget was $25,000.

We found a three story house within easy walking distance to the school, to the church, to the park and even to the shopping center.

We also had bus transportation. It was a perfect location for a thriving
family. Dick and I went in with the realtor and I was pretty disappointed.
The house was a rental property and had not been well maintained.
There was linoleum flooring even in the living room. I didn't like it at
all. It looked kind of dumpy. My husband went down to the unfinished
basement, looked up into the rafters, checked out the electrical wiring
and announced

"The house has good bones, the work is mostly cosmetic. I can easily
fix everything that might come up."

Dick, as he used to say

"I'll just shake up the old money tree" was able to secure a mortgage.
He was a hardworking, ambitious young man. He showed great promise.
The kind of guy bankers love to lend to. My mother loaned me $5000.
for the down payment. I would write up a dozen postdated checks
of $100. I was using the baby bonus money I used to get from the
government. It took about five years to pay that off. You see my father
had a lot of money for those times but never believed in giving, only
loaning. He said

"It's a financial arrangement man to man. You got to let a man keep
his pride. A loan isn't charity."

My parents and our best friends helped us move in. While the former
tenants moved out the front door, we were bringing our stuff in through
the back door. As the lady was taking her last box out, she just happened
to mention in passing.

"Oh don't be surprised if every once in a while you happen to see a
few ants in the house."

Everyone pitched in setting up the bedrooms, the bathrooms, and
the living room and dining room. The kitchen was all ready for the next
day's breakfast. We ordered take out food and everyone sat in the grass on
blankets in our own back yard. I was very proud. When I put the girls to
bed Marie started to cry. She wanted to know

"Why did daddy give away my other house. It was so much more
beautiful than this place. I don't like it here."

I explained about renting versus owning etc. Who cares right! Then
I started to cry because I didn't like the place either. It was so old and
dingy. What a shame! Poor Dick was so angry with us and I don't blame
him.

"We were spoiled rotten girls and had absolutely no idea what great things he would do here to turn it into something beautiful."

He was right. I had never seen him build things because everything we had in the past was relatively new and we had been renting. I hadn't realized that when he was eighteen he had helped his father build an entire house in Pierrefonds. They only got to live in it for a couple of years. Unfortunately the bank had repossessed it when his father declared bankruptcy. I did my best to apologize in the best way I knew how. I made love to him in our bed, in his new bedroom in his new house.

I can tell you that my husband was a master renovator. There was nothing he couldn't do. We were on 43rd avenue for ten years and in that time he built us a modern oak kitchen, totally finished the basement into a practical family room with wall to wall shelving and upgraded the upstairs bathroom. He laid beautiful slate tile in the dining room. He had also built an extra large, roofed, back porch and a patio with a BBQ pit. We also had a six foot high privacy fence. I helped out by doing all the painting. I loved doing that kind of work. My Dick always cleaned up after himself. I, on the contrary, hated to soak and wash out the brushes and rollers. Instead I would throw everything into a garbage bag and buy new ones as needed. What was flattering to my husband was that my married girlfriends would come in and always say to their husband.

"Oh Dear! look what Dick built! Could you do something like that for us. Maybe you should ask him how to do it?"

The guys would tease Dick and say

"Hey stop being so bloody smart, you're making us look bad and my wife won't stop nagging me."

My husband used to tell me that he would tell his co workers or clients.

"I have to go home to work now!"

His boss had a great bonus plan set up which was very helpful. Rather than cash which could be spent just 'silly Nelly', he added Dick's name to an existing company account at a local building co-operative. All the building materials and tools for household renovations were paid for by the company. That was a great saving for us and assured that we would stick to the plan. For our twenty fifth anniversary my daughter had collected pictures of those decades and put them in an album for us. She captioned all of Dick's building projects as 'Real estate, something to keep Dad out of Mom's hair.' Actually those were very happy times for me. The house was always in a construction mode. The advantage was that Dick was at home, not out in a bar with his buddies. We were doing something very positive together. What was great is he never seemed to mind it either. I think he was proud of his accomplishments. I never ceased bragging about his expertise.

Another thing we did, as a family, was plant a summer garden in the spring. My father and mother helped and the girls learned to appreciate nature's own. My sweet Meme used to walk over from the senior center with her beau and help me collect the vegetables for the meals of that day. They would gather a few things for themselves and have lunch on the back porch in the shade. Our back yard became the neighborhood playground. I didn't mind. I was happy the girls had many friends to play with. I could keep an eye on everyone from a distance. I got to do a few things for myself those first two years. Dick had agreed to give me one evening off. He would be home to get the girls to bed. Once a week I had an evening ceramics class which I just loved. A few years after, I took a typing course at the junior college. I was so pathetic. I got just the basic passing grade which was thirty words a minute at touch typing. I have always contended that there was a mistake made in my overall education. After completion of grade nine, students were offered to proceed to the secretarial program or university prep. I, since I was to become a teacher chose the latter. Yet surely we could have all used one less Latin course and taken touch typing instead. When I went back out to the work force, in the late 70s, the first question was always

"Do you type?"

I always answered yes. Luckily no one gave me a typing test. I would have failed. When I was in my late thirties, the CEO of the company I worked for had me compile a special sales report. I had completed it and he approved. He said

"That's great, just what I wanted. Now you can just type that up and we can co-sign it and send it off to the client." I answered

"Sir, I can wash windows and prepare sales presentations but I do not type!"

He called his secretary and gave her instructions. PHEW! That was a close call. I think he surmised that if he was paying me a salary to be a sales administrator he wasn't going to see me waste my time typing. Look at me now. I'm typing this book. Wonders never cease!

One winter my mother helped me get a job at a leather goods store across from the children's' clothing store at our local mall where she worked. Dick had to be home Thursday and Friday before 6 p.m and Saturdays so that I could go out and earn some pin money. I got dressed well and even did my nails. The job was very boring, consisting of dusting glass shelves and selling handbags and accessories. It was especially tedious in the summer time because everybody would be outdoors enjoying good weather and I was stuck in a store. The air conditioning was a plus though. Dick and the girls got to know each other so much more and I got a little bit of independence and freedom. One evening my former school principal Ms D'Amour came by and purchased a handbag. She was thrilled to see me. I was also, but a bit shy. It had been five years since I had left teaching. See if you choose to, you can even go missing in a small town. It was all my fault. I had been too embarrassed about my first pregnancy and chose to avoid people. That was such a huge mistake on my part. Do not ever close the doors on good employers or professional contacts. Check in with them every six months. You never know what they may have available for you. They can't read minds. 'out of sight, out of mind.' I have found, with experience, that very often your personal lives do not reflect your hire opportunities. If you were very good at what you do, supervisor will ignore the past. As long as there is nothing illegal, all should be OK. Ms. D'Amour asked

"I had no idea you were working? When did this start? Why didn't you call me? I can use your help at the school. When can you start substitute teaching for me?"

I was so thrilled to be acknowledged. I replied

"I have no one to babysit the girls during the day. That is why I haven't gotten in touch. This was more convenient."

Well we hugged each other goodbye and I promised to keep in touch with her if ever things became more manageable. You'll see real soon why turning back to teaching was, unfortunately, not in the cards for me.

I really enjoyed that home and neighborhood. The ladies were mostly 'stay at home' wives. Even though I was courteous with four of them, whose children played with my girls, I did not feel comfortable getting to know them on an intimate level. I think I had had my fill of that from the apartment building gang. I still had my friend Maureen with whom I spoke every day, via telephone. My parents' house and my Meme were all within walking distance. My three single girlfriends still came by and visited with me and the kids or met us for Saturday family outings, such as a visit to the zoo. They used to say

"Oh yes, I'd like to have kids if they were born as three year olds and behaved as well as yours do."

I never envied them their single status. At that time, I was quite content in this role of wife and mother. I enjoyed taking the girls to the park two blocks away where they could play for hours and we could have a picnic lunch and walk back in time for afternoon nap. We even had a membership at the community swimming pool where we went every day, in the summer, to cool down. I never needed a car because we walked everywhere. Marie's new school was two blocks down from our house. We had elected that the girls should go to a French school because we wanted them educated in both languages to uphold the tradition of my family's heritage. Politics in Quebec were getting a bit racist. It was best to prepare for our daughters' futures in the event of any possible changes. The first day of school my younger daughter and I walked the oldest down to school. We were all holding hands. This was such a big deal for me. Typical of all moms I shed tears at the school yard gate as we were leaving. The second morning as we started off Marie let go of my hand and said

"I don't need you anymore. I can do this by myself."

That pretty much defined who Marie was and still is and the relationship we have. She is a take charge kind of an individual and successful. I always wanted a self assured child willing and able to meet the challenges of life. I have always believed

"Better a child be over confident than less."

The long weekend holidays were spent on the road. Dick's parents had moved to Sudbury. The children were already in their pajamas and the girls and I had had dinner when Dick got home. The car was packed immediately and we were on the road no later than 7 p.m. We would arrive at 4 a.m in the morning. Dick drove all night. I stayed awake to keep him company and luckily the kids slept the whole way. We never travelled in the winter time it was way too dangerous. We did this three times a year May, July and October. Those trips were exhausting. The girls were quite awake and chipper by the time we settled in. Dick went straight to bed and I usually waited until the girls' naptime just to make sure they weren't too much of a handful for their grandparents. We all shared a small bedroom in their trailer. Luckily there were children Marie's age for her to play with in the trailer park and Trudie didn't mind because she was being loved to death by her granny. My father in law chose retirement early due to serious heart problems and concurrent surgeries. Dick always seemed to do what was right by his parents, I thought. I know his father never gave his children any praise or appreciation. It's sad to try so hard and not be acknowledged. I guess that was the German way. Perhaps it was a given by the generation of that era. I think even my husband's behavior towards me had been pre-programmed a long time before he married.

Christmas time was celebrated at out place. His parents would come and live with us for a month. Dick and I would give them our bedroom. His father had to rest a lot. This way, the kids wouldn't be in his way. We slept downstairs in the basement. We didn't mind. The kids could play with their things and we only had to open and close the hide a bed as required. I'll never forget going to check on the turkey I had thawing in the sink of the laundry room to find that the 'bird' had been attacked by our two cats. The 'beasts' had managed to tear into the cavity and feast on the heart, liver and gizzards and some of the neck. It was gross! I was so angry yet scared to death about what my father in law might have to say. I called for Dick who checked it out and started to laugh. He said

"Who cares, I won't tell my father if you won't. Anyways he won't know the difference once it's cooked. I'll just throw this stuff out. Nobody will be the wiser."

Then there was the time the eldest daughter left us a note on a pretty crooked Christmas tree. The note read

"Mom and Dad cats jumped on tree and knocked it down to the floor. I heard it while you slept through the racket. I pulled it up as straight as I could. Love Marie"

She had managed to pick up all the fragments of broken balls and cleaned up. She was a good kid. She would have felt responsible to fix this problem. You see the decorating of the tree was Marie's domain. Dick put up the lights and I placed the higher decorations but that girl painstakingly took each strand of tinsel and applied them to the branches. To this day she is known as a perfectionist and their Christmas tree is still her 'baby'.

Just a couple of weeks after another serious surgery my father in law still wanted to fly out and spend Christmas. I was really nervous about having a recovering heart patient in the house with all the usual goings on at that time of the year. We always had our meals in the dining room. The kitchen was too small. Eating in the dining area did teach the children a feeling of manners and decorum. I even had semi classical music playing during the dinner time. It helped us relax and we could catch up with the events of our day. One lunch time, my mother in law had prepared everything as per usual. My father in law had finished his large meal of sausage and cheeses and breads and hard boiled eggs and had just lit up his Cigarillo. I got a whiff of it from the kitchen. Next thing you know Marie comes tearing into the kitchen screaming

"MOM!! Grandpapa just died. His head fell on the table and he's dead."

My mother in law came down from upstairs with a bottle of smelling salts which she immediately put right under his nose. Miracle! he came to. The children were shocked and started to jump around cheering. Dick's mother stretched the old man on the living room couch and tucked a pillow under his head. She explained to the kids that

"Grandpapa should not have had that cigar after such a big meal."

The house returned to it's normal rhythm. It was nap time, so my father in law was escorted upstairs by his doting wife. The rest of us went down to the playroom. Granny was a huge help when she came to visit. She loved every minute of her stay and was always helpful. She had the girls baking gingerbread cookies and making costumes for the Christmas pageant and practicing their lines. She always read the nativity story before we opened gifts. She cooked a few of my husband's favorite meals and always took up mending the odd pieces of clothing I of course was too inept to fix. I enjoyed her company. I, unlike so many others, had a really positive relationship with my mother in law.

I used to always think

"Well at least I know Dick will have to behave better for at least a month while his parents are here."

That, though, was not necessarily true. I hated the couple of weeks before the construction shut down for the Christmas holidays. There were so many office parties during those weeks. Naturally Dick attended everything. His suppliers provided a cornucopia of booze. Every other night boxes of wine bottles or cognac or gin or vodka or scotch were brought home and lined up against the furnace room wall. By the new year my husband had acquired a stash of free liquor to last at least three months. Other people with that amount would probably have enough for a year. He loved to brag about all the friends he had in the trade. My in-laws and the kids were sleeping upstairs and I would watch TV until he got in. By catching him at the door I could direct him to our bed downstairs so that he wouldn't bother the others. It was always so late. One time he drove into the driveway at 2:30 a.m. The headlights of the car were still on shining through the living room drapes. I looked out and my husband was slumped over the steering wheel and the car was still running. I put my boots on and went out. I opened the driver car door. I tried to wake him but he was out cold. I turned off the engine and left him there. I went back into the house and set the alarm clock for 6 a.m then I went to sleep. In the morning I went back out to the driveway and woke him. He came in went downstairs and slept until the kids went down to play after their breakfast. I never told his parents. He and I never talked about it. What else is new? To this day I swear the man 'was born with a horse shoe up his ass'. Then again what is the old saying 'only the good die young'. I can only say, that although Christmas is mystical and sweet just as it is claimed to be, I truly dreaded the holidays. Everything was always so stressful. Only the happiness of my children kept me on an even keel.

THE BOYS' ARRIVAL was totally unexpected. There are so many things in one's life that are unpredictable. I can't be the only one where circumstances, even out of your own sphere, can turn your whole life as you knew it totally upside down and inside out. Six years after we were married Dick and I, who had two girls, ended up having two girls and two boys. This all happened in the space of a couple of weeks. Dick used to tell people

"Oh the boys are Jo's. She just never told me about them before we got married."

Everybody would get a big laugh. This is the real story.

I think it was early summer of 1974. Dick got a phone call from his brother in Pennsylvania who told him his wife had died that morning. I asked my mother if they could take care of the girls. We would be back as soon as the funeral was over. Max's wife had for many years tried to carry pregnancies to full term but unsuccessfully. Now they had an adopted son and she with the help of medical science had been able to give birth to a boy baby who was nine months old. Dick's brother had left for work at the garage station early Saturday morning. The oldest child was looking at cartoons eating his cheerios. His mom was still in bed. Sammy, the baby, awoke and started crying. The dear mother got up, walked around the foot of the bed and fell to the floor never even saying a word. Overtime the baby's cries became screams. Michael tried to wake his mother but couldn't. He got up from the floor, went to the other bedroom and pulled his brother out of the crib. He sat the baby down between him and his mother. He was a smart five year old. He went and got a bottle out of the fridge for the baby and more cereal for the two of them to munch on. After a while, no one knows for sure because no one was there to witness, Michael decided to go downstairs and tell the neighbor his mom was still asleep on the floor and she wouldn't wake up. Luckily that whole building was made up of very familiar, good people. When the lady found their mom she called Max at work and the ambulance. Max's wife, the mother of his sons, was declared dead upon arrival at the hospital. She was in her mid thirties. We were told she had had 'a hole in her heart'. Either way the wording needn't be all perfect. It had probably been a heart attack.

Dick and I drove out and arrived eight hours later. By the time we got there the family lines had already been drawn. My brother in law's wife's family was already arguing about having their say about the funeral requirements and preparations. His mother in law in her grief became an even greater dominatrix and the whole family took her side, naturally. Dick went with his brother to take care of all the arrangements. I stayed behind to take care of the boys. This poor woman had been born and reared and had been a nurse for at least a decade in their small town. Her family insisted that there be a three day wake in order that all the relatives from out of town and the members of the community be able to pay their respects to the family. Max just had Dick and me. We made sure Michael did not attend the wake. I only brought the boys to the church for the funeral and we returned back to the house immediately afterwards. At that time, even though I had experience with children, I really hadn't detected any serious grieving on Michael's part. This was all new to me though. We explained the basics

"That mom had gone to heaven in the sky and would not be back but that his Dad was always going to be here for him."

That seemed to satisfy his five year old mind. The baby wasn't aware of any change. He was well fed and pampered and played with. I sang songs to him, read stories and rocked him in my arms while he drank his bottle at bedtime. What more could a little guy want? As strange as this might seem Michael was figuring we were having a good time together. Auntie and uncle Dick were visiting. What he seemed to miss the most at the time was his girl cousins, our daughters. He couldn't understand why they hadn't come down. Dick and I had to get back to Montreal, he to work and I was starting to worry about leaving our daughters in the care of my mom for too long a period of time.

When the dust settled if it ever really does in those tragic circumstances, time proved that Max and the boys were having a really hard time of it. Max had to coordinate child care for the baby in the home and kindergarten for Michael and his two part time jobs. The passion his wife's family had exhibited at her death did not translate itself into fulltime child care for the grandsons. It never ceases to amaze me how selective some people are as to what they can contribute to the help and healing of a family in distress. Dick took another call from his brother later that summer. Max called to ask if he and the boys could come up and spend a week's vacation with us. He and his wife, a year prior to her death, had discussed his reapplying to work in the American Navy. The recession had damaged his opportunities as an electrician, in the private sector. There were no jobs available. The Navy could provide a more secure financial future for the family. His former wife had agreed. He liked his work in the Navy and had been a much happier man. His wife could manage his being away six months of the year. She had her friends and family in town and now had their two sons to keep her company. She gave him her complete blessing. Soon after his dear wife had been put to rest, Max was notified by the USA Navy that his reapplication had been approved. He was going to have a full time job on the ships.

Now there was a major problem. How could he go back into the navy and be away six months of the year when he no longer had a wife and he had two boys to raise alone? Max and the boys came up north sometime in August. He did all of his driving at night also, guaranteeing the kids would sleep through. The cousins had a great time together. There was so much for everyone to do, the community pool and the park were going to be put to great use. My brother in law took care of the baby, changing diapers and bath. The kids played outdoors until nightfall. The adults had a BBQ steak dinner with wine. The conversations were very intense. It appeared that Max wanted to accept the navy's offer for the position. Nevertheless, when he had approached his wife's relatives for child care while he was away on deployment, he hit a brick wall. There were only the grandparents who could avail themselves to the task. All the other members had their own kids already in school and working full time jobs. The elders said they would consider taking the baby because he was their daughters 'real' son but they couldn't take the oldest boy. He was a handful and two kids was way too much for people their age. Max would have to find someone other than the family to raise him in his absence. He mentioned a friend who might consider it because they had a teenage daughter still left at home, who could assist them in providing care for the oldest boy Michael.

I let the men clear up the kitchen and I went up to bed. I heard their distant voices on the back porch but could not make out what they were saying. I was still awake when Dick came to bed. I just couldn't sleep. The dinner conversation had so upset me. I guess I'm super sensitive when it comes to children. We laid down beside each other holding hands. We relived the day and the words his brother had spoken. I said to Dick

"This is the worst thing I have ever heard. This is awful, to select children based on who is a 'real son' as opposed to adopted son. I've never heard of such ignorance. Oh! I stand corrected, your old man had said the same thing when Max and his wife had brought two year old Michael to meet his grandfather. They had driven all the way from Pennsylvania to Sudbury for a celebratory family reunion. We and the girls had driven there from Montreal. Your younger sister and her new husband had driven there from British Columbia. When Max showed your father the adoption papers, your dad said 'It means nothing. The boy is not of our blood.' I was disgusted then and I'm more disgusted now. What kind of a sick generation are these people?"

I was really ranting. I'm the only one who can actually rant in whispered tones. I mustn't wake up and frighten those sweet children sharing bedroom floor space across the hallway. Then, as if directed by angels, I turned over and looked into Dick's face and said

"We cannot allow this to happen. These boys' mother died two months ago. Their dad said 'it was OK, he was going to be there for them.' Now he needs to go away to work. We cannot let this happen. All these boys have is each other. They cannot be separated. We can take care of them. I don't know what papers Max and we have to sign. This is the only right thing to do."

My husband looked into my eyes and asked

"Do you think YOU can handle it?" I answered

"Of course I can!"

It is after many years that I now understand his question. This additional task was to be born by me single handedly. I will vow as God is my witness I did not regret taking in those two children. I was never able to call them 'my sons' in respect for their dear mother. But to this day I like to call them 'MY BOYS'.

Strange emotions are consuming me now. It is what I think a space time capsule moment could feel like. I have hooked up to Internet Face Book (2012). I have been corresponding a few times with Michael, my oldest boy, over the last few days. He is doing very well. He turned out just fine, tall, handsome, a chef no less. I'm proud for him. His guardian angel, Mom, has been keeping an eye on him. I'm glad I have succumbed to use this medium, as a connection tool, to all these fine young people who have been in my life. They are all a little older now than I was when I had the pleasure of raising them as my own kids. It is such a feeling of relief for me to know that they are all working hard and still play hard and seem to be able to enjoy life. My youngest boy has had a rough road to walk. He has managed to have two beautiful families in the last ten years. He sacrificed his own interests and devoted himself totally to the well being of his children. He seemed to be in the shadows for a while. He's probably trying to catch his breath while he proceeds to create a new canvas of himself for the future. Personal mosaics are trickier because there are so many pieces, unlike abstract that have such large, sweeping brush strokes. I miss the boys so badly. I wish I could call them and have them over for supper tonight. That would be only in my dreams.

Back to the past. The following morning we spoke to Dick's brother and made him an offer we knew he could not refuse. He was very happy. We started to try and figure out how to get all of this done before we were to announce it to the children. There were our daughters, having to share a life with cousins, to consider and Michael's leaving his roots. I think Max left the boys with us and headed back to Pennsylvania on his own. I'm not sure. Knowing myself I probably decided there was no need for the boys to be underfoot while their father got his career and all the boys requirements for an undetermined stay in Canada arranged. All was going well. The cousins, my two girls and two boys, were getting along most of the time. I think the children's' ages were Marie 7, Michael 5, Trudy 3, and Sammy 13 months, give or take a year. Baby Sam only seemed to show difficulty adjusting, at bottle feeding time. I would tuck his right arm under my left arm and had his head resting on the left side of my chest. I would cradle him in that fashion while he drank his bottle. I was used to doing that with my girls when they were babies. It was a cozy way to stay connected and helped the children relax and be calm for a little while in their busy lives. It also gave me the opportunity to slow down and sit still. Sammy rejected the embrace completely. I found out that he and his mom would lie in the bed together and his mother would breast feed him. After she had died he was old enough to hold his own bottle. That's what his dad had done with him. Well I held fast to my plan and after a week he was acclimatized. I was really happy to have that special time with Sam. The older three were very busy kids and this gave me a break.

Max drove back up to Canada two weeks later. The trunk was packed with suitcases of clothing and every Fisher Price toy imaginable. Apparently his in-laws did not like his decision at all. Even though no one there would offer that kind of help. The grandparents had no qualms expressing their great concern at Max's leaving his children with Canadian 'people'. As opposed to what, separating both boys and leaving each one with 'A Hole' caregivers?

I was angry but satisfied that we seven, two fathers, one mother and four kids would win out in the end. Anyways by the following summer a few of these so called Pennsylvania relatives and friends came up to visit the long, lost boys and naturally stayed at our place. They were just checking us out and enjoying a lot of that Canadian hospitality. I suspect that was their motivation as well as getting a cheap vacation out of the deal. What happened in PA. didn't interest me. We parents had to get organized for the house. Max and I went through he Sears catalogue to order the extras that would be needed to accommodate the 'motley crew'. He bought two studio beds for the girls' room and a dresser for the boys' room. The boys were going to use the great customized bunks Dick had built. Max asked me what I would like for myself. I was surprised but did not hesitate. We purchased a dishwasher and a '8 Track' sound system. Everything was delivered before Max headed back to the USA navy to begin his first deployment in September. After the men had set everything up, we explained to the children that

"Max was going back to work on the big ships. The boys would be raised here with us. That eventually, if Max met some special lady they could get married and he would be able to bring the boys back home to live with him in the States. In the meantime he would be coming up to visit every time his ocean trip was done."

Well I know now as my seven year old grandson, very recently, has taught me

"Nana I don't know what I want to do next summer? I can't even figure out what I want to do this weekend"

So to Michael the idea of 'eventually' could never be on his personal radar, not yet. Baby Sammy, as long as all of his needs were being met, was too young to comprehend 'loss'. Actually the kids were too excited having all these great new toys to play with. In fact the speech took all of five minutes and then they took off, out the back door, to play in the yard. That evening we three adults went over birth certificates and legalized written authorization from Max to have us as designated caregivers for his sons. There were documents from the US navy for health care coverage. There was no legal custodial arrangement set up. I'm sure we all slept better that night. The challenge was to be tomorrow. Max was leaving, away for six months. I was confident. I just needed some sleep!

Thinking back now I know how organized I would have had to be to run that household efficiently. Luckily my experience as a teacher came in very handy. I have always been ruled by time so adhering to a schedule would have been of the essence. Another point I believe to this very day is

"A family is not a democracy. You may express your opinion and I will take it under advisement. I am the leader of the pack. What I say goes."

Another of my famous sayings was

"Three strikes and you're out" or "If you think you're stubborn you haven't seen anything yet."

You might have notice I use the word I not WE as in father, mother. That never was the case. Child rearing was my job, be it two girls or two girls and two boys. Dick did admit once

"My girls turned out OK because my wife raised them."

In a way, that indifference to the task can prove helpful. Not withstanding that physically taking care of the children was exhausting, emotionally and psychologically I felt capable and knew there would not be any interference or arguments about the task at hand. The greatest challenge came in the area of the dynamics between my older daughter and my older nephew. Michael had difficulty in adjusting to a group setting.

At first glance everyone got along just fine. Trudy was a quiet, self contained child who would rather observe than participate. Sam was more her kind in temperament. She and he would spend a lot of time in quiet play, like Fisher Price village and looking at books. On the other hand both Michael and Marie were frenetic, more interested in highly physical, super, active play. They were able to fuel each other up. There was only a couple of years between them but my older daughter's staying power was a thousand times stronger. You see she had been accustomed to street play with children ranging in ages from six to twelve. She was our neighborhood 'tom boy' and darn proud of it too. She took care of the little ones and did them no harm but she was also able to hold her own with any school or street thug. I encouraged her feeling of toughness just as long as she stuck to people her own size and did not start the fight. I had had to hang out with aggressive boy cousins and it is good that a girl can hold her own. Keeps the boys in their place. Michael, on the other hand, was raised for four years as an only child. They were in a complex where there were no children his age. In those days daycare facilities were not in vogue. His dear mother was very protective of him. He was a coddled boy. Things such as cutting his own food and tying his shoe laces or dressing himself were foreign to him. His mother would have derived pleasure in doing those things for him. I did not. It might have been more expedient to do it but I felt he had to learn to be self sufficient, like my girls. I set up an immediate coaching program. He would test my patience to it's maximum limit. I never gave up. Eventually the boy did. Playing with his siblings or with the kids on the block was challenging for him. He expected to be given the advantage of 'new kid on the block requires special dispensation'. Children don't respond kindly. Most of them don't welcome the interloper until he can prove himself worthy to be in 'the gang'. There in lay Michael's dilemma. He would always start something but got in too deep and couldn't get himself out or accept defeat. His response was to start crying foul and enlist the help of an adult. It's better known as being a 'cry baby'. Several weeks went by and I always intervened and tried to explain to Marie to go easy on the guy.

"His mother has died and he's not used to living here and needs time to adjust. She was the oldest and should be more understanding and bend a little." Finally the eldest said

"Mom I don't care that auntie died. That's really too bad. But he's always starting trouble and I'm always getting blamed for everything. Well I don't have to understand. It's all wrong and it's not fair. So you watch him from now on cause he's a real trouble maker."

Consider myself told by a seven year old.

I spent a lot of time in the hospital emergency requiring stitches for those two older kids. Let's see if my memory serves me well. There was a time when Michael and Marie were at the park, two blocks away, attending morning youth activities in the recreation center. They were rehearsing for a play and Michael had decided to throw on a costume which consisted of a woman's dress and floppy hat. He was doing his usual 'goofball' routine, skipping around the room and tripping on the long hem of the dress. The other kids thought he was hilarious. The more they laughed, the harder he tried to entertain. Then one more misstep and doesn't his head land against the metal frame of the double door at the entrance of the building. It had been left open to cool the hall down. Apparently the crash was so loud even the counselor had to turn around and check out what had happened. There was my boy sprawled out looking like a sacrificial lamb with blood pouring out of his skull and onto his clothes. Marie was beside him trying to console him. I'm at the house with the two younger kids. The doorbell rings and there is Marie with a police officer by her side. There was an ambulance and a police cruiser parked in front of the house. I ask

"Jesus where is Michael?" The officer answered

"That's why we are here Madam. Your daughter told us they couldn't go to the hospital because you wouldn't have a way of getting there and that you had two more kids at home that you couldn't leave alone. The boy is in the ambulance and we are here to pick you all up to come to the hospital together."

It took me five minutes to get the navy health card and scoop the two youngest into my arms. Well everyone was thrilled. The kids were riding in an ambulance with the siren going. I was scared shitless

"What will Max say when he finds out?"

Apparently some head injuries look worse than they are, because the scalp bleeds a whole lot. It didn't take too long. The other three kids kept busy in the waiting room. I went from one to the next making sure everybody was OK. To them it was an adventure. Luckily the hospital was only a five minute taxi ride home. I must remind Dick to give me some emergency cash I can keep in the house for other similar situations. I had a feeling this would not be the last one. My older nephew is now forty. He does not wear dresses and has a crew cut. Last time I saw him in 2004 he still had that prominent scar at the top of his forehead. He is a funny guy. He still enjoys entertaining his friends and colleagues with his one liners, just like a stand up comedian.

Another time Marie and Michael were coming back around 5 p.m from the 'Grovehill' toboggan run. This was another place they could get to on foot. It was ten blocks away. We were really fortunate in those days. The children, if they were old enough, were able to play at the park or the pool or the snow field and be safe from predators. Were they safe from each other? I can't be too sure. I always sent my kids with the words

"You guys have yourselves a great time. Remember a lot of people know us and are watching over you. If you get into trouble they will call me guaranteed. So be good."

All the 'at home' mothers, that was just about everyone, were organized into a neighborhood watch. We all kept an eye out for each other's children. I was at the living room window watching my two 'wild cats' walking up the street. They were shoving each other into snow banks and took turns pulling the toboggan. All of a sudden my oldest girl is running, pulling the wooden sleigh and I see Michael take a running dive for it. I kept watching and twenty seconds later I see Michael standing up with a lot blood running down his mouth and chin. He missed landing on the toboggan. As he was ready to grab it, my daughter yanked it away fast and his face landed on the bottom of the wooden frame. I put my boots and coat on and told sweet Trudy and Sammy, my angels, to stay at the window and keep watching me. We got back into the house and I carefully washed my oldest boy's face. The front teeth were still there. Thank God! Unfortunately, within a month's time, the two adult front teeth turned black. Michael had the repair work done since the last time I saw him, in 2005. I saw several pictures of him on FB with a broad smile and there are brand new front teeth.

I think Michael might have been planning a come back trick for a long time because it worked. He did get Marie back right where it hurts the most, the heart. There were two guests visiting from Pennsylvania that week. It was late afternoon and we were having a cocktail. My daughter asked if she could go out for a while and would be back in time for supper. I was just about to serve dinner and realized the girl hadn't come back yet. I sent Michael and Trudy to go check out on the street. She was nowhere to be found. I was getting annoyed but decided to go ahead anyways. No more time to waste. The guests helped to get the younger kids to bed and I asked Michael where he thought his cousin could be? He answered

"Well she may be at Patrick's house. She had a date with him earlier. Patrick told me to tell her to meet him at the park" to which I replied

"Where does this boy live?"

My husband was not home, as usual, and I had no car so I jumped on my bike and peddled to the park. The park was empty. It was dusk. I was really getting upset and worried. I remembered Michael had said Patrick lived on 39th avenue which was really only the next block over. I headed out there and found my dear daughter sitting on the curb with her bike on the ground. She was just sitting there staring at a house across the street.

"What are you doing here? I've been worried sick"

She stood up and put her head against my chest and started crying

"Michael said Patrick told him to tell me he was going to meet me at the park at 4:30 p.m and I waited there. He never showed up so I came to his house to see him and ask him why he didn't come? But he hasn't come out of the house yet."

I was so angry

"Forget it get on your bike. We are going home now."

When we came in I excused myself to the guests and said I had family business to take care of. Michael explained that he might have misunderstood about the time or the place or the day. He was hedging and hawing. I knew darn well he was lying. Finally he admitted he had made it all up. He knew how crazy his cousin was for Patrick and he wanted her to look stupid. I told him he was grounded from the park for two days and would have to spend his time in the back yard with all the little kids. He was to apologize to Marie in front of the whole family and our guests. Just another chapter in sibling encounters. There are too many to enumerate. At this juncture in our lives, my crew is old enough to remember what they want to and how. It's sad to say I did revert, in some instances, to the use of corporal punishment on my nephew. Michael, when a young man, asked me

"Did you know I never wear a belt? Do you know why? It's because it reminds me of all the lickings I used to get." To which I replied

"Oh sorry about that but look how great you turned out!"

He said another thing to me though when he was much older and I had offered a heart felt apology for my letting him have it too hard, too many times

"I've been living with a friend who has three kids. If I had some of my own, I would raise them the way you did us." Phew forgiven!

School days presented their own peculiar circumstances. Michael was going to remain at kindergarten level. There was enough for the boy to adjust to without having to learn reading and arithmetic. It would be repetitive but his personality would best be served in a more relaxed setting. He was a really jumpy kid. Always jittery like a Mexican jumping bean. One of his chores was to take out the garbage. He would drag the green bag down the driveway. The bag would tear and pieces would slip out one at a time. Then he would drop off the half empty bag at the curb. He would turn around and walk past the litter without picking any up. I honestly believe he did not see the mess. My husband saw this, coming in one night, and there was hell to pay the next day. I then monitored the take out garbage detail. I know none of it was intentional, I am sure, but that behavior is very frustrating to a parent. In my day it was defined as hyperactive. Today it is diagnosed as ADHD. We didn't have opportunities in our day to access information. The solution was "keep the kid under control". Another time, he was goofing off while carrying his dinner from the kitchen to the dining area and tripped. The plate of spaghetti fell on the carpet. Michael ate his supper off the floor that night. Then he had to shampoo the area with soap and water. He never spilled anything again. My method was kind of military style. Everything was orderly and routine was respected and upheld. There was very little deviation except on the weekends. Michael went to the English Protestant school six blocks away. He spent most of his time after school running the distance home because there was always someone after him. I would stand on the front porch waiting. He would turn the corner at full gallop with two boys in hot pursuit. I would step down and start walking towards him. The bullies would stop and turn around. Interestingly enough that set of bullies would not return but there was always another new group after him. He was either taunting guys or liked to practice running. He sure as heck didn't confide in me. He was grateful though and did follow my advice. In his case it was

"Don't fight him. Just run like the wind boy!"

Marie, on the other hand, was a take charge kind of gal. She went to the French Catholic school. I'm sure if she had attended Michael's school, he would not have ever had to run home at the end of the day. There was a brat on our street called Gordon. He was a real 'prick' excuse the expression. Even I hated his guts. The boy had scrawled FUCK all over my driveway overnight. I went over to his house with a bucket of soapy water and a brush and spoke to his father. He got his son on his hands and knees and had him scrub down his mess. He took it out on my eldest daughter of course. She could hold her own. They were very competitive. The role of Alpha on the block had to be shared and neither one of them liked the idea. They played street hockey to win. There was nothing neighborly about it. Luckily one of the dads was on shift work and was usually home to referee the 'apres' school games. One day Trudy came running into the house screaming

"Marie is really hurt, there's a lot of blood." My poor children, the criteria for their being able to whine to me about injuries is, indeed, if there was blood. My philosophy was if there is no blood it can't be that bad. I never thought of broken bones. I tell you nowadays I would probably be called a 'bad mother'. I found my girl on the sidewalk with an egg the size of a lemon on her forehead. Apparently she and Gordon were playing chicken on their bikes. He was at the top of the street, she was at the bottom. Neither gave up. Rather than collide head on she swerved and hit the curb. She lost her balance and went flying onto the sidewalk. Off to the emergency we went. The doctor tried to console me by saying.

"Don't worry better the bump be outside of the brain than inside."

I was given instructions as to what to observe in the event of a possible concussion. Luckily nothing worse happened. When Dick came home that night I explained everything to him. He tried to reassure me, and it didn't work. He said

"What do you want to do? shackle her to the bed post. She plays hard. She's bound to get hurt. You'll just have to get used to it."

There it was! Dick's attitude "What me worry!"

My girls were really good in school. The older had adjusted quickly and made several friends. She was loyal to all of them. She only got into trouble twice with school authorities. The French school grade six was having what was known as a 'field day'. They were all heading to downtown Montreal using public transportation, buses and Metro. It was just before 5 p.m and Marie wasn't home yet. I was getting worried. I called the school and the secretary mentioned that the students had returned an hour ago and had gone home, except for some who were kept in detention. Marie was one of them. I told her I would be right down. I arrived to find her in the classroom with a couple of others. Her teacher explained that she had detention because

"While she was on the Metro she was talking English to one of the other students and that is forbidden. My daughter had been warned but still persisted. Ergo her punishment was staying in after school."

I could not believe what I was hearing. I told the teacher

"The first and utmost responsibility she had when they got back was to, at least, advise the parents that detention was taking place and that our children would be home after 5 p.m. I was taking my daughter home now and would be in touch with the principal tomorrow for an appointment to discuss this matter further."

To this day I can't believe the toilet Quebec was flushing itself into, at that time. The political language legislations were Fascist and this gave vent to many 'anti Anglo' sentiments expressing themselves openly in day to day life. I did inquiries with the PTA regarding language rules established by the school board. The regulation was that 'all students attending a French catholic are to speak only one language that is French in the school, in the classroom and in the school yard.' I met with the principal. I had only two meetings with her in six years so I was welcomed. She was not on the defensive but she was prepared. She was aware of the regulations. That school event was considered an educational school activity and consequently subject to school rules. Therefore the use of French was to apply. I respectfully countered.

"The public transportation system is not a school property. Forcing students not to speak English in public is 'Fascist' like. I'm sure if a teacher wishes to enforce political legislation she could always apply for a position on the language police force. Public school activities should not be used as platforms for prejudice. The school should be proud that it does provide bilingual opportunities. It is to your credit that this can take place."

She smiled. We did both agree, though, that the parents should have been notified. Those were the times in Quebec when the political climate was such, that everyone was leery. I had been raised fluent in both languages and that I passed on to my children. If my husband had remembered his German we could have had girls who were trilingual. I had tried everything possible to comply and also maintain independence. There was a law enacted which did not permit my daughters to be transferred to an English high school because their primary education was in French. I circumvented that by enrolling my girls in a private English academy. I sometimes wondered if my blond hair, blue eyed, pure Arian Trudy would have to have her hair died dark brown and use dark brown contacts on her eyes in order to be 'acceptable'.

The second daughter was different. She was a quiet child, spent a lot of time observing rather than participating. Coming up behind Marie and Michael she was to say the least, cautious. When she was older she had said to me

"I always watched what Marie did. If she got into trouble for it, I made sure I never did it."

Trudy started kindergarten at the same school as her older sister. Every day she had breakfast and brushed her teeth. She would put on the clothes that had been laid out for her the night before. She looked really cute. Marie and Michael went ahead and we followed with Sammy in tow. Then, all of a sudden she started to vomit. We would walk back home. I would call the school and advise them we would be late. I would change her in something less pretty and we would start off again. We would take her into the class, give her a kiss and then head back home. Eventually the throwing up ceased. I met with the teacher for the Christmas report card. It was far from stellar. It was just kindergarten, no big deal. The teacher advised me that in her opinion

"Trudy should be taken out of the French school and put in the English school program. She is totally uncooperative and uncommunicative. Marie had been very active and responsive in class. This was completely different."

I took the time to explain my younger daughter's timid nature. I replied

"As a former teacher I know that comparing the sisters was not good practice. It obviously has prejudiced your assessment. I will continue to keep Trudy at Therien school and your job is to insure that she is capable of meeting the basic standards. If at the end of the year those are not met than we will consider an alternative for our daughter. I will drop by the principal's office now and mention that we are taking your opinion under advisement. I will request that the principal also follow up Trudy's progress. Well Trudy did finish kindergarten in French and achieved all the requirements. She was passed up to grade 1. That fall there was a PTA meeting. A few of the parents were chatting. We were comparing notes about child development for the better from one year to the next. Apparently several of the children of the last year's class had suffered stomach or bowel problems or bed wetting or vomiting. We decided to send a letter, co signed by those involved, to the principal. We were advising vigilance and caution for the present kindergarten children. Based on the facts we had shared, it was evident our children had suffered stress and anxiety while in the care of a specific staff person. I was proud because that kindergarten teacher had been offered early retirement. She had been working with that age group for just over two decades and completely burned out. I surely understand how that can happen. Trudy finished her grade one class with an above 90% average. It was a great lesson for all of us. Ours was not a family of quitters.

Sammy was at home with me helping with household chores while the other three were in school. He made the beds in the morning by walking from the foot of the bed to the head pulling the bed sheet and blanket behind him, then lay them down. He was only two. Another job he loved was emptying the dish washer. He would take a piece, dry the drippy ones up and stack everything on the counter by category. Corel ware was very handy to have. He would then pull up the stool and spray the counter top with cleanser and wipe away until everything got soaking wet. He would then get a dish towel and dry everything up. He was a very fastidious child. That's why I think the DNA is hard wired from the get go. Sam, when given the opportunity, was displaying the engineering mind he had inherited from his grandfather in even the most mundane of tasks. He was a pretty calm child. After having handled a situation with my two eldest I would turn around and breathe a sigh of relief when I would see Trudy and Sam. They were the polar opposite of the first two. Sammy, as we called him, had only two temper tantrums that I can remember. Both events had to do with his stubbornness. That I know is in the German DNA. One case was over his refusal to take, much needed, cough syrup. After much struggling, the job got done. He had totally lost it. I had to cancel playtime and bring him upstairs for bedtime by throwing him over my shoulder. The other incident was over ice cream. I must have taken a bowl of ice cream to him five times just to be refused and then asked for some again. Then I realized this was a game. The other three kids thought this was hilarious. So he played it to the hilt. How to drive a parent stir crazy and score points with the gang. Well over the shoulder he went again. Luckily he got the message in two tries. I did find myself thinking the grass was greener on the other side of the fence. The older kids were in school full time and I was 'stuck' at home with Sammy. He wouldn't be starting for another year. I even wrote a letter to myself about it. I was hoping to get a jump on the future. My destiny happened soon enough. Another momentous, swift shift was to take place. Do you know the old saying

"Beware what you wish for!" Another chapter coming up real soon.

All I know is if things are good don't hurry them up. Just enjoy, savor the moments.

I was really so busy, never a dull moment. On the weekends we were on outings or people came to our house. Instead of four being all over the place we were six. Dick's boss was really great. After learning that Dick had to take two trips to Brossard with the kids because the company car, a Mercury Comet, was too small he decided his contribution to the expanded family was to bc, a station wagon. He was my hero. What a vehicle! The back seat reclined flat so that all four children could lay down in the back and sleep all the way home. There were no seat belts or children car seat requirements in the 70's. Marie, when she was older, referred to Dick as a 'weekend Dad'. I loved having him around. I missed him so. I so needed to get out of the house. We had several trips together, especially on the three day civic holiday weekends. We usually went to Orillia at my younger sister's place. It was only a five hour drive. Everyone got along very well. My favorite was the trip to British Columbia. It was to be a family reunion. Max couldn't make it because he was at sea. We brought our babysitter Valen to help me with the children. Max paid for her airfare and that of his two boys. This was very exciting for Dick's mother and father who had retired to their eldest daughter's farm. There were nine grandchildren ranging from about four months to fourteen years and nine adults, quite the clan. The family had a lot of room for all of us. Michael and his younger male cousin were both frenetic so you can well imagine, they got along really well. The westerners were very relaxed when it came to discipline. I'd have to do damage control when we got back home. Marie loved the farm animals. She had to clean out the chicken coop every morning and gather the eggs. She never complained. She did a lot of pony riding. In fact she loved it so much she was able to travel back on her own when she was thirteen. She was a dependable young lady who had earned the trip. I was so happy. I was able to be with the kids and adults all the time. My mother in law and the babysitter and I shared the care of the children. It was so much easier on me. My husband and I even got a week's vacation in California visiting with three of our dearest and longest lasting friends from our youth. We went to so many places interesting places. I know for sure we enjoyed each other's company.

He seemed to like being with me then. Maybe it was having children that seemed to get in his way of our being together. That's too bad though. It's not as if I would allow them to disappear forever.

There is one trip with the seven of us together that definitely needs mention. If nothing else but to purge myself or a warning to anyone else to

"Do not do this".

We had planned a trip to Walt Disney world. My brother in law was going to come up to Canada and he and Dick would share the driving. The two oldest kids had had the chicken pox the month prior. I was tied up, in a musical beds routines, trying to keep the two youngest one from catching it. Our bedroom became an infirmary each patient sleeping in my bed and I in theirs. Dick used the 'hide a bed' in the playroom downstairs. I swore, as the summer vacation was approaching,

"I don't care, if Trudy and Max get the chicken pox I will wrap them in blankets and sneak them across the border. I will not let anything stop me from having my vacation".

Well God must have heard me because there we were one fine morning at the beginning of summer heading out in the station wagon. Dick was driving I was in the middle, Max was riding shotgun and four kids in the back seat. The men would alternate driving each time we did a pit stop. That was only every four hours or so when the gas tank was close to empty. We got to get out, stretch our legs, go to the washrooms and order a quick lunch. The men were in their zone. I and the children were very uncomfortable being confined. I don't know how these men did it. They could actually shut out the cacophony taking place behind them. I'm sure I don't have to explain what it's like being a kid, having to share a car seat with a sibling. It brings back nightmares for all of us. At one point the fighting was getting so bad I actually had to put Michael against the back door, separated from the other children by a row of suitcases. The days were long almost ten or twelve hours of travelling. We got to pull into the driveway of a friend of Max at dusk every night for a sleepover. The seven of us hit Walt Disney in peak family travel time. We all enjoyed the little rides for Trudy and Sammy. The older kids and their fathers had a blast on 'Space Mountain' and other great rides. When they were doing their thing the younger ones and I sat on benches, in the shade, people watching. It was the first time I was exposed to very fat people with pizza juices dripping down their forearms. It was pretty gross. We didn't stay overnight. I know for sure I and the little kids would not have been able to do another day. We left at night fall for Fort Myers beach where my older sister had rented a cottage for us right beside hers. She and I were to have a sea side family reunion for a week.

That was the good part of the vacation for Dick. He would go out on a small sailboat and we would loose sight of him. I wondered if he was going to Cuba. My older sister and I got along alright considering. My brother in law would spend the day at his parents house. Trudy and Sammy and Michael were on the beach in front of our cottages. Marie was in the ocean with Annabelle's boys. I think, most of the time, it looked like they were attempting to drown her. Luckily she was really strong. My sister's husband read them the riot act early in the game. He was a great disciplinarian. All the kids listened to him. The first afternoon my sister and I were together getting dinner prepped and she asked me

"What kind of a relationship do you and your brother in law have?" I was puzzled

"I explained I was more like the nanny. He mostly hung out with Dick. Why? What kind of question is that?"

Check this out. My crazy mother had told my older sister to be careful and not be too shocked by Dick and I and Max because

"I think they have a 'menage a trois'."

I started to roar so hard I almost wet myself. She started to laugh also.

"Our mother is certifiable. I'm glad you got that out of the way early. Now you won't have to waste too much time getting freaked out."

What I loved the most about that location, was sneaking out to the screened in porch at night. When the other six were out cold, I would stretch out on the cot and be lulled to sleep by the sound of the surf. Sad to say all good things must end. On the trip back, I finally got the fathers to agree to stop in at a decent restaurant. I really wanted to sit down and take the time to order and relax, to actually sip coffee from a real, non-Styrofoam cup and use real cutlery rather than plastic. It was lovely! We got to the Canadian border and I had to use the bathroom for an hour. I had a really bad case of the runs. I obviously had too many MacDonald happy meals. I didn't go back into those fast food places for at least three decades. That was, until my grandchildren insisted it had to be the best meal in town. That was the case, only, because by then that company was giving out free toys to bribe the kids into their establishments. I was so happy to get back home. I would never complain about needing to get away again.

I think we all got by, whatever that means. I know I did my best. As all children have a tendency to do when we grow up into adulthood, there will be critics. I hate to tell you all

"Frankly my Dears I don't give a damn anymore"

What I have accomplished with and for my girls and 'my boys' are the greatest achievements in my life. This I brag about. When I was a child I was told God kept a book, a record if you will. I know I have gold stars beside my name in regards to child care. If I had a choice between my having a great marriage or my having happy children growing in to self sufficient adults, I would choose the latter. This is who I am and have always been. I prefer the company of children to that of adults. The little ones, unlike the adults, can reciprocate the love you give them one hundred fold.

THE BOYS LEAVING literally broke my heart. Tears are streaming down my face now as I write this. I never took my brother in law seriously about his getting married and moving the kids back to the States. Why would he want to do that? He had his own unhindered career. The boys were secure. Why mess things up? He definitely was interested in marriage because he asked four women to marry him in a space of four years. The first three did not accept the proposal, the fourth did. Mind you when he was a much younger man he had asked two girls to marry him before he did meet the third lady. Diane did become his wife and the mother of the boys. Maybe he was a hopeless romantic. I have learned one thing while developing wisdom in my old age is to never try to get into someone else's head. Impossible, the work is way too frustrating. I do think that the so called quest for a second wife might have been just as much a search for a step mother for the boys, if not more so. So my take on it would have been that it would have been more of a proposition than a proposal. The first lady was the young daughter of his best friends in Pennsylvania who had offered to take in Michael originally. She decided Max was a little bit too old for her, almost fourteen years, and Michael was fourteen years her junior. It just wasn't going to work. She wanted to have fun in her twenties. I can see that. Relief poured over me. She had even come up to Montreal for a short vacation and stayed with us. I guess that occasion was enough to convince her. The second woman was an acquaintance of mine. This fine lady was a university graduate, career woman. I would have trusted the boys to her any day. She dated Dick's brother several times when he would be on shore leave in Montreal. She did know the boys well and they her. The two of us and our mutual best friend Carol went out to dinner one evening. I felt I was brokering a deal. She felt very guilty for not accepting but said the reason she refused the offer was

"Max is too needy. I don't love him and I doubt he does me. I mean five dates does not constitute a relationship. I don't want to move to the USA and be 'stuck' with two boys while my husband spends six months of the year on a ship out at sea. It just wouldn't be right for me or for them"

I understood everything she was saying. We three toasted to her having made a very logical decision. My friend did marry for the first time when she was fifty. She had a built-in family, a husband, who had three adult children and three grandchildren. She is retired now and very happy playing with everyone. She still is a very wise woman.

The third woman I did not like. She was a colleague of my girlfriend. Carol loved hooking people up together. She was what was referred to, in those days, as a match maker. This one's name was Arielle. She was a divorcee with one daughter. Max was in lust with this one. That's ok I knew all about that feeling. When Max came up on leave, he stayed at her apartment instead of at our home with his boys. He would make what I can best describe as play date appointments with his eldest son Mark. The 'douche' thought Sammy was too young to go out with them.

I cannot begin to express to you the anger I had for my brother in law's behavior towards his sons and even me as their caregiver. My husband didn't care either way about the impact this had on his nephews or me. I learned that this indifference to others and not seeing the big picture was definitely a prevalent self serving, male trait in that family. They role modeled their father. I will try my damndest to depict what happened, unfortunately, too many times.

My husband would get a call from his brother on a Friday night letting us know he had arrived in town and he would be by Saturday morning to play with the boys or take Michael out for breakfast with his girlfriend and her daughter. The 'woman' never came to our house for family events. That was ok with me. They had a 'thing' going on. She was keeping things separate. Made sense to me. My nephew Michael was up and fully dressed on the Saturday morning, at the break of dawn. He would have his breakfast and wait for three to four hours for his father to show up. He would have his face against the living room window pane waiting for the car to pull in to the driveway. I would have to placate him and get him involved in some things the other kids were doing just to distract him. Oh God! I knew his heart was aching every time. I was fuming in side for the pain my brother in law was inflicting on his son. Dick would finally call his brother and tell him to

"Get over here. The boy is waiting for you."

Max would arrive, play around with Sammy for a little while then take Michael out for lunch and bring him back two hours later. The family, adult males in his life were very poor role models. His dad and uncle were both absentee fathers. They just kept, inadvertently, pounding away at this boy's self worth without realizing the long term damage this could have. Instead of learning a lesson from the pathetic way they had been raised, they chose to perpetuate the cycle of indifference. Eventually that third relationship fizzled out. Nobody knows what happened. Carol did say her girlfriend wasn't interested in having to marry and mother three kids, her own daughter was enough. My opinion was good riddance to bad rubbish.

My buddy, Maureen, had been divorced for a couple of years and had met a military man. He seemed ok. He accepted the fact that she had three kids and they decided to get married. I was to be the matron of honor. Max was going to be up visiting that weekend of the wedding.

Maureen's cousin needed a date so she was introduced to Max at one of our usual gatherings. The couple looked real fine together and had a great time. Max and lady number four started to date pretty seriously while he was on leave. He made a lot of trips North that year. I knew Barb. She was divorced with a daughter and had a good position at a Canadian bank in Montreal. She knew how to get around and had been around the block, if you know what I mean. She liked to party. Having her mother to take care of her daughter, who had epilepsy, was really handy. We all used to bump into each other once in a while at Maureen's house. Max invited Barb to visit Virginia Beach and check out where he lived. They were gone for a few days. The phone rang one Saturday evening and it was Max telling Dick he and Barb had decided to get married and would Dick like to be the best man. Dick put his hand on the receiver and told Maureen, her husband and me what was said. I shook my head and started to tear. We could only hear one side of the conversation. Dick seemed to be getting angry. The conversation ended with his yelling

"Ok! I'll do it but only because I know I am the better man."

Dick and I and cousin Maureen and her husband agreed the boys were not to be told anything. Before Max returned, I had made sure that I explained to Dick what I thought should happen for the transition and that he had an obligation to me and the four kids to make sure Max complied. Dick agreed with every thing. When the engaged couple did come back to Montreal I insisted that, this time, Max live at our house with his sons. There was to be no shacking up on the South shore. Any dating with Barb was to be in the evenings after the boys were tucked to bed or during the day with family activities that included all the children, her daughter as well and his two sons. We were never involved in any planning discussions as to the feasibility of the boys moving from our home back to the USA. Max and Barb had planned everything and our input was not necessary. He had made up his mind that our comments were just to be regarded as negative and an interference to their new family's happiness. Everything would be just fine.

So this was the game plan as explained to us, in detail, by Max. Barb did not attend these sessions. Her cousin probably warned her to butt out and let the two brothers work this out. Talk about the two most inept men to plan the future of two boys. The blind leading the blind. I was to comply of course. Keep everything on an even keel. Watch over the boys to make sure the transition went over without too much bedlam. At least Dick was kind enough to appreciate all my concerns and at least pass them on to his brother. Max said

"I'm going to be deployed in September so we will marry in the summer and move the whole family to the States just before school enrollment. Everyone will, at least, have a couple of weeks to settle down before I leave for six months on sea duty." my reply was

"What's the hurry. If you must get married, so go ahead. You can head off on your deployment in September and come back after the six months. The new school year will be almost over and at least when you take the boys back you will be there to help Barb and her daughter and the boys get acclimatized. You would have six months on base and she won't need to be alone doing all of this." He explained

"She is perfectly willing to do it this way. Her mother has even offered to come down over the winter and help her take care of all the kids. It will get her out of Montreal for the winter months. I have a huge network of navy friends and services ready to help out. Barb will get to meet everyone. That is what we do in the Navy. Wives get used to husbands being away and keep each other company"

I couldn't continue. I did freak out though and had a hissy but to no avail when he said

"I will be going back and forth to the States often in the next several weeks to get everything in order. Barb will be taking the boys to the family cottage with her on the weekends. While I am away Michael and Sammy will get to know their new step mother and all her family. They will have a lot of fun and other cousins to get to know and play with. It will also give Dick and you a break from taking care of them. You and Barb can plan it all out, pick up early Saturday, returning Sunday evenings. It's going to be great"

I couldn't believe what I had just heard. I had to coordinate, in my brother in law's absence, weekend visiting privileges with the new wife and step mother of the boys. I felt so sick to my stomach, I had to excuse myself. I really thought I was going to throw up. My girlfriend Maureen, Barb's cousin, felt really bad for me. What would happen to the boys? All the head way that was made here in Canada with us after their mother had died could probably fall by the way side. There was absolutely nothing we could do. The boys' extended American family from Pennsylvania, who had accepted us a couple of years prior were happy the boys were coming back to the states. Nevertheless they were worried about loosing contact with them because of the new step mother. Honestly their selfish concerns were the least of my worries.

I think I had lost part of myself, for good after all of this. I wonder if spiritually or psychologically, a human being can be ripped apart like one could tear off the heel from a loaf of crusty French bread? Can the heart, which is anatomically divided into four parts, actually loose a part? That spring I knew I was not thinking rationally. I made decisions that in retrospect had absolutely no logical sense. I took my usual course of action as previously shown in my life. I was not going to allow myself to get depressed over the leaving of my boys, actually in reality the sons of Max and the new stepmother. I mentally programmed myself with that new definition. I will busy my days with busyness. I told Dick

"I need to get a job to act as a distraction. Perhaps out of all the people you know someone would hire a housewife with thirty words a minute typing skills."

He agreed to ask around. It never occurred to me to call Miss D'Amour, the principal at the school. What a shame! That's what I mean about senseless behavior. I talked to my mother about the solution to my slowly creeping problem of depression. She resolved to find me a day sitter to watch the four children, maybe someone old enough who could cook meals and do some light household chores also. A couple of weeks later I had a job as a receptionist in a construction company where one Dick's friends worked. The only difficulty was it was an 1 ½ hour commute morning and late afternoon. So what! I had done that before when I was eighteen years old. No Problem! The fact that I was thirty three with four children was not relevant. I can do this. The only thing that really scared me was the typing! What is still amazing to me is no one tried to intervene, slow me down. I undoubtedly came across as so much in control of the situation that those close to me probably thought

"She seems to be taking it rather well. Everything looks ok."

I was very adept at masking my rage and sorrow, especially for the boys' sake. I was a train wreck waiting to happen. I should have just stayed home and played with Sammy. Instead I became a manic bus transportation commuter to a job I hated. The babysitter would arrive early. My husband drove me to a specific bus stop that would be quicker and eliminate two transfers. By the time I got home at 6 p.m, I served supper and listened to a litany of complaints about the sitter.

"She ate a pound bag of French fries and hardly gave us any. She didn't play with us. She watched T V all day. She kept all the windows open while the air conditioner was going. Her cooking was God awful and on and on." My husband said

"I was allowed to continue working as long as all my other household work didn't suffer. I was to cook all the meals in the future. This was just a temporary thing anyways until the boys were gone. Then we wouldn't need a babysitter and our life could get back to normal."

Spoken like a true German chauvinist pig. Luckily a neighbor came to my rescue. The company he worked for was interviewing for a new receptionist. I should apply for the position. He would give the personnel department a good reference for me. A week later I started a new job in a lovely reception area, no typing required. It was only thirty minutes away by bus.

Thank You God. I started July 1978.

I'm exhausted just thinking about the pace. I can so relate with all the parents in our present, western society. As you can well imagine things were moving right along in my brother in law's romance. A life which unfortunately touched us all because of the affects it had on the boys. The family had been made aware of the change in their father's status. There was no negative reaction. I spent an inordinate amount of time explaining the benefits, a much larger family in Canada and in the states, more cousins, more presents at Christmas, great weather, a beach to go to, a membership in a club with a swimming pool. I really laid it on thick! These conversations were short and sweet. Keeping an excited, positive front was extremely difficult on me. Once when I was mending the hem on Ritchie's trousers he sat beside me and leaned in and asked

"Who's going to fix the holes in my clothes when you're gone?"

The child was getting it. I think the boys were trying to fake it too. Weren't we all supposed to be as happy as Max and Barb were. Wasn't this what it was really all about. Max, a military man said 'jump' and we said 'how high'.

Dick and Max's mother flew in for the nuptials and stayed a month. The sitter was given a short, paid leave of absence and my mom in law was able to help with the kids. The whole family had the appearance of solidarity. There never was any discussion about feelings. What? This German family did not do that. The wedding and reception went without a hitch. The boys, handsome in their suits were in the wedding party along with Barb's daughter. Mark was the ring bearer. Dick stood up for his brother and was seated at the wedding party table at the front of the hall. My mother in law, the mother of the groom and the parents of the bride sat at a designated table to the side. My daughters and the boys and their new step sister all sat together with the elders. They were to keep each other company.

"Where was I?" you ask.

I was at the last table at the back of the room along with another couple who were friends of ours. I had been ostracized. The message was put out there, loud and clear for me and everyone else in the hall. I was officially to be kept out of the picture from now on. I had been put in my place. Excellent move by the new step mother. My best girlfriend, at the time, who was also Barb's cousin was very embarrassed by the 'faux pas'. After the meal and all the speeches and toasts were done, Maureen and her husband came and spent a lot of time with me at the back of the room. We left the reception earlier than the others. I used the excuse, which was the truth, that the children had had a very long and busy day and needed to get to bed. Dick, his mother, our daughters, the boys and I came back to the house. The newlywed couple were heading off to Virginia for their honeymoon and were to be away for two weeks. The groom's sons and the bride's daughter were not invited to join them. I was back on duty for the assignment of taking care of my boys.

Dick's mother was very impressed and happy for her eldest son. When I told her how I felt about all of this she addressed my concerns by saying

"I don't know why you are so upset? After all they weren't your sons to begin with. They belong with their father."

The rest of the summer was rough. The boys went to Barb's parents cottage every weekend. They came back every Sunday way pass their bedtime. Naturally, they were wrecks. I knew all about that family's cottage life. The summer before Maureen had invited me and the kids over for a Saturday fun in the sun and sleep over. It was a camp, a couple of bedrooms with lots of bunk beds. I was sharing a hide a bed in the living room with Maureen when her uncle came stumbling in at 2 a.m. My girlfriend said

"Don't say a word. If he knows someone is awake he'll come and talk their ear off."

He walked by, stood over us than proceeded into the bathroom where I could see him open the medicine cabinet and begin drinking most of the contents of a bottle of mouthwash. That wasn't much of a shocker because my mother used to drink cough syrup. The gang sure knew how to party. I understood, after we had bought one that, in so many cases, is what cottage life is all about. That Sunday night Barb had called from a payphone at a garage asking her brothers to come and get her. On her way home to Montreal she had driven the car into a ditch. That had been a year before she met my brother in law. What a winner! So you can see why I was so nervous leaving the boys with that gang on the weekends.

The week days were miserable for all of us. The boys had to be completely reprogrammed. Michael was more hyper than ever and argued about everything. He would brag about his weekends where he didn't have all these rules to follow. He could stay up by the campfire until all hours of the night. He even got to serve his uncles their beers. They just had to ask and he got everything for them. He was damn proud of it too. Michael was nine years old at the time. The uncles used to think Sammy was a wimp. The kid was only four years old. They recommended

"I should try and toughen him up a bit. He's not used to the rough housing and cried a lot over there."

The meals were just one refusal after another,

"Didn't like this, won't eat that."

The girls and I were getting really ticked off. There was no recourse. I wasn't going to get involve with Barb and tell her to keep a more watchful eye on them and not let them run wild. My girlfriend said it would be of no use. It was at times like this that I felt ashamed because I was actually looking forward to being just a family of four. The week of the move came upon us quickly. Max had taken most of the boys things to their new house in the states. He would load up the car every time he made a return trip. I decided to plan a block party for everyone to say their goodbyes to the boys. It took place the afternoon before they were to leave. Max and Barb and her daughter were going to pick them up the following morning. Everyone had a super good time. There were about thirty of us. My parents and neighbors and good friends understood how difficult this was for me. The whole focus was on the boys and how proud everyone was of them and wishing them good fortune. Everyone was going to visit them at their new place and go to the beach. These folks were just wonderful. They had known the boys for four years. Their sentiments were sincere. Finally at sunset everybody left. I got the kids ready for bed. Michael was the last one for me to check on. When I knelt down to straighten up his pajama bottoms he started to beat up on my chest with all of his might. His clenched fists just kept pounding and pounding on me. He kept screaming in my face

"I knew it. I knew you never loved me. How could you let me go? You never loved me."

I let him wail away on me until he began to get so worn out he fell to the floor crying. I took him into my lap. I said with all the fortitude and calm I could muster

"I couldn't keep you. I wasn't allowed to say

NO, YOU CAN'T TAKE THEM! Your father wants you and Sam to be with him now. You can be sure of one thing though. I have always loved you. There were hard times but we did ok. We all managed together to get through them. I know that no matter how old you get I will always love you. You're my oldest boy. That will never change no matter where you live."

I laid down beside him in his bed and stayed until he fell asleep. I checked on Sam and my daughters. All were sleeping. I went down to the playroom. My husband had cleaned up after the party. I remember collapsing on the floor and began weeping like someone had died. I think maybe it was me. My husband came and lay down beside me. He rocked me in his arms. It probably took me an hour to calm down. We never spoke. I had nothing left to say.

Here I go again now! Tears sliding down my cheeks like a stream.

The following morning Max and his new family arrived. Dick and Marie and Trudy and I kissed Michael and Sammy goodbye. Max shook hands with Dick. He took the boys and put them in the back seat of the car. The gang from the street came out of their houses and stood on the curbs waving away as if my boys were royalty. We all kept waving as the boys did the same from the back window of the car. The car turned left at the street corner. That was the last time I saw my boys for several years. Why that is I really do not know? My mother in law, in Vancouver, used to call quite a bit and tell us all about the Virginians.

"I told her we never got any news. She mentioned that Max had come up to Montreal with his family at least once or twice a year to visit with his wife's family. My friend Maureen would say she had seen the boys. Yet Max never called us or brought them over to visit. That really made me angry. How we could have responsibility for his two sons for four years yet were not worthy of a short visit once in a while just to stay connected. I can only presume that the new step mother and their father wanted a clean break, no connection, no interference. The navy man would have agreed because my feelings would not have even occurred to him. Finally while Max and his family were visiting his mother and the clan in Vancouver she happened to tell him

"You should be bringing your sons over to visit with Dick and the boys' aunt and girl cousins. To leave them out is not right. They are part of our own family."

The message either sank in or he knew his mother would be checking with us. It doesn't matter. We got to see the boys once a year after that. Now thirty four years later I keep up with Michael on FB.

Life was back to normal. Our daughters benefitted from not having extra people needing my attention. My husband was out extra money his brother gave him every month for the care of his sons, which I never saw a penny of in four years. The good thing was he wouldn't have to put up with so much racket. It took me several weeks to adjust. I kept setting the dining room dinner table with six place settings. Then I would correct myself and put the extra cutlery away. Dick decided I didn't need the baby sitter anymore. The girls were both in school. Marie was eleven and perfectly capable of taking charge of the house and I worked only thirty minutes away. If there was an emergency I would be home in 10 minutes by taxi. You notice still, the whole deferring of family responsibility to me. I will admit now that my decision to get this job, in the long run, was actually a very good one.

"There is 'life after death' no matter how you define it. No matter how you define death or life. Each traumatic circumstance seems to bring about a bit of both."

This little job, having some income and especially meeting new people that apparently thought I was pretty good was to be the salve I needed to heal. I worked for that company from 1978 to 1993. When it came to work, my husband didn't pay much notice. I made sure all my responsibilities were met regarding our daughters and the domestic chores of the home. During those years I had been promoted from receptionist, clerk to assistant to the sales administrator. The sales manager called me his 'girl' once. I told him I didn't like that. He then started to refer to me as his 'right hand man'. I was pretty proud. I used to talk about our projects a lot. I thought I was important. Dick said

"I preferred you more when you were just a receptionist" or the other wisecrack was

"When you earn as much money as I do, then you can add your two cents worth"

In fall 1998, he got a third DUI and Ontario took away his driving permit for thirteen months. I had to quit my job to be a driver to him for that duration.

His client base was all over Eastern Ontario. On the other days, we had to get to his office which was thirty miles away. I would also have to go back at the end of his work day to pick him up. There was no appreciation. It was as if it were a given. I had had two part time jobs when that happened. His response to me years later when I said

"I had to quit my job because of you!" was

"Oh anyways! It was just a little job." I remember this scene so vividly. We were sitting in the living room on River Road looking out to the water in the distance. I had asked him about his day, which was always of interest to me. I asked him

"I hope you don't find me too boring since I quit working. I don't have anything really interesting to talk to you about?" his reply

"Don't worry about it. I'm kind of relieved actually. Now I don't have to listen to you go on and on 'blah, blah, blah!' about all your staff and every little detail of your work day."

It never ceases to amaze me how he always had to belittle me. He was a BULLY through and through. Luckily the people, at the few companies I had worked for, have thought I was a good worker and a nice person. I won't dwell on my working days. They were never the 'be all' of my existence. Suffice it to say that I worked very hard and got good promotions with decent pay. The paychecks were accounted for. There was enough money from my salary to provide Marie and Trudy with private school and university educations and let's not forget the weddings. Plus OH YA!, my favorite spending extravaganza. My little paycheck was able to cover the costs for an Island of the 1000 Islands for twenty eight years. I think I did OK!

"The pride in my being able to provide those contributions to my family cannot be diminished. It is all deep in the core of my being, protected as if in a fortress."

I am not a proponent of joint bank accounts. There was his money. There was my money. We each had financial responsibilities to meet. The only difference was, I was a saver. My husband used to call me 'the squirrel'. He'd always come to me to pay off income taxes owing or California legal fees to the tune of $4000. etc. There are just too many here to enumerate. You get the picture. If Dick and I had had a joint banking account, we would both have always been close to bankruptcy and in over draft. Luckily I was able to spare myself that embarrassment.

CHAPTER 14

THE 80s—ISLAND GHOST STORIES

The boys were settled in the USA now. The girls were thriving. I was calmer. I was doing rather well at my job. This was the time when woman's lib or better yet the 'feminist movement' was establishing new norms in hiring practices. Women were finally being recognized for something more than just a piece of fluff on the assembly line or in the secretarial pool. I started as a receptionist and after nine years became the first female manager for that company. I was proud. I brought all my educator, organizational skills as well as my nurturing skills to the table. I spent most of my time working harder than a man in the same position. I also had to always stay on my toes, looking over my shoulder, trying to prove to the men that the general manager had not made a mistake in promoting me. I had a saying when it came to a woman interacting with male counterparts.

It was "COVER THINE ASS", not only sexually but professionally.

It was worth it though because I see that a lot of toxic circumstances have been removed from the work environment. Yet the arch rivalry between less than competent men and their able female colleagues still seems to be raging on. You would think that having a new, super busy job and two children and a distant, weekends only husband and father and a needy mom and dad living down the block, would have been enough on my plate.

Heck No!

My girlfriend, Maureen now living in Ontario, calls one evening and says

"Oh since you guys are coming down for the weekend, how would you like to go see an Island of the 1000 Islands that is up for sale now?"

"An Island are you crazy? Nobody can afford that. We had agreed to consider purchasing, maybe, a mainland property on the river where we could build a couple of cabins"

"Oh it's going to be fun. The weather is supposed to be good and we really don't have anything else to do."

"OK see you Saturday morning early."

My friends second husband was military and he had been relocated to a beautiful part of the world. It was idyllic for summer, family fun. In the late 70's, this area was still not commercialized. It was truly pristine. I used to call it "God's country". My father had cruised down from Montreal every August for at least two decades. He and my mother would go from dock to dock at the Canadian provincial parks and enjoy three weeks of peace and quiet. The original plan was to hopefully provide Maureen and Bruce a small place where they could enjoy part time freedom and get away from the rigid confines of the army base. Dick and I loved the idea of cottage life rather than boating and thought investing in Ontario was a much better idea than in Quebec. That way, the two girlfriends and all the five kids could still keep in touch on weekends and vacations. It really was just a lot of chatter, so we thought. I wasn't too serious. I figured you needed a million dollars to buy an Island. My girlfriend was adamant.

"We found something you won't believe or be able to resist."

Just thinking of a boat ride in the Islands was good enough for me. So the following day we drove two and a half hours and met a real estate agent in Guan and came to visit Islands E & F. A week later we four and the five children between us became Islanders. I was so proud. I knew it would be difficult but we were securing a piece of Canada. It was incredible to me.

In the fall of '78, before the final purchase paper work was completed, we were given permission to return to the property. To our astonishment we found this beautiful house, a replica of the wealth and opulence of the 20s, to be a product of years of neglect. What a sad house it was! The land had originally consisted of three small islands. The original owner, Mr. S, a wealthy coal baron, had the small islands connected by pouring tons of rock from the nearby quarry. The shape of the final, almost one acre property was in that of a horseshoe. The original owner was a betting man. He owned several racing horses. The house was built by itinerant workers from the British Iles who had immigrated to Canada and worked for a stipend and room and board. There were, also, servants to work in the service of the master and his family. These were not slaves. They were free to leave anytime they wanted. These were the family's usual town staff who would take over the duties at the cottage during the summer vacations. Life was grand in the summer. The whole area was inhabited by wealthy men of commerce and academia from the University in Kingston. The rich played, the poor worked. I had the honor of meeting the descendants of both the very rich and the poor. Their stories were fascinating. The wall street crash took place in 1929, Mr. S lost his fortune and apparently the only thing that was still mortgaged by the bank was the Island property. The home was rented out to several different summer residents. It 1951 it was eventually bought by a Dutch couple with four sons. He was a professor of music at the university. Story has it that the boys were really wild. That's kind of funny to hear now, because to my recollection most of the children spending the summer in the 1000 Islands were all on the wild side. The pleasures of swimming, the sailing, the canoeing, the fishing, the parties until dawn were all conducive to exciting, crazy times. In fact the adults were no different. It was indeed an enviable place to be. The 'townies' resented those 'rich Island kids' and used to try and befriend some so that they too could partake in this great life. The Dutch couple's family was all grown up by 70s. As was customary in those days the children had left for greener pastures in other parts of Canada. Island E was to change hands again. Here we come!

Our arrival was memorable, etched in my mind forever. We opened the back, kitchen door and all nine of us walked into the dining room. The shellacked tongue and groove pine walls and ceiling were coated with spider webs. There were many hornets nests. I even found the skeleton of a bat on the top of a door frame YUCK! The house and property had been totally discarded by the owners. Our neighbor used to rent the house once in a while until he inherited his uncle's island. He would do his best to maintain it while he was staying there. He did that because he, having been born and raised in the village, had a remarkable respect for the history of this area. It is sad to think that people can loose interest in their home, but it happens. I was to learn that myself decades later. This was to be the 'clean up of the century'. We worked all through the weekends of October. The weather gods were kind and generous. The men and the children worked outside chopping down trees, clearing shrubs, picking up kindling and securing docks. We girls got brooms and mops and swept and scrubbed until everything started to shine again. You see the house did not have any electricity or running water at the time. We would get buckets of water from the river, pour them into cauldrons on the wooden stove and wait for the water to get piping hot. We didn't really wait. There were several pots boiling at the same time. One was always ready for use. Another useful thing about that exercise is, the kitchen was kept warm and toasty. That's where the nine of us would gather to warm up and get cozy.

It gets dark early at that time of the year and crossing the river can be dangerous, especially to novices. One Saturday afternoon we made a last minute decision. We decided to sleep over. People seeing us now would have thought we were crazy but we were so excited and happy. The men went back to the mainland to get a couple of buckets of chicken. The house was really toasty because Maureen had the fires going all day. She was a tiny woman. I was easily a head taller than she. I would put things up on the pantry shelves and she would come and take them down and put them on the lower shelves. Yet, she was a force to be reckoned with. Maureen was afraid of nothing. She could drive trailing the boat, back it down the launch ramp. She could run the boat. She was a pro at everything. Her husband was in the service, so when he was going to be away she wanted to make sure she was totally self sufficient. I, on the other hand learned nothing of that. Thanks to Maureen's coaching, I did overcome my fear of fire and became the official fire maker for a couple of decades. That first night was remarkable. We even had the five kids stand and sing 'O Canada' before going to bed. That became a custom of ours. We were so proud to have the privilege of owning this land. There were lots of old wrought iron bed that would squeak every time you rolled over. We used carpets that we had beaten clean outdoors, just hours before, to cover the children. The five slept together in the center room. They could keep each other company and their body heat could keep the room semi comfortable. We adults had gotten into some sherry so we weren't too cold. We tossed a coin for the master bedroom. Dick and I got that one on the west side and Maureen and her husband took the east wing. The darkness and the silence of nature at that time of the year is awesome. I remember, so vividly, that I could see my breath as I exhaled in the dark. It was lit only by the reflection of light from the stars and the moon just out the window.

The sale transactions seemed to take forever. Being 'city folk' we had difficulty comprehending what appeared to be a lackadaisical attitude of the locals professionals. For instance someone would say

"The document won't be ready for at least a week because we have to drive all the way to Brockville to get it registered"

Ok! that town was thirty minutes away. What's the big deal? We Montrealers were commuting twice a week for two and a half hours. Hot shots! You know the kind. No disrespect intended. A lot of people around here still feel that way. What's the hurry? It's how far? They are good people, the 'salt of the earth'. The weekend of November 4th, 1978 we were able to celebrate our joint ownership. We toasted with cheap champagne in plastic cups. The kids just ran like hellions through the whole house, up the kitchen stairs, up into the attic, back outside, back into the house, up the living room stairs, over and over again until they were left breathless. They were all tucked away in their new sleeping bags and out for the count by nine o'clock. I had stuffed the bottom of the bags with towel wrapped hot bricks. It was an 'old world' trick I had learned from a Hungarian lady at work. Theory was they kept the inside of the bag toasty so the body could be less chilled. It was mild enough that night so that Dick and I were able to go for a paddle around the island. It was our eleventh year wedding anniversary. We were able to look into the various rooms that we had lit with candles. It was truly a spectacular sight. The house was majestic again. It was evenings like that one that we would be able to enjoy and share together so many times over. They always helped to ease the pain of sore muscles and all the tension from the city jobs. That Sunday the men put up the shutters and the house went totally black like a tomb, remember no electricity just a flashlight. That is a really weird feeling! Now our house was battened down, ready for the winter. More than that, now she had the smells of cleaners and an aura of family life. We were two families that so deeply respected it's grand past. We were more than willing to provide it with a future of laughter and joy. 'The Island House' was to be lonely never more!!

The following Spring we four Montrealers headed out to Gan in the hope that spring might have sprung early. Mid March and believe it. Yes! incredible the ice on the St. Lawrence river was actually gone in that area. Only river rats or cottagers or islanders or all of the above can actually appreciate how fabulous that is. We were like the homing pigeons. We had to cross this mighty river to our summer home. Bruce's boat was launched the third week in March. We ignored all the warnings the locals had given us.

"It's too early. You never know what you'll find at this time of the year. Things could freeze overnight. The boat might not start. You're all alone out there."

All nine of us were in our winter gear. The kids had their snowsuits on. It was cold. The trip would normally be just under ten minutes. This was, to me, like crossing the Atlantic in the Titanic. Bruce was running the boat. Dick was on the bow leaning out using a boat paddle trying to push some loose ice floats out of the way. I must tell you I was scared but exhilarated. The kids thought this was awesome. As we approached the island we saw a person walking about. My urban paranoia got the best of me and I imagined a vagrant or thief or both. I tell you it didn't take me long to figure out that no one but us crazies would go out on the water that early in the season. The landing dock was gone and we had a huge holding tank that had drifted up on the west beach. Here I was screaming

"Where's the dock? The dock is gone!" My dear husband tried to reassure me, in a stern but gentle voice

"SHUT UP and RELAX"

All I kept thinking to myself is I've spent all this money and now I can't even get on my land. The so called trespasser was Jake. He was the caretaker of a huge mansion on a neighboring island across from us. It was his habit every year when the ice broke to check on all the properties in the area and give the owners a call in case of serious damages. The twenty thousand gallon tank had broken away from some other island and landed on our shores. Our crossing dock from the boathouse to the island would never be found. It had probably drifted off and could be caught up in some ice jam down river. We would have to build again. Dick made his way into the horseshoe bay at the front of the house. We tied the boat down very close to the rock wall. The kids were able to crawl off the bow unto the lawn. We thanked Jake for his vigilance. He and several other river men kept a careful eye on us city slickers. They all became legends in our time. There is still a great deal of folklore being written about them even years after their deaths.

I'm not one to write much about scenery and stuff. I usually even skip through it when I am reading a book. I have always thought I would never be able to do the beauty of nature justice. This though I must share. I'm going to close my eyes and visualize. You can do the same. There had been a violent North Easterly storm. We call them 'Nor'easters'. The towns people along that whole seaway corridor had suffered the tragedy and damage from a storm that would go down on record as being the worst in twenty six years. That's is one of the reasons we love old timers for, the weather history. The water was very high and moving extremely fast. You can't even imagine the speed at which these currents are flowing. The waves were at least two feet high. That would explain why, after two days of constant rocking, those large items like docks and tanks and even boat houses managed to break free. The ropes or the cables just got frayed or stretched and wore out. The water was carrying hundreds of ice floats down river along the main channel. We were very lucky because our Island was sheltered by two others whose retaining walls would always take the brunt of the pressure of the water and the multitude of debris speedily floating by. It was like watching, from a distance, the floats at a Santa Claus Parade. The noise of the howling wind and the crashing of the ice against the retaining walls was like no other symphony in the world. The smashed ice turned into thousands of shredded, frozen particles that just flew up and across the beach. They could lay there for a week until the weather got warmer and nature's own ice castles thawed into a puddle. The trees were weighed down with iced covered limbs. The branches were shining and glittering with the rays of the sun. We went back to town after a couple of hours. There was nothing to be done now without tools and equipment. We came back the next day and the men were able to pull the 'work horse', an aluminum boat, out of it's watery grave to dry on land. Luckily the motor was stored in the work shed. We were very dependent on that beat up old boat. It proved itself worthy of our respect several times. The men were able to build a new dock with timbers that had been found by Bruce in a friends barn. OH! ISLAND LIFE. You either love it or hate it. I was often anxious and frightened but honestly I was always exhilarated.

Between the four adults, there were approximately forty relatives, elders, siblings, cousins and let us not forget friends. We were so proud of the island and loved to share it with everyone. Most weeks of July and August were booked solid. Maureen had stopped working and had a fourth child, a daughter. She was up all that summer. It was convenient because our daughters were able to stay at the island with her gang during the week while Dick and I worked in Montreal. Marie has horror stories of having been the chief slave and gofer of that time. It was not unusual that ten or twelve people would be staying in the house during our absence. The attic had been converted into a dormitory where all the kids slept. The other six rooms were for adults. It was a full house indeed. We would assume that the week guests would leave by Friday. Unfortunately that was not the case. They would stay over the weekend just to be able to catch up with our news. It was very disturbing because the last thing we wanted after working a full week in town was arriving with twelve people meeting us at the dock, all jabbering at the same time. No rest for the wicked. Some folks were great. Others were never invited again. Many thought because they were vacationing that they didn't need to help or even contribute financially for food or gas for the boat. Everybody wanted a ride up river or wanted to go waterskiing. We did love to oblige. We truly wanted them to remember their stay with fond memories. It's interesting to me though that a few assumed we were well off because we had bought an island. That was not the case. We were four working islanders and one was on maternity leave. Eventually we had a piggy bank sitting on the credenza with a 'gas money' sign glued to it. Friends and family members started to get the message and left us a couple of twenty dollar bills for a five day stay.

We did have what would best be described as an unusual guest, or should I say boarder. At first we thought the phantom was the spirit of the original owner of the estate. The first time we ever took note of something quirky was when I volunteered to take care of my boss's dog during my vacation. She was to be in Hungary for two weeks. The dog's name was Snoopy. He was an old, curly haired beast with 'will nots' stuck to his bottom. When he came out of the lake he always smelled so bad the kids would scatter. He would run after them for fun and the game went on and on. Everybody cringed at the idea of this dog being allowed in the house. There was a small adjacent room, off the living room. The only thing in it was a turn of the 20th century church pump organ. That is where this stinky dog could spend the night. Throw an old blanket in there, close the door and let him sleep. Unfortunately the house was more than a little bit lop sided and the door could never quite close completely. It never quite made it to the door frame but was definitely jammed against the old pine floor boards. The adults headed up to bed through the kitchen stairwell so as not to alert this dog of our presence. It had to be about 2 a.m and I heard some organ sounds. There was no music played just a deep, hollow sound. Then I could hear Snoopy dog whimpering and I just rolled over and went back to sleep. The heck with this noise. We all woke up early in the morning which was customary. There at the bottom of the living room stairs was Snoopy barking his joy at our being up and about. We were stunned! The door to the room had been open wide. How did that dog get the door open? Over breakfast we all asked each other question like

"Did anyone let him out because he was hollering? Did you hear anything weird going on downstairs?

Maureen was the only one who said she thought she had heard the organ also but figured it was the dog. The rest of the time that Snoopy stayed with us, he got to sleep outside. I didn't care what my boss thought. This was the country and I was not going to have anybody's dog rob me of my sleep on my flipping vacation, no less. A few other circumstances left us all, including a couple of guests, with a somewhat creepy feeling.

We could be sitting in the living room by the fire and someone sitting in the corner would say

"I'm getting the creeps. There is something at the top of the stairs staring down at us."

My mother would be sitting on the front lawn and say there was someone in the attic looking down at her.

"Probably the kids", we would say.

Dick woke up in a sweat one night. He couldn't breathe. Someone, a shadow, was leaning over him, with two hands pressing down hard on his chest. It took his breath away! A twelve year old guest saw a young girl in a white nightgown coming down the kitchen stairwell while she was going up. We were playing cards in the kitchen and I had to go get some paper out of my desk in my bedroom upstairs. Remember, no electricity. I was very comfortable walking through the house in total darkness. We always had light coming through the windows from outside and the bedroom doors were always kept open. On my way down the hallway back to the staircase I put my hand down on the oak banister rail and I felt a hand push my right shoulder. I held on tight and turned my head around and said

"What the hell!"

Nothing there, but I distinctly felt someone try to shove me. Once, I was awakened by the sound of a bouncing ball on the attic floor over my head. I took the flashlight, climbed up another narrow set of stairs to check on the kids. They were all asleep. Another time it was a doll baby stroller that I heard rolling, back and forth, overhead. I couldn't believe one of the kids could be playing at this hour of the night. I went up and checked. All five kids were in a deep sleep. I used to hear cats meowing and there were no cats on the island. We adults kept these stories among ourselves. We spoke with our neighbor James who had rented the house for a few summers. He recounted his experiences. He began

"We had thrown a big party. Everybody had crashed. I was awakened by the sound of a woman crying outside. I walked out in the damp night and thought the weeping was coming from the gazebo, at the point. I thought maybe one of the ladies got put off by one of the male guest and decided to take refuge in the cabin. I lit up a smoke, walked towards the guest house. I stepped up the stairs and the crying stopped abruptly. I opened the screen door. There was no on there."

He told us that local folklore speak of a legend of star crossed lovers. The original owner had four daughters. One fell in love with an itinerant worker. That was definitely taboo in those days. The Island family was wealthy upper class. The young man was hired help. The two just do not mix. The so called liaison was disapproved of by the family. The young man apparently hanged himself from the rafters in the gazebo. My Dear Aunt Madeleine lived in that cabin when she came to the island for some well deserved R&R. When I told her of this story, my aunt who was deaf and a divorcee said

"I'm not afraid! He can make all the racket he wants I won't hear him anyways. As long as he is gentle he can stay in the gazebo as long as he wants."

The two of us hunched over and laughed so hard we thought we were going to pee our panties.

I often wonder if the spirits actually could play or weave a web in our daily goings on. The relationship between our friends was often volatile. In turn, ours with them had become strained. They had moved to Montreal from Kingston and could not afford the trips to the island. Maureen, since she was at home taking care of the family, was defaulting on her mortgage contributions. I chose to cover those because I sure as heck did not want the bank to give us any grief. She was a good friend. I presumed she'd get back to work as soon as her last daughter was old enough. The end of the season arrived. I took out the financial statements of island renovations expenses, which were to be split half and half. Dick had installed brand new electrical work and modernized the plumbing. He even got us a brand new hot water tank. We were finally modernized, thanks to all his hard work and dedication to our basic comforts and to the house. Our partner started to make excuses as to why he thought he should not have to pay his share of half of the expenses. He claimed

"They were not at the cottage as much as we since they had moved back to Montreal and were no longer only thirty minutes away. Their contributions should be reduced. Dick was not having to pay for his gas because he had a company car. Dick had a company building fund. The actual costs of renovations was not cash directly coming out of his pocket." He proceeded to claim that

"After all we were a two income family with only two kids. They were a one income family with four kids."

I could not believe my ears. Had this man no pride or was he just thinking he could con us with all the bullshit. I was so fed up with the whining I finally asked

"Can you not afford this land partnership?" he answered

"No I cannot and neither can Maureen. We think the island should be sold." My response was

"Over my dead body, I didn't buy an island just to have it sold three years later. We will get it appraised and see what it's worth."

Dick and I covered all the cost of that season and prepared to have an amicable dissolution of the contract between them and us. Bruce figured this could all be done between the four of us. We could come to an agreement and all four of us would sign a document confirming everything. He would have drafted it up on a paper napkin if he could have gotten away with it. It got pretty tense. I paid for the appraisal. The property value came to not quite $4000. more than we had originally paid. It was imperative to me that I must have a lawyer involved in all transactions. I hired Dick's company lawyer to represent us. Our partner had to get his own. That really annoyed him. I called it

"The cost of doing business the right way."

The whole transaction was settled in this manner. I gave them cash for half the real estate profits accrued over those few years. They took back the boat which they owed. I did not have them pay me back the $4000. they had borrowed from me for their down payment share on the original purchase. I negotiated with my bank for a new mortgage for the present value of the property. Imagine way back then in 1982, I got that mortgage at 18.5%. Come hell or high water we were to be the only owners. I feel bad to some extent. I have always maintained, that Maureen had to do what she had to do for her family's sake and I did what I had to do for mine. I strongly recommend against any partnerships on any purchase between friends or family, unless they are legal transactions. Personalities, circumstances and finances dictate the outcome of the relationships. Each of which usually change over time. It is a very high risk and expensive situation. One thing about me is I will give you my time and all the energy left in my soul to help you but when it comes to my hard earned nickel

"Don't mess with me!"

The winter season was busy as usual. It was hard for me, a little bit tight, to be paying for a property for five months of the year when we never set foot on it. The Island was now my baby, my responsibility. It was my gift to me and my family. When I think about it now, there is no denying, the Island was something I did for me, myself and I. When they say now to women

"Take care of yourself"

I actually did that way back then. The very thought of spring and opening up the house brought me such a high. I put up with so much crap at work but it was all worth it when I got that paycheck every two weeks. We owned a piece of the Canadian landscape. It was February, my colleague Iris was over one evening. Our husbands had gone to shoot pool and grab a few beers. She asked me about the ghost stories. Many Italians have always had a belief system in the spirit world, the evil eye and other such superstitions. She said her grandmother in Italy was very sick and wondered if we could find out how she was doing with the help of a Ouija board. I told Iris I didn't have one but we could cut up little squares of paper and write the letters of the alphabet on each and see if it works. We had absolutely nothing better to do. We just felt like fooling around, an amateur séance. My eldest daughter who was around thirteen joined us at the dining room table. We had placed an inverted wine glass in the center and had lined all the letters around it in a semi circular position. Iris put her right fingers on the glass stem, asked her question but there was no movement. We three, after a couple of tries each, started to giggle. This was crazy. We were being so silly but we were having fun. Marie was sitting to my left with the window behind her. Iris was sitting across from me. I placed two fingers of my right hand on the bottom of the wine glass. I had such a strange thought so I verbalized it and said

"You must be so cold out there?"

I was thinking about the ghosts on The Island and how freezing it must be in that house. Then all of a sudden the wine glass with my fingers on it started to move just below the letters. It moved ever so slowly, first to the right then arching back again towards the left. The three of us were dumbfounded. No kidding! My sweet daughter asked

"Are you good or are you evil?"

The glass moved to the letter E, than moved to the letter V, then moved to the letter I. The glass, then, went flying off the table to the left side of my face and smashed itself to pieces on the wall behind me. My daughter's and girlfriend's screaming was what brought me out of my trance. I shouted angrily

"What is wrong with you people?" Iris answered

"You looked awful a minute ago. Your eyes turned back in their sockets and all we could see was the white. Then you woke up."

You have never seen three women move so fast out of the dining room to the living room. Even my German Shepherd dog was leaping up and down at the front hallway door seeming to want to get out of the house. It was crazy! Well it did not take us more than a second to get our act together. We put all the letters in an ashtray and burned them. Then I put on my boots and went out to the end of the back yard and buried them, including the ashtray, in the deep snow. It was the last time I ever attempted to consult with the Netherworld. I must say that is not quite true. A couple of years later, due to additional bizarre occurrences, I had to seek out the help of a trained Paranormal psychologists.

One night, at the Island, during a fantastic thunder storm I got up to close the bedroom window. There was a strong gale blowing over the sill and the rain was coming in. It wasn't late, only around 10:30 pm. I closed the window and leaned on the sill. A lightning strike hit on the west beach and there under the willow tree, stood a man. He was at least six feet tall and really thin. He wore a set of overalls dark in color, I guess maybe black or dark blue. His face was looking up to the house. His hair was cropped very short, like a brush cut and he had a 'Lincoln' beard. You know narrow at the side but fuller at the chin and jaw line. I'm sure I blinked. I must have because immediately the figure was gone. I turned around, got into bed and told Dick all about what I had just seen. I asked

"Can you believe that?" He said

"Sure. I believe in extra terrestrial, why not ghosts. Nobody really knows for sure what is out there in the universe."

Neither one of us was afraid. I fell asleep thinking, maybe it was that itinerant worker's spirit looking for his lost love. The vision sure looked like a laborer of olden days.

Another time, Dick and I together encountered what we think was a spirit. We had finished a great steak dinner and were out walking the grounds checking on everything to make sure all was secure for the night. It was dusk and as we walked out of the boat house we saw a dog, a beautiful totally white dog on the spit of land. The animal looked at us. Dick and I looked at each other. The short hairs on the back of my neck were standing. Then the dog turned around and started to walk across the lawn. We followed. My husband asked

"That's not Tammy?"

"Can't be. She should be in the house in her bed in the front room. I'll go check. You follow the dog. I'll be right back."

I ran into the house and found our German shepherd sound asleep. She was fourteen years old by then and retired early. Now, I know exactly how she felt then. I came back out and Dick was in the back of the house by the kitchen gallery.

"Where's the dog?" I asked

"It disappeared! I'm not kidding you! It came around the side of the holding tank to the back. I was several feet behind it. As I came around I saw the dog was nowhere. That was just a few minutes ago." I suggested

"Let's start looking. He might be under the house or behind the shed or maybe just swam off. The dog must belong to someone and got lost. It happened once before remember with that Beagle who had jumped out of the fisherman's boat and swam up to our island and was there when we got back from work. He had a collar with a telephone number on his tag. We called it and then the owners came by and picked him up. Maybe this is the same thing?"

We looked over every inch of the island. We called the dog. Dick even crawled under part of the gallery with a flashlight, trying to spot the animal.

Nothing! We gave up and headed up to bed shaking our heads. We concluded it must have swum away. Even though neither one of us had heard him go into the water or any dog paddling noises. At night those sounds would have been easy to identify because everything is so acute.

The next day we headed back to Montreal. In the marina as we were unloading our boat to pack up the car we saw the beast again. Dick pointed out to a perfectly white husky sitting still on the tailgate of a truck. We both looked at each other and wondered. In the month of November of that same fall, my dear Tammy dog had to be put down. I miss her so badly. She was a true friend. I have never been able to replace her. To this day I think the 'white, Husky German shepherd like dog' was the spirit of Tammy warning us of her demise. Maybe it was coming to get her that night and we interrupted. My curiosity was aroused after Tammy's death. I did some research in ancient aboriginal mythology and I found that apparently the wolf is a common spirit that roams the northern lake lands. Actually, I like my story better.

Spring has sprung. It's April. Time to pack ourselves up and leave Montreal on the weekends to go across the mighty St. Lawrence and open up the house. This time, thanks to the Island king's hard work the previous year, we could install electric heaters to warm up the bedrooms. I would stoke up the wood stove and fireplace for coziness. It was great having just one master of the estate. I truly missed my girlfriend Maureen and her kids. It was weird walking around not hearing the cacophony of voices. The twin boys used to run a lot in the house or fall in the river, by accident. There was always boys clothing, drying on a makeshift clothes line above the wood burning stove. It didn't matter how often we yelled at them to

"Stay off of those rocks. They are very slippery. You're going to fall in."

They fell in! There were a lot less guests that year. Our girls were able to stay at the Island over the summer. Dick and I took separate vacations. Each of us were able to be at the Island with the girls for two weeks at a time. In addition to that my aunt Mado and my mother in law each stayed for three weeks to help. So all the bases were pretty well covered for the girls' summer vacation. Dick bought a beat up boat and trailer in Montreal which we were using for island commuting. It eventually was called 'Patches' because Dick had sideswiped a neighbor island and the right side of the boat had to be re fiber glassed. That side was never painted to blend in with the rest of the boat, ergo 'the Patches'. I was blamed for that incident because Dick claimed he was blinded by my flashlight as he was coming between both islands. He was going full throttle, meaning full speed. Luckily he was close enough he was able to steer it into our boathouse.

There was always something going on with the boats. One afternoon Marie was coming back from town with Trudy, granny and a boy cousin from B C. The motor conked out just minutes away from our place. After several futile attempts at getting it going again she decided to jump out of the boat. She swam to our island, got the dingy out of the boathouse and rowed back to the disabled 'patches'. She finally managed to tow the boat and the occupants back home. Sometimes the engine was flooded and we would just have to wait until it recovered. Trudy had an experience coming back from a neighbor's place one night. I had a trained ear for river noises. I looked out the window and there was Trudy standing in the stern with her arms wrapped around the engine block. She was steering the boat with her body. The cable connecting the wheel in the front to the motor in the back had severed. She made it into the boat house safely, great steering! I tell you our girls were really brave. The following morning we called Dick in Montreal and told him of the problem. To this day he still claims

"There is nothing wrong with those boats. I never have any problems with them. It's just that the girls don't know how to run them properly."

No empathy! Nothing! Ever! It was always somebody else's fault. He just loved to lay blame. The fact that he never had the boats professionally serviced at the end of the season is totally irrelevant. The more I write the more I realize what a pathetic specimen he is. Most men are wired to help the 'weaker sex' which we three ladies were not. Most men have an innate mechanism to want to protect women from harm. Every winter I would ask Dick to have the boat checked out and ready for next spring opening. He never did. He would just ignore me. His philosophy "What me worry?" was entrenched. I worried enough for both of us.

I, as I have mentioned, do wonder if spirits contribute to the mood of a house. Can their influence have a negative impact on the inhabitants of that dwelling? Judging from the spooky movies, they might have. I can't confirm or deny that from my own personal experiences. It would be almost too ludicrous to presume that our marital problems were directed by phantoms. Things were getting rough around the edges between Dick and me. Perhaps I should say for me. Dick just kept on doing his things and I and the girls just had to adjust. I became less patient and more combative. I started to dislike company coming. I never did have the capacity to drink excessively. The few times I have been totally hammered, I just threw up each and every time. That was a great deterrent. After everyone had gone to bed I would get out of bed and go back downstairs and check all the ashtrays, inside and outside to make sure the cigarette butts were all out. I would pour buckets of water on the burning pit where inevitably Dick had had a bonfire going. Everybody had a 'blast'. An island is great for rowdy parties because the police can't come to your house and tell you to quiet down. The cops do not cross the river at night unless it is a maritime accident. The neighbors can complain to you all they want. They usually won't though because more than likely they are doing the very same thing on the weekend. One summer I chose to make myself my own separate room. I was really fed up with Dick's snores bellowing in my ears every single night. I used to have to get up twenty minutes after he came to bed and move. Why not have my own room where I could get some peace and quiet and much needed sleep. My aunt and his mother said that was not a good sign.

"A woman is supposed to sleep in her husband's bed" I would answer

"If she can get to sleep, right!"

My belief was that once my husband got the sex he wanted, I was lucky to have the luxury of going to any other room I chose and just sleep and not being poked at later for yet another quickie round.

The room I chose was in the centre of the house, beside the master's. What a name, master bedroom. I turned it into a real girlie, girlie room. The walls still had the original four inch studs running vertically and horizontally along the two main walls. I was a voracious reader. Our friends would bring books and leave them or take a book away and bring it back. I called it the 'book room' because there had to be at least one hundred paperbacks filling those narrow shelves. There were three large windows facing west and outside were the branches of ancient oak trees.

You could actually see the birds and the squirrels nesting. I had lavender potpourris and miniature oil lanterns for ambience. The bed linen was white with small floral designs reminiscent of the French country provincial style. I slept in a fifty year old iron framed double bed. Gosh it was uncomfortable but sleep I did. It was my sanctuary. My daughters knew their dad was a loud snorer. They were not at all surprised at my private night quarters. When too much company came I forfeited my room. No one was the wiser. That was the style in those days. I was starting to collect my own 'skeletons in the closets'. I confided in no one. By then, the girls each had their own rooms at the far end of the house. No one was sleeping in the attic anymore. I used to get this very fine, cozy feeling when I was resting in the book room. One night I was sound asleep. A hand was slowly making it's way from my wrist to my forearm, to my shoulder. The sensation was so gentle. It was like a feather. I felt such a rush of heat through my whole body. I could actually feel the blood flowing in my veins. It felt warm to me. It was kind of like that slight shuddering feeling a woman has after she has orgasm. I felt the hairs rising and I immediately awoke and sat straight up. I thought Dick was beside me. I was really going to give him heck for disturbing me. Yet there was no one. The bedroom door was still closed. I rolled over to my side, looked out the window to the starlit sky and went promptly back to sleep. That occurrence took place a few times and I liked it. I had my own secret lover and didn't care. It was always a simple stroke, a caress. I happened to mention the story to Iris and another colleague of mine. We used to try to get out to dinner at least once a month. There was very little time for chatting at work, not the juicy stuff anyways. Iris' friend gave me the name of a medium that they both frequented once in a while. She would make an appointment for all three of us. It would be fun. Sure why not! I always find it interesting to note that even though French Canadians are baptized Catholic there was always this underlying interest in the supernatural. Taboo can be so cool.

The consult was late in the afternoon. I climbed the outside stairwell to the third landing. I rang the bell and was greeted by a woman in her late forties. She led me into a dimly lit room. It was tidy but there were volumes everywhere, even on the floor, neatly stacked along the wall. There was a fragrance of incense. She sat down in a straight back chair and asked me to sit directly in front of her. It wasn't at all what you would imagine. Not at all a gypsy boudoir, more like a professor's study. She told me to think of three questions and wait quietly. I watched her inhale deeply three times and exhale. She seemed to be transforming herself into what I do not know. That spooked me. Then she asked me what it was I wanted to know. The very weird thing about it is this French woman was speaking fluent English to me without a trace of an accent. I proceeded to tell her my stories. She confirmed that there was a ghost.

"His name is Arthur. He will not harm you or your children. There are about forty-five other spirits in the space around the Island."

She took another deep breath, exhaled slowly then her eyes opened and she continued our conversation in French. She could not tell me his history. This kind of disappointed me. She recommended that I get in touch with someone who could exorcise the spirits in and around the house. It is best to purify the environment. The session took less than an hour. I left feeling no differently than when I had gone in. A couple of weeks later a salesman colleague of mine came to my office. His name was P'tit Bout Langelier. That translated would mean 'short stuff'. He had heard through the grapevine that I had ghosts at the cottage. News really gets around fast in the office once you let it out in the open. His wife was a student of Parapsychology at the University de Montreal. She was in her third year. He wanted to tell her about my stories and see if she could or would consider being of some help. I spilled the beans to Andre. He then spoke to his wife who then called me directly that vary same week. We chose a date for them to come over and stay with us at the Island house for the weekend.

It was early July and M. and Mme Langelier were to be the only guests that three day weekend. The family and I were looking forward to their visit. We were fascinated by the concept of having someone with Jeanne's powers with us. Our curiosity was definitely aroused. We did want to get to the bottom of this if possible so we could resume our lives without too much external distraction. Having ghosts was not frightening to us. It was more of an inconvenience or a nuisance. The Thursday of that week Andre came to my office to tell me that his wife and he would not be able to come to the cottage because she was ill with an intestinal flu. I was disappointed but we could always defer to another time. Dick and I and the girls settled in the Island house on Friday evening. The phone rang around nine. It was Andre asking if they could come by tomorrow for noon. His wife was still quite sick but insisted that she come. She had a very strong premonition that the situation had taken on some urgency. She would explain when she saw us. The following day I welcomed them and ushered her upstairs to a bedroom so that she could rest after the three hour drive. A half hour later she was at the screen door of the dining room and wanted to talk with us. She explained Parapsychology to us and what her studies entailed. She talked about numerology and Dick wanted his done. She took all the pertinent details required to draft up his chart. I then took her on a tour of the island and the house and we all contributed our facts on the history of the property and our experiences. We had dinner and at nightfall we all headed upstairs together for the night. The following morning all of us talked about the good night rest. All except Jeanne, that is, who had been up most of the night.

We all poured ourselves our first cup of coffee. Jeanne began her story.

"I had heard very loud and aggressive sounds in our room. I left the room because I did not want my husband awakened by them assuming he might hear them also. I came downstairs and curled up on the living room couch. The noises followed me. I concluded the spirits were manifesting themselves only to me. Otherwise the whole household would have been awakened and wandering and wondering. This show of strength was for my benefit. I think the spirit knew I was coming this weekend. That would explain why I have been so ill and retching all week. The ghost wanted me to stay home in Montreal. He knew his staying here would be threatened by my visit."

Jeanne explained that I was the principle enabler. I was welcoming the ghost through my acceptance of his presence. Spirits are supposed to cross over. Some do not, due to unfinished earthly business. This one was gentle with me but obviously was dangerous to everyone else who tried to sever his contact. My husband was a rival. We were, also, supposed to be very vigilant about our eldest daughter because prepubescent girls are easily vulnerable to influences and can be targeted. As long as I permitted this ghost to stay I was inevitably leaving open a portal for other, much more evil ones to enter our space. She thought that extras had been enlisted during the night to create all that racket in order to try and scare her off.

This was to be the course of action to be taken to excise the present beings. I was to take a picture of each room including the gazebo and the boathouse and the slave shack. There was to be absolutely no human in any of the pictures. I unfortunately don't remember what the reason was for that. Maybe it's that aboriginal concept that the soul is stolen when a picture is taken. I really don't know. After having done that I was to go through all these rooms and speak to the spirits. I was to tell them

"Turn around and face the light. The light will guide you. You're business is done here. You don't belong here anymore. Nobody here knows you. Everyone you know has already crossed over and is waiting for you. Turn around face the light. Let the light guide you."

She also said that all the comic pictures in the attic and the photos of cats and castles and whatever from the turn of the century were to be removed. She explained that the meowing of the cats might have been generated through the many pet pictures. The irony of the cats was that in the 90s the island had five cats staying there. They were our daughters' pets. We used to call the Island 'cat camp' during July and August. The house was to be turned into our home by clearing all the mementos of the past eras. I can honestly say I was rally relieved once she had explained everything to me. Jeanne spent the afternoon doing Dick's numerology. That is a really long and exhausting exercise. They must have been together for three hours. She and her husband spent that night in the kitchen listening to music and playing cards. She did not want to be in the other rooms. Andre was so loyal to his wife. Some people thought she was a kook. I disagree. I witnessed physical and psychological manifestations taking place in her, that could not be faked. It's no wonder she was always skinny and sleep deprived. It's true what some people who have the 6th sense awareness say

"It could be a curse rather than a gift."

Dear Jeanne called me that week after we had returned to Montreal to tell me she was completely over her flu bug and had slept for sixteen hours straight when she got home. I told her I would absolutely follow though with her instructions and see her in the fall after the closing of the Heritage house. I would bring her the pictures then. I remember now going one step further. This is amazing I actually see myself. I went to each compass point on the Island and laid in the grass and made, instead of snow angels, grass angels. I said the same prayer Jeanne had taught me.

Early November I met Jeanne and a colleague of hers from the university at her home. The three of us had dinner and looked at all the pictures. I explained them to her friend and retold our story. We cleared the dishes and sat out on the back patio for our coffee. The two ladies were seated together on the swing set. I was across from them. There was just a slight swaying. The ladies were telling me that special incantations were going to be told over each picture. This was going to be done several times. They were going to bring them to the university and get their professor and fellow class mates involved. I was listening attentively. All of a sudden, I went totally deaf. I could see their lips moving but I could not hear a word they were saying. I heard a male voice instead speaking to me in English. The voice said

"Don't listen to them. They don't know what they are saying! They are just trouble makers"

I covered my ears with both my hands. The ladies stared at me quizzically. I opened my mouth and said to them in French, because they were not bilingual

"I can't hear you. A man is talking to me now as I speak to you. He keeps repeating this stuff about you. Oh my God now I'm really getting scared."

The two ladies joined hands and chanted something. The voice stopped. My hearing returned to normal. I asked

"What just happened?"

"He followed you here. He is no longer at the Island. He is with you."

They showed my how to ward off a presence as soon as I get a psychic sensation. I am to put my arms together, left inverted and right laying on top and I am to press into my solar plexus. It is supposed to be the center of energy. I am to say my favorite prayer which is the 'Our Father'. I am to continue in that fashion until the feeling dissipates. They believed me to be a channel. I have had to do that a couple of times since. Now for the good news everyone is waiting for. Whatever powers the mediums and Para psychologists used, they actually worked. The following spring there was not a single para normal occurrence. The house and the land was ghost free. I and no one else had any experiences for the duration of our ownership. I think.

The Island was home to me. The first eighteen years we packed the kids and pets in the station wagon, every Friday right after work for eight months of the year. Other than being afraid of some pretty dangerous crossings I was very contented. The daughters started part time jobs when they were sixteen. We fought and won to keep the property in early 80s. Dick and I were separated for about ten months during '84 but kept the island. He got a super huge raise in '87 or so and the mortgage was paid off. What a party we had! Now we knew the bank couldn't take it away from us. My eldest daughter even had a Toronto film company come and make a video about our beautiful area for a tourism journal. They visited our island, took movies in and out of the house and interviewed my daughter and husband. I wasn't there during the event. I was not invited. Oddly enough I was just expected to clean up the house and make it look charming and welcoming as per usual. Cheap shot, I think! Already my daughter and my husband were displaying their combined inabilities to take an interest in my feelings. The name of the video was called 'Island in the Sun'. Maybe after I'm dead the daughters will have the video converted to DVD so that my grand children can see how fabulous I had made our home look. Dick had been asked by the interviewer

"What brings you back here weekend after weekend to what seems to be a lot of work?" to which my husband replied

"Being here for two or three days is like being away in the Bahamas for two or three weeks. I cross the river and then sit here on my front lawn looking back to the town. I think of Greta Garbo's famous saying 'I want to be alone!'."

In '92 Dick started a new job locally and lived at the Island. The property had to be remortgaged. Our younger daughter lived there also. The oldest was living with a man who was a local. He later became her husband. I was the lone Montreal/1000Islands commuter. The property had to be remortgaged and insurances policies had to be cashed in order for us to stay out of the poor house. The relocation, in my opinion had been a financial disaster. Every February, Dick would go into a screaming rage and try to convince me to sell the Island. I refused. The game plan was that we were to retire there and winter in Florida. I would be dammed if I worked this hard to let go of my home. I paid for that place every month and our rentals in Kingston until finally our Quebec house was sold. I really believed this home was to be passed on to our daughters and their families. Finally in 2000, my father died. This will sound absolutely awful and I don't mean it to be, in the least. At that time it was quite fortuitous. My dad could not have planned it better. He left my sisters and me a very sizeable inheritance. I was able to pay off the Island and all the debts, such as my husbands lines of credit, our cards etc. The debt accrued over the eight years since we had left Montreal. I was able to give our daughters some financial assistance. I even had lots left over to invest for our future retirement. That was just ten years away. Life should have been rosy. No way!! not when you are living with a drunkard.

Adult daughters have little tolerance for a drunken father. That is ok. It got to the point where the oldest and her husband, Dick's now best friend, were hiding their wine stash because 'Dad' was going though it like water. There was a time when our daughters told me they were not going to be coming to the Island as much in the future because they sure could not expose their children to 'dad's' drunken hissy fits. My suggestion was that they and their husbands spoke to their father directly about this. Maybe that would help him better appreciate the needs of the whole family. That never happened. In fact after one really frightening night tirade incident, my eldest daughter's husband just got up the next morning, woke Dick up and they took off to play golf just as if nothing had happened buddy, buddies! In fact when my oldest asked him if he had talked to 'dad' the man actually said

"What's the point people are going to do whatever they damn well please anyways"

I spoke to him the next day just about every incident. He did not give a damn. He did not believe me.

"If it was that bad the kids would talk to me directly. I was making those things up."

Now I understand why he felt that way. I wasn't the only enabler in the family. The stress was indescribable. One fine February, of course, I happened to mention to my husband that I would like it if we laid hard wood flooring in the city house. The five year old carpet would have to be replaced anyways. The area was perhaps twenty feet by twelve feet. He said

"NO! I can't afford it" to which I replied

"Well if we're that broke we just might as well sell the Island?"

That was a rhetorical question. I had gotten into the habit of baiting him. When you get that way, you are in an ugly relationship. It's like your turning verbal fighting into a contact sport. It's very dangerous. He replied

"I've been telling you to sell that damn island for years." I stared at him, dumbfounded.

"I was just kidding"

"I'm not"

"I can't do that. If you want this done you'll have to do all the arrangements yourself."

That spring Dick contacted a realtor. I insisted on having two agents to interview and we would decide who could best represent us. The guy, selected by my husband in my opinion, was a local sleaze bag. He never sold the island that season. That was a reprieve for me. The following spring my daughter Trudy took me around to see a few other life style options. Common sense dictated,

"That since you had cancer three times in less than seven years, that you are alone at the Island during the day pretty much seven days a week, and we the daughters would not be able to take over the care of the property, it would be best for you to continue to pursue the idea of selling."

In 2006, I chose another realtor. One offer fell through. The second did not. There was only 10k between seller and buyer. I was holding out. My realtor called me in the late afternoon and said that I could meet him at his office to sign the papers to close the sale. Dick had just called him and said he accepted the offer. I never had a say in the matter and I was not going to start arguing with the realtor.

THAT'S IT, THAT'S ALL. END OF DISCUSSION!

That beautiful 'Island in the Sun', my home for twenty eight years, was sold in fall of '06. Dick and I had travelled high and low in the region to find something within a thirty mile radius of the city, yet still on a mainland waterway. We couldn't agree on anything. Dick found a large city property with a swimming pool and a lanai. The house had lots of room to entertain and have the grandkids visit for sleepovers. I loved it. I had worried a lot about finding something special for Dick so that he could transition easily from no longer having the magnificent Island. This was going to be just fine for us. I spent most of that time of my life at this home also still waiting for Dick to show up sooner than later. The only difference is I had great neighbors with whom I was able to chit chat over the fence and with whom I could begin a friendship. I would be busy mowing the property as were the two male neighbors on either side of me. Inevitably one would ask

"Where's Dick today? Still golfing?"

After a while they stopped asking because they knew their snoopiness bugged me. That was eight months of the year probably most days of the week. Twelve months later, in fall of '07 after forty years of marriage I filled for divorce. I finally concluded, it did not matter where we lived. Dick was not going to be home. He just needed a place to crash. Do you see the puzzle pieces coming together?

A good man never destroys the hard work of a well deserving woman. A good man protects and defends a deserving woman. A good man supports a deserving woman's dreams and ambitions, especially when their happiness is her only goal. That's what partnership is all about. My husband was not that kind of man. There are several films about the 1000 Islands. People come from all over the world to take boat tours to see the magnificence of the St. Lawrence river. A local man had said

"People chose the 'River' as a place to work and play and rest but in the end the 'River' chooses you."

I can only conclude that my husband's absence and his wanting to sell the property was definitely a sign of mental instability. See I'm still making excuses. There is only one true reason. He was an absolutely unappreciative, self absorbed idiot.

CHAPTER 15

SEX, DRUGS, ROCK & ROLL

I DON'T KNOW WHY everybody tagged the 60's as the decade of sex, drugs and rock & roll. Anyone, who has done a lot of reading, knows this has been going on since the beginning of human civilization. Sex was always there but kept on the QT. Drugs such as marijuana or cocaine or meth were not commonly available. On the other hand opium goes way back to the time of the Romans even. It was definitely in use and of course there was always alcohol, the legal drug. Rock & Roll might not have been invented but women were seduced with different kinds of erotic serenades. Heck pornography in Italy or in India can be seen in all the art and sculptures and on stone wall carvings. I hate to disappoint anyone but it wasn't about American morals gone bad. Lack of restraint just went public. The following text will undoubtedly sound like ramblings. That is exactly what it is.

There are so many things I don't have answers to. My conclusion is simple. The older I get the less I know. Does that mean that our 60's generation has not, in all these decades, acquired any wisdom. My grandmother's opinion was revered. She knew all the secrets of life but unfortunately did not share them. She only recounted the good stuff. Those life lessons were the skeletons in the closets. In those days it was considered disrespectful to 'speak ill of the dead'. If I could have known those truths I'm sure I probably could have avoided getting into a lot of trouble. My parents' opinions were heard and respected but definitely not adhered to. We were the first generation to openly profess that

"WE know it all".

Was there more sex and drugs in the 60's. Well I know for sure there is more sex and drugs now in the 21st century. "How do I know that?" you ask. Well! in those days when a girl had her first menstruation her mother would tell her father, middle class people, my only point of reference.

"So & so has just become a woman this week."

The father would put down his newspaper and reply

"That's good."

And proceed to reading the daily news. A young woman, by the age of eighteen, would have probably dated for a couple of years and marry her high school sweetheart. She would not have had sexual intercourse with him prior to their wedding night. How is it possible for most girls in the early to mid 60's to have been perceived as 'promiscuous' when they only did 'IT' with one guy? Some of these couples are celebrating their silver (50th) wedding anniversary. The ones I know aren't having any sex now, either.

Then there is I, from July1966 to August 1967, that is thirteen months in case you are into your third martini and are having trouble counting. I had sex with three guys, without being on the pill even. What a crazy 'promiscuous' young woman! The third one I married because I was pregnant. Well we were engaged, if that really matters much. One couple, out of two, married for that reason. They were called 'shotgun weddings'. Apparently if the statistics are correct 50% of those couples got divorced. I stuck it out for forty years because I wanted to prove a point. I wasn't like everybody else and I refused to be a statistic. We would be 'forever'. Then there is my older daughter who started to express her sexuality, sooner than I. I used to say she used to display her sensuality on her shirt sleeve. She managed to have six live in, live out partners or friends with benefits, that I know of. The others, a mother really doesn't want to hear about. So were the late 80s sexier than the late 60s. Are you keeping up with me here. You can't stop me. I'm on a roll. I know my younger daughter had three 'love interests' guys. She confided. What she did away at university I am not privy to or I have forgotten. You see the evolution of conversation taking place from the time I couldn't tell my parents I was pregnant in 1967 to the time my daughters were sharing their love life with me, during the 90s. Now this is what really blows me away. My older grand daughter, went through a phase where she would take photographs of herself trying to be provocative and seductive and post them on the internet. That was at the cusp of adolescence. Luckily it did not last long. Unfortunately the pictures are floating up there in cyberspace. I always used to say to my girl students and my daughters

"If you're not selling, don't advertise".

Hormones not withstanding! We are now in the early 21st century yet I feel we are slipping backwards. Young girls still think they can be validated by getting the attention of a male. The families should be teaching the young women about privacy and just a bit of discretion please. They should be bolstering self image and enforcing self worth through athletics or activities in art or dance. I do not envy the parents of today. There is so much more to be vigilant for. When I was in my forties I, used to ask myself

"If they are doing @#@#, at sixteen what will be left when they are twenty six?"

Now the experimentation is starting at age twelve. 21st century media is thriving on what is known as the early 'sexualization' of girls. I hate to be the bearer of sad tidings but are these girls ever going to be disappointed when they experience the real thing and find out it's not such a big deal after all. I read a F B posting from a young teen male who stated

"Such and such a dance club was the best place to be at in town Blah! Blah! Blah!. All the shanks together in the same place at the same time. You better bring at least five condoms if you're headed there this weekend."

I guess I should be encouraged that the guys have the common sense to use protection. That's about all I can say from my perspective about sex regarding our three generations. To speculate any further or even pontificate, for that matter, would just be a waste of my valuable time.

I'll get personal and confide. I was what would be referred to as a late bloomer. I had menstruated late. I didn't start hormone surges until I was sixteen. When I was in college, Mr. B had tried to stroke the inside of my collar bone through my winter coat collar. He was trying to get to a breast. I freaked out. Good catholic girl that I was. I remember, when I was fourteen, necking with a guy in a snow bank thinking how bloody cold and wet and uncomfortable I was. I found his lips to be mushy and yucky. His advances sure as heck did not have the intended effect. I guess today I could assume he had full lips, rather than skinny lips, which can be a good thing. I learned that from experience as I matured. Just like kissing a guy with a soft mustache rather than the bristly kind. How does one tell a man you're married to

"I don't like kissing you because your upper lip is too prickly and it doesn't feel sexy."

The European bus driver sexual experience was the same every time. Maybe that's why his girlfriend of four years broke it off. Mr. B, I couldn't rate because three times does not count. Mr. K on the other hand was hot. Either that or I, at the ripe age of twenty two, was finally being inundated with hormones. I think a good lover actually enhances the libido.

Heck if the sex is hot what woman would refuse it unless she had medical issues. But 'hot' is all relative and has a different connotation for men and for women. There in lies the conundrum. My husband and I were very compatible in that arena. We both had minimal experience. He claimed he was a virgin when he met me. He definitely made up for lost time.

Dick was a porn enthusiast. I'm really being very polite. He actually was obsessed with porn. He even threw a porn movie party in our apartment. It was supposed to be with another couple. When the doorbell rang and I found out it was my husband's work colleague I decided to abstain. My girlfriend and I spent that time in my bedroom watching T V. When Dick moved his stuff into our apartment, he brought his twin bed, a desk and some one hundred Playboy and Hustler magazines. I sure as heck couldn't object. I was, after all, the liberal girlfriend who had loaned the guys the projector for the porn movies at the stag party. By the time we had bought our first home and this was to be the third move, I asked.

"What are we keeping all these magazines for?" He replied

"I have always wanted to plaster my bedroom ceiling with Playboy centerfolds. Now that I have my own house I just might be able to do it."

I decided, since I always packed and unpacked everything by myself when we moved, that I would save all the centerfolds. The actual magazines I put in garbage bags to chuck out to the curb. My best intentions were not well received. Who cares? Dick was still buying porn so he just had a new batch of literature to accumulate. I didn't really care one way or the other. I just did not like clutter. Ten extra boxes of magazines I sure as heck did not need. By the way he never did paste all the pictures of nude women on our bedroom ceiling. It was only like in my thirty fifth year of marriage that I noticed there were no more skin mags in the house. Then I realized porn was on the internet for free. So why should my husband waste money on magazines. I didn't know in those days that obsessive interest in pornography might be considered 'questionable behavior'. I, having never lived with males (Dads do not count) thought

"I guess this is normal."

Looking at the pictures was not a turn on for me but reading all the articles was. My favorite was the Xavier Hollander advice columns. I learned a great deal about sexual practices from those articles and experimented with what I had read. My husband and I reaped the benefits of those tutorials. They helped me acquire a lot of confidence. A teaching colleague of mine who had been married for ten years and had three children once said her husband believed that there was just one kind of great woman. He had said

"A lady in public but a hooker in bed."

Over years of practice I became quite the artisan. My husband many times, because of his constant exposure to pornography had to be, how should I put it, entertained or seduced. Porn is very difficult for a wife to compete with. Performance, if it were to occur had to be helped along or enhanced with a titillating show. That is where Barry White and his tapes became very useful. I could do anything to that singer's voice. He and Isaac Hayes were my turn myself on, sexy music. It always baffled me that my husband expected sex without any stimulation to the woman. I guess that's what porn does. It's not interactive where as love making is. My husband would say

"Do you want to fool around?" as he rubbed a semi boner on my rear end as I was washing dishes. I would say

"Why don't you say "Do you want to make love? It's so much sexier" he replied

"What's love got to do with it?"

Check out Tina Turner's song "What's love got to do, got to do with it, just a second hand emotion."

I don't think I'm shocking too many of you. I'm absolutely sure this has happened to many. There are occurrences that I do question now. I did not have the wherewithal to wonder, is this normal or not? I just didn't have any reference points to compare to. I wouldn't even know where to Google the information in this day and age? I have checked on the concept of conjugal rights and they go back to biblical times. Sexual intercourse, how and when and how often is to be the husband's prerogative. Now being a feminist from way back I need to ask this question. What about the wife's rights to say NO? There in lies the contradiction. If the man is the 'boss' and has the rights in his favor then what chance does a poor woman have. Many a woman has had to put up with very bad sexual experiences with her own husband with zero recourse. If the guy isn't good or does not fulfill his sexual responsibilities to her, is she allowed to take a lover. I don't think so! I'm sure if a guy had a frigid wife, other men would feel sorry for him and many would condone his extra marital liaisons. On the other hand if the roles were reversed, a woman would be condemned.

There were several things I did not like. For instance anal intercourse only had to be experienced once by me and it was to never happen again. If I had needed a laxative I could be using a pharmaceutical product. Don't let anyone con you. It hurts like heck. I did not hesitate to vocalize my total disgust. Oral sex was precarious. Both of us enjoyed receiving but neither of us enjoyed giving. I would have to be half in the bag to go down on my husband. It was, how shall I put it, distasteful. My husband did not like my female scent, no matter how often I bathed. There were some odd things, experimental would be the most descriptive word. This seemed unnatural. My husband inserting different phallic shaped objects inside me to see how much I could expand. The Polaroid camera came in handy for those pictures. They never were full body nude poses of me. There were only vaginal shots. That was never attempted again. I certainly could not have known without doing these things that they were not for me. Where does a wife draw the line? Often there seems to be this threat of a fight if one doesn't comply. The last thing any mother wants is to wake up the children. You just go through the motions and hope it will be over sooner than later.

My husband had ideas and I went along with them, for a while. We met another couple at their house and started playing strip poker. It was fine until I was the only one loosing. I obviously was never a very good poker player. I was down to my bra and panties and bingo something has to go again. Dick started laughing. I started crying. I wouldn't do it. I couldn't do it even though I knew this couple very well. Underwear is one thing but nudity, no way. My girlfriend's boyfriend, not my husband, came to my rescue. He got up and got me a blanket so that I could continue to play but covered. Wouldn't the proper thing to do have been for my husband to have stopped the game. One more hand and I was down to my top and quit. I had a hissy fit and walked out of the room and locked myself into the bathroom. My girlfriend brought me my clothes and I got dressed. My husband and I headed back home and never said a word about it ever. Rest assured that was my first and last time. Another couple, very good friends of ours suggested we join them for an overnighter at a resort. The kids would be with babysitters and we could all have a fun 'get away'. We all had dinner and then the ladies got into their newly bought sexy lounging wear and the guys were in their underwear. There was more booze. Before you know it we were all on the king size bed watching a movie. My girlfriend started the conversation on couple swapping and we all kidded around. Then it hit me right between the eyes. This was going to happen. I was sandwiched between Dick along side of me in front and her husband along side of me in back. She was along side her husband. I was really embarrassed and nervous because both guys had erections. They didn't mind one bit. I sat up really quickly and went over to Maureen's side of the bed and started to explain that I thought swapping would be a bad idea. She said

"Well it would just be for this one time, just for fun" I countered

"What if I like it so much with Perry or he with me that we get together again on our own."

"That's not going to happen we all friends here. We don't want to cause trouble. It's just for fun."

"But that's the point we don't know, really know what any one of us will do after we go home tomorrow. I just won't take the chance. I don't want to put my marriage in jeopardy. What I don't know won't hurt me."

The husbands had each gotten naked and retreated to their respective armchairs. They were watching a movie and sipping their cognacs. My girlfriend and I ended the debate and she and her husband opened the door to their adjoining room and we all waved goodnight. Dick and I ran ourselves a deep tub bath, a real treat. Next we hear all this yelling and screaming and crying next door. Our friends are having a mega fight.

We heard the door slamming and everything was quiet. Dick and I went to bed and made love a couple of times. Love making we both enjoyed and doing it alone together. I knocked on the door the next morning for breakfast wake up call. Perry answered and said his wife had gone to the car to spend the night. I got dressed and headed to the parking lot. The two men went down to the dining room for breakfast. I brought her back to our room and ran her a bath. She explained they were fighting about his wanting to get it on with me and she got furious. I reassured her that that was never going to happen. I had warned her about that kind of stuff. To be honest I wasn't playing the saint card here. Quite the contrary I really liked Perry and I don't really know what I would have done in the future if I enjoyed being with him sexually that weekend. I was putting the brakes on all of us, especially me. I have found, because I have known several to whom divorce has happened, that a marriage break up whether it be after four years or forty causes severe trauma to the human spirit. I can honestly say I have never had crushes on my husband's friends. They were probably too much like him. As I was maturing I was getting very leery of the type. Most probably though, was that I still loved Dick more than anything.

I learned a very hard lesson, the difference between lust and love. I had believed that my husband always lusting after me was a sign of his love for me. My father had said to me at least three decades ago

"When the lust goes out of the marriage which it naturally will, a man and a woman had better be friends."

I figured Dick and I would always get it on. I should have inquired more. It was never explained that a man's body looses the ability to perform sexually as the aging process takes place. The word impotence was never even whispered. It's hard for me to pin down when it was exactly that I started to wonder if Dick's love for me was waning. I never thought that he might have a woman on the side. You would wonder why I was never suspicious because he was gone at least four nights a week. His absences, so he claimed, were usually a result of his going to night school at the university. Though the classes finished at ten or eleven, he still had to head down to the pub. Once there, he would socialize with writers for the daily newspapers and stay until the bar closed. There was always a good debate to be had there. He would come home, have a quickie and fall asleep. I really did not like that. You would think that he would leave me alone since I was asleep. No he had needs. It would only take five minutes, no big deal. Conjugal duties there you go. This will sound crude but I sometimes have thought that my husband just needed a body to ejaculate in. Add to that a good mother for his children, a financial partner and a great little homemaker and I fit the bill completely. I keep being reminded of the adage we had in those days that if a man got all the sex he needed at home he would not need to have extramarital affairs. I had never seen my husband being flirtatious with my girlfriends. I had seen a couple of women hit on him at a few parties but he seemed to ignore them, turn his back to them and keep chatting with one of the guys. I was never worried. This feeling of confidence was reinforced in the oddest way. A new credit manager had been hired at my company. She introduced herself as Coco. She was a tall 'red head' and we would be doing a lot of work together. She happened to notice the name plate at the desk and asked

"Do you happen to know a Mr. K?"

"Yes why do you ask?"

"Is he your brother?"

"No he is my husband! And how do you know him?" She replied

"Oh I'm sorry, we never even knew he was married. My last job was at Carrier Montreal for years and he came out with us a lot. Oh no! don't worry he didn't fool around with anybody he just liked to drink and play cards. They used to have some pretty serious poker games going on."

Can you imagine the relief I felt knowing he was just gambling and drinking instead of screwing around! I sometimes wonder if I was not a little crazy. Then there was the time two ladies from my church congregation were visiting. I was undergoing some cancer treatment at the time and they would like to come by and keep me company. They decided to wait around so that they could say Hi! to Dick. He didn't turn up until close to six. Pat jokingly said in her heavy Celtic brogue.

"Where have you been Dick, we've been waiting for you for hours now?" to which he replied in his usual sardonic manner

"Oh I've been around but at least I don't bring home any venereal diseases." The two ladies and I looked at each other and shook our heads in dismay. He so loved to shock. The ladies excused themselves and left. I went into the kitchen to prep supper. My husband poured himself a drink and went down to the playroom to watch the news.

You are probably wondering why I didn't fight. Honestly, if I had fought on each and every occasion Dick did his thing, our lives would have been a war zone. I had finally tried that technique after sixteen years of marriage and he was still totally indifferent. I no longer wanted to be so stressed out and frightened by him. I also didn't want our girls to be exposed to this constant tension. I think, or I was hoping I could teach him a lesson once and for all. I had filed for legal separation when the children were in their teens. He called every night at the dinner hour and saw the girls every weekend. We lived apart for ten months. His mother's and his boss's incessant pressure made me reconsider. He was considerate for eighteen months. He tried to consider the needs of his family but then went back to being his narcissistic, self absorbed self all over again. I have concluded that Dick's personality was not conducive to family life. I know for sure now after doing enough study that those kinds of individuals, be they male or female, are totally incapable of feelings for others' well being. They neither possess conscience or remorse. Their personal needs will supersede the best interest of anything or anyone. These people are hard wired that way.

I will be frank. By then I was no longer in denial. My realization of this came through my 'school of hard knocks' lessons, yet again. Trudy was in bed, Marie was out with friends and I was waiting up for her and for Dick. At 11:30 p.m the door bell rang. I looked out the front window and a shiver ran down my spine. A police cruiser was parked in front of the house. I opened the door and there stood Marie and a police officer. She had been found sitting, on a park bench in the west end of town, with two other guy friends of hers. The officer said she had been charged with loitering. The park was restricted, closed after 11pm. The boys who were over eighteen were charged with drinking beer in public. She had not been drinking. Thank God for small favors. We would be getting a notice in the mail with the date for her appearance in court. I closed the door. She and I talked and then she went to bed. I was so upset, embarrassed, and angry. It is indescribable what a sinking, hopeless feeling I had when not only does my husband get in trouble with the police but now my elder daughter was doing the same thing. This I was not going to put up with. I waited until Dick got in. It was 2 a.m. He was loaded, of course. He didn't care.

"We would all talk about it tomorrow. Now he had to get to bed because he had to work in six hours." I answered

"So! like I have to work too".

"Just don't bother me with that stuff now"

I could have run away from home then. Interestingly enough, while our daughter was in the park at age seventeen with two boys who were drinking beer, her father was just down the street at a bar, walking distance to home. We did go to court a few weeks later. Marie's case was dismissed because the lawyer was able to prove that there was no signage at the park indicating park closure times. The judge walked his dog there on a regular basis and agreed that that was indeed the case. So you want to know what the response was on the part of daughter and her father.

"That wasn't so bad after all. Luckily the police had made a stupid mistake." All I had to say to my daughter was

"Don't you ever make me have to loose time from my job to take care of your problems. I have just lost a morning's pay because of this.

You will make sure that until you are eighteen you are to be in the house before 11 p.m. After you are eighteen you can just get yourself a lawyer when you are in trouble."

I had for years made excuses that the only reason Dick didn't like coming home after work was because we had little kids at the beginning or later that we had had four kids in the house. I figured surely as the girls were getting older he and I would spend more time together developing common interests. That was not to be the case. If nothing else we became more distant. His overt dislike for my needing more company and attention from him and my loosing more and more respect for his indifference to my needs and concerns were the building blocks for the wall going up between us. Sexually, we both became disinterested. It was pretty hard for me to be motivated to put on a sexy show for someone who, when he came to bed, was usually loaded. There is nothing I hate more than my man trying to crawl on top of me and having trouble inserting a limp penis inside me. Better yet penetrating me with a 'semi' and after a dozen thrust, slowing down and collapsing on top of me. The worst was having to be forced to give a BJ and getting smacked repeatedly on both sides of the head because the expected response was not happening due to the fact that OH YA! I was doing it wrong. The epitome of sexual distancing is the 'doggie' style. The penetration is deep and quick. Yet the partners never once get to look in each others eyes. That method became common with us. We were at the point that the feelings reflected in our eyes were probably best concealed. It was, needless to say, a highly impersonal act but the job got done.

By the third decade of marriage, the sexual pairing became non existent. Having had successive years of radiation and chemo therapy to fight cancer, I usually had to go to bed earlier. I was always so tired. My husband never came up to tuck me in. He would stay up until well passed midnight. One thing I do know about myself, for sure, is that in those days I always did think the best of people. It would never have occurred to me to imagine bad things about my husband. My naivety astounds me. There were always subtle wise cracks hints about strip clubs and pole dancing. The remarks just flew right over my head. The most fun I had was in what I referred to as my 'afternoon delights' on the weekends. The children, when they were older, would be out visiting friends or at the park. I would get the tunes going and put on a show. My husband and I would have enough time for private moments. He would be sober and attentive and we would enjoy pleasuring each other. Thinking of those times brings a grin to my face. The last time we made love was the summer of 2000. You wonder how can she remember that? We were celebrating my having received a sizable inheritance. We were at the cottage, the mortgage for which had been finally paid off. All the credit card debts were cleaned up as well as my husband's line of credit. Relocating to Ontario had been a financial fiasco but now we were free and could have a financial cushion invested. My husband was thinking of opening his own company. We were able to plan permanent renovations to this grand old house of ours. It was a memorable time for me. When I was young, I kept count of how many times we would make love and darn proud of it. As I entered my fifties I was counting how many times we hadn't made love. Month after month would go by. Then year after year would go by. I can only speculate why. Was it the fact that my husband was on cholesterol medication? His sister even recommended we use the blue pill. She and her husband did because he had serious back problems and they were only in their forties, too young to give up their sex life. My husband said

"There was no way he was going to walk around with a 'boner' for four hours."

I suggested I could be his manager and have the ladies line up and take advantage of his predicament. He didn't like our laughing. His little sister said

"You can cut the pill in half use a lower dosage" He yelled

"No way I'm not taking anything"

This is what I mean about conjugal rights being pretty one sided. If the husband doesn't want then the wife can just go without. Another reason he could have been turned off by me was that I had cancer and had both breast removed over a period of two years. I had gained at least thirty five pounds as a result of oral and infusion chemo treatments. For a man who most often needed visual stimulation all of his adult life to be sexually aroused, I was to say the least 'a sight for sore eyes'. I was a truly pathetic looking specimen. Looking at myself even turned me off. You see the continuation of the pattern of always self-blame.

I did try to broach the subject a few times. This was very daring on my part. I really wanted us to be able to correct the situation. I was very lonely. There were two instances where I approached my husband and in all innocence asked

"Why don't we make love anymore?" to which he replied, as God is my witness.

"Because you always have to climax and it takes too long. If we just had regular sex we would have it a lot more often." I then said

"But I thought good sex was about insuring both partners were satisfied"

No comment. I'm such a glutton for punishment. The next time I asked,

"Surely you must need a release, I know I do. I don't know how you can stand going without. I don't know how you do it?" brace yourselves, he answered

"Memories and masturbation!"

Can you imagine! What kind of a human being would look at this wife square in the face and say something like that? He didn't even blink. I just turned away. I couldn't look anymore. This man was real sick. He was a bully and a sadist. He took pleasure in inflicting pain. Belittling me was his way of controlling me. By the time I had filed for divorce I had been celibate for eight years. That is a very unhealthy place for a woman like me to be at for too long a time. I must say though I am surprised with myself. This is the longest sex conversation I have ever had in my entire life. I'm sure you probably have your own ideas of what the 'bastard' was up to. I often hoped that I could know. Either way did he have several women, several men? Who cares? Even if aging slows a man down, there isn't anything a loving couple can't deal with if they really choose to. I know having had two breast chopped off due to cancer did not make me appealing. I was, no doubt, repulsive to my husband. It was pretty hard to compete with porn beauties when I no longer even looked like a woman. I refuse to accept that I or breast cancer were completely what was at fault here.

DRUGS played a very miniscule role in my life. I was first introduced to 'pot' by Dick who had purchased a dime bag from my girlfriend's husband who was a habitual user. Dick was going through a major sales pitch trying to convince me this was going to be great. I had not yet seen anyone on 'weed' so I didn't know what to expect. I was nervous because our baby was in the next room and I was hoping she wouldn't wake up and need me for something. I trusted my husband. An hour after having shared a joint I started to see things, weird things. While I was kissing Dick, I happened to look over to my right and the end table lamp looked very small to me. I have to try to explain. It was as if I were a giant standing up and using the lamp as a chess piece. That got me really spooked. Like the one in the Jolly Green Giant commercial. Next thing I knew I was envisioning the top of my head being severed in two with a huge crevasse running from my front hairline to the back. I stood in the shower running cold water on myself, as cold as I could stand it, in the hope of getting rid of this frightening feeling that I was stuck in. I hardly slept that night. I made sure Dick was kept awake also with all of my anxious ranting. What was supposed to be a relaxing, mellow experience ended up being a total 'downer'. Dick had made inquiries the next day about the quality of the weed. The 'pros' confirmed they had never had ill effects from this batch. It was a few weeks later that we realized that the diet pills I had been prescribed by my GP for post baby weight loss were an amphetamine. No wonder I was freaking out. What a mixture marijuana and speed!

Authorities are concerned with drunken drivers and so they should be. Nevertheless there is an additional menace on the roads. There are so many senior drivers on pharmaceutical drug these days and several people are driving high on soft drugs. My experience driving on 'pot' was funny at the time but not wise. We were at friends for dinner. There was a lot of booze and 'grass'. Dick was, as usual loaded, so I decided it was better if I drove home. One good thing about my husband being on 'weed' was that he was not aggressive and much more mellow. The fact that he even allowed me to drive us home was historic. I was very careful on the twenty minute run. It was 3am the streets were deserted. It was only when I got to an intersection close to home that I realized I was impaired. I stopped for the red light, no problem. My husband told me to move up a bit because I was too far away from the intersection. I had literally stopped the car at least thirty feet from the white line. Luckily, it was 3 a.m and the street was totally deserted. I never drove stoned again. My husband was on the road in Montreal most of the day. He did tell me a couple of stories about seeing drivers using a pipe while driving during the middle of the day. Once, I had helped a neighbor out when we had our first house. He had broken his ankle by falling in his driveway. I had taken him to the hospital. He even grew his own 'pot' in his back yard against the garage wall. There was a time he had even suggested we grow our own and we could all dry the branches up in the cottage attic and collect the seeds the following year when we re-opened. He was a habitual user. We partook with him and his wife on those Saturdays we might be invited over. They did not have any children. I remember getting stoned and sitting on the floor in a yoga pose, probably listening to some C C R, beating away on non existing drums. I was also staring into their fish tank and mistook the gold fish to be piranhas. I was not impressed and didn't bother partaking anymore. It wasn't a 'Saint Jo the Catholic Bitch thing', I just didn't enjoy smoking grass or using hashish. In fact, once, when my husband was complaining to this very same neighbor that I was such a square the man came to my defense. He said

"Leave her alone. Jo is high on life."

He was right. Once we were invited to a party by one of Dick's buddies. We walked into the apartment and all the lights were out. We were taken into the living room and there was a circle of people sitting around what looked like a bucket with flames shooting out of it. Whatever the gang was getting high on I didn't want to have anything to do with. Doing dope and throwing plastic kitchen catchers into a fire and getting all crazy was not my idea of a good time. We were out of there in minutes. There is one thing I am sure of and am not ashamed to say, I wish my husband were a user of marijuana instead of an alcoholic. At least the moods would have been less volatile.

I get a feeling Dick's experience with dope was more extensive. I can only go by what I noticed. It would seem like the tip of an iceberg. Or as my dear Aunt Madeleine would say

"Where there is smoke. There is fire"

That is why I have concluded, part of my maturing, that he was very familiar with drugs. It's impossible to know what someone is doing when they are away from you for eighteen hours a day. I do know that a guy can get into trouble during the night or during the day. More than likely though if he does have a job it more often eliminates daytime trouble. If the husband is not home from 6 p.m to 1:30 a.m four nights of the week and does not call home, a wife can only presume something is just not right. The first time I found a cube of hash was in his winter coat pocket. We had only been married a couple of months. I was cleaning out our hallway closet, switching winter clothing for spring wear. I would take heavier pieces to the dry cleaners. I naturally checked in all the pockets to make sure nothing was being left behind. Actually, I was always looking for a ten or twenty dollar bill. I was a 'stay at home Mom', no income. I took that sliver of dope and flushed it down the toilet. When he came home that night I confronted him. He was so angry with me. I made it very clear that I would not tolerate any dope in our house. It was several years after when I realized there was pot at the cottage. My mother in law was staying for her usual month vacation. The kids were playing outside and Maureen and Granny and I were having a tea after dinner. Dick comes sauntering down the stairs with a lit joint in his hand. He's sitting in his usual place at the head of the dining room table taking a few tokes. My girlfriend and I were so shocked. Why would he do something so stupid? Did he just want to annoy his mother? What was he trying to prove? This was his mother's response

"Dick! I don't like that you smoke. It is so unhealthy but what I hate most is when you smoke those disgusting French cigarettes. They stink."

Her son, the crazy one, went into fits of laughter and had to leave the room Poor, dear, old lady thought he was smoking Gitanes cigarettes. She didn't seem to have a clue he had been smoking marijuana. He was so happy he had been able to trick her. He was thirty four years old for Pete sake. But that was my husband just a total juvenile. The next time I found 'grass' wrapped in foil in our dresser drawer. I threw that out also.

I became very suspicious when Dick's behavior, other than the usual boozy horror shows, became bizarre. Unfortunately I had no proof of anything. The answer to my questions would be

"Ask me no questions. I tell you no lies"

A close business associate of my husband bought a house on the other side of our street. It was a private sale Dick had helped broker between our neighbor friends and his associate. Dick had known this couple for a long time. Everybody thought this would be great. We would loose one set of friends but gain new ones. Unfortunately this relationship proved to be in my opinion, toxic. After Jason had moved across the street, Dick started to come home more often. He didn't stay home though. He walked over to Jason's place. He still didn't come back in until 1 or 2 a.m. I know a stronger or angrier woman would have walked across the street, gone into that house and raised bloody hell. His wife, my so call friend, had said the three guys are just downstairs listening to music and talking shop. The third guy was a boarder, another very close friend of theirs. Hell! all these people were so close. They were 'tight' alright. The guys downstairs were getting high on dope and the woman upstairs was getting totally loaded on her sherry. Everything was a big secret of course because possession of any substance was illegal. God forbid I should ever find out what was going on considering my bias regarding drugs. Apparently my older daughter said Jason was also doing cocaine at that time. They used to get it at the 'Maple's Inn' in Pointe Claire. How my oldest ever knew this stuff, I don't know. That certainly would explain my husband's odd behavior. I don't wish this on anyone. I already know, though, that so many of you and your children are living the nightmare now. A mother is known to do anything to save a child from the danger of a tornado or flooding. Be vigilant, watch and hear what is going on. The question I ask you moms out there is

"Why not do everything humanly possible to protect your children from their parent's addiction? Get them out of there!"

I thought as my girls were getting older that I would be able to get some decent nights sleep. That was not the case. One night I hear water running. I thought I was dreaming and for a minute allowed myself the luxury of ignoring it. Then all of a sudden I sat bold upright in bed. I swung my legs off the bed and ran to the bathroom. The door was partially open. I pushed it and saw Dick passed out with water up to his chin. The water was at the edge of the side of the tub and ready to spill over any second. I turned off the tap and pulled out the plug. The water started to drain. I went back to bed without waking him. One thing I learned the hard way is

"Never wake up a drunk. You never know what creature from hell will arise."

There is a very old saying "Let sleeping dogs lie".

The next morning nothing was mentioned. Incredibly Dick was able to get ready, have breakfast and head out for work. Then there was another time when my daughter Trudy came screaming into our bedroom. I asked

"What are you so upset about? What's wrong?" Through her tears and wailing she was able to say

"Daddy is at the bottom of my bed all curled up in a ball and sound asleep and he's naked Ma, naked!"

It would be so much easier for me if I could get an explanation or some questions answered but that will never happen. My therapist told me quite a while ago that even if I asked my husband the questions, the answers more than likely would not be truthful. To some there are probably comments like "What's the big deal he was out drinking or playing card or smoking dope. It's not like he was a murderer?" to that I say

"If that was the kind of life style he preferred than he should have cut me loose a long time ago. That way I could have had a chance to meet someone nicer and with whom I was more compatible."

ALCOHOL was Dick's drug of choice, a major addiction. It eventually took over our whole lives. His behavior was such that the concept of my 'walking on eggshells' became the norm. The older daughter claims he never got to her because she could hold her own with him. Yet the younger daughter and I took a great deal of mental abuse from the man. I know there is 'Alanon' to help family members of alcoholics adjust, but I think these organizations are missing the point. We should be teaching families the ways and means to get control over the outcome of their lives and prepare for the eventuality of self sufficiency. In fact when I was finally on my own I met two women who had been married to alcoholics. They and their children had used the services of that kind of support group. Both women said it did not do them any good. Nothing was changing so they escaped with their children in the middle of the night and created new lives for themselves and their families. Alcohol is called a disease. Yet to me I don't see it as such. Cancer, Parkinson, MS, are diseases. None of us who are fighting these incurable illness asked to get sick or intentionally do anything that made us ill. Yet an alcoholic will willingly take that fifth or six round of liquor and continue until he gets drunk. That to me is addiction. In this day and age there is such an uproar on cigarette smoking or obesity. Yet alcoholism is threatening the stability of families and communities on a daily basis and everyone is hushed.

This is the sequence of events as I know them from my husband's youth to recently that I know played a hand in his being a drunk. Let's call 'a spade, a spade'. Everyone is pussy footing around these days. We regular guys are supposed to put up with everybody's weaknesses and try not to hurt their feelings. Well enough already! In my father's day alcoholics were called 'drunks' or 'alkies'. There were degrees or types of drunks, for instance there was the happy, funny drunk, the mean drunk and the falling down drunk. In my experience my husband could be all three of those in one given day. The following stories of his youth and family background were recounted to me by Dick. I never saw his father inebriated. His dad had a spoonful of 'Captain Morgan's' rum with his afternoon cup of tea. He also liked to serve us each a little six ounce bottle of wine with a twist cap which he placed at the table setting to the right of the wine glass. This was a weekend dinner time ritual. His mother, when with us at the cottage, did indulge in a 'Bloody Caesar' before dinner and a glass of white wine with dinner on the weekends. I had attended a few of their social events after I was married but my in laws were always sober. If there were any relatives on either side that might have contributed to an addictive personality disorder it would be impossible to say. I do know that his maternal grandmother had committed suicide in the 1930s. His mother had told me that her brother, sixteen, and she, fourteen, had returned from school one afternoon and found their mother with her head inside the gas oven. The story is that this woman, his grandmother had not loved his grandfather. It had been an arranged marriage. Many years later, she had fallen in love with a another younger man and her husband would not give her a divorce. She became very depressed obviously and despaired. My mother in law, when Dick and I were first separated in '84, was always

"Afraid that he may do something desperate like her mother had. Maybe there was a pre disposition to depression in their family."

Dick's father was away a great deal, travelling all over British Columbia working on construction projects. He could be gone for weeks. It seems Dick had a friend he used to hang around with, whose father was a heavy drinker. This man would drive the boys around town to wherever they had to get to and always had a 'fifth' of booze in a brown paper bag which he drank from, while driving. You have to remember drinking and driving was fairly common then. In fact in certain rural areas around this town, guys are still 'brown bagging' their beers or liquor. My husband used to brag about teenage drinking exploits in high school, such as cases of beer stacked up against the kitchen wall when his parents were away for the weekend and drunken beach parties. He apparently was not a ladies man. Girls would call him up more as a friend seeking advice on how to get a date with another guy. When the family moved to Montreal he was enrolled in his first year at McGill U. The legal age for alcohol was twenty one. He hung out at the Pierrefonds tavern and shot a lot of pool. He and the guys he hung out with obviously had false ID cards which were very easy to come by. The crowd was rough and wild. My husband failed his first year at university. His father was able to get him a job immediately with an electrical contractor. In those days you didn't need a university education to be hired. You were an apprentice and received hands on training. The days he worked. The nights the buddies shot pool and got drunk. In a period of two years, he totaled his father's VW and a company car. There were no regrets. They were just accidents. Like I said it was a fast crowd and bragging about surviving wrecks seemed to be a badge of honor. Believe it or not in the mid 60s when I was driving we were told if we got in a car accident and the police arrived to file a report you'd better not say the other driver was driving drunk because the insurance company would not pay. I never got into an accident so I don't know how true that is.

The job he had when we were married was with an HVAC contractor. Mr. G was a dedicated private business man. His own father had led his family out of Poland during the Nazi invasion. He chronicled the stories of their trek in his memoirs. An amazing story which mesmerizes me to this day. I have saved it so that my children and theirs can see how courageous mankind can be. When they finally arrived in Montreal, Mr. G did not even speak English yet he managed to work and pay his way through McGill. He graduated in engineering. He and his wife are devout Jews. They were extremely good people, dedicated to hard, professional work. They offered constant contributions to their family and community. The reason why I have spent time describing Mr. G is because he, though only ten years older than Dick, mentored him and trained him in that specific trade. He kind of adopted my husband as a brother. He rally saw how intelligent Dick was and used that to enhance his success and that of the company. Mr. G was not a drinker. The Jewish faith has strict guidelines about the use of alcohol.

Unfortunately the company failed and Dick was out of work but only for a couple of days. He was really smart and was developing an increasingly larger network which was able to acknowledge and appreciate his expertise. He was establishing a good reputation in the city. The next company he was hired on was in the same trade. It, also, was a family run business. The owner was English, another graduate engineer. Dick was Mr. B's right hand man, also. There was one subtle difference between Mr. G and Mr. B., Mr. B was a drinker.

My mother had a very old saying

"Dit moi qui sont tes amis et je te dirai qui tu est." "tell me who your friends are and I will tell you who you are"

Dick had a gang of buddies who were all heavy drinkers. They had all started like he had in their teen years and were not showing any signs of letting up. Now an older man, a boss, another professional mentor was setting an example of a relaxed norm when it came to booze. In fact Dick had told me several times that the owner would open his office bar after the staff was gone at 5pm and they would have several scotches and go over the day's work load. He was even given an expense account. All the heavy drinkers in the industry would meet for a liquid lunch or after work. The credit cards were used for client entertaining expenses. At that time the vodka martini tumblers were in fashion. It was becoming easier and easier to sustain an alcohol addiction when you didn't even have to pay for it out of your own pocket. 'Birds of a feather flock together'. One Christmas the boss Mr. B and his wife had come over to our house for some drinks. They were to meet my husband's older brother and his sons. The adults were all to go to the Hilton hotel for the company dinner. Dick had just made it in with all the gift bottles he had gotten from his suppliers. At the hotel, we had finished a fine dinner when all of a sudden Dick just passed out into his desert plate. I just didn't know what to do. I froze. The boss called the maitre 'd over and whispered something in his ear. An attendant came over with a wheel chair. Max and the attendant put Dick in the chair and wheeled him out to the front entrance. He still had not come to. I followed in tow so ashamed. Max drove home. The next day nothing was mentioned. If Max spoke to Dick about it, I wouldn't know. That was the last time the boss took us out for dinner. They did invite us up to their summer cottage for a weekend and a few times for drinks at their house. Mr. B had a fully stocked bar in the playroom downstairs. Those occasions seemed normal because both Dick and his boss were in the sauce so that made it OK and it was in the privacy of their own home. Nobody was watching. Dick left that company after several years because the boss had decided he was going to make his new son in law the manager of operations instead of Dick. He said he wanted to keep it all in the family. My husband was very disappointed.

By then Mr. G was back in business and had asked Dick to join him again and so he just moved back in with him and his brother. He made him vice president of that company and that year Dick was president of the Association of Refrigeration Engineers, Montreal chapter. He was the youngest ever elected. Dick's early forties seemed to be his best. I was so proud of his accomplishments. You would think he would be happy. Yet that dark cloud lurked always ever so close above us. It did not take long before things started to unravel. A few years later, there was a falling out between Mr. G and his brother who bought out Mr. G for a large sum of money. Mr. G invited Dick to join him in opening a new company together. My husband chose not to. He wanted to stay so that the existing company would be able to continue and produce work for him and the other employees. The recession hit hard. There was less work to be had and the competition was fierce. Company cost cutting measures were implemented. Dick's expense account was cancelled. A few months later the new company owner, the younger brother, without warning or discussion, decided to slash salaries by 25%. This was the end of the gravy train. Dick decided that we were moving to Ontario. Everything we did seemed radical. We did not think things through thoroughly. Since we did not have conversations on issues it became apparent that the move was going to be a knee jerk reaction. He moved in '92, I followed in '93. We had debt galore and only half the combined income we used to take in. The company Dick was hired by was again family owned. The boss was ultra conservative English. The company car was the owner's wife's former car. There was no expense account. In fact Dick was reprimanded once because a client had called to tell his employer that he could smell beer on Dick 's breath during the meeting. The rule of thumb was no drinking during the work day. My husband would have to realign his thinking. Firstly, he was insulted at being put down. He was going from the sublime to the ridiculous, a large network of established clientele in a major Canadian city with double vodka martini lunches to a government town with very little industry and a brown bagging lunch policy. That is enough to drive a drinker to more drink. His life style had to change. When I finally moved there a year later he actually had to come home for supper because there was no where to go. The old gang was no longer. At the beginning, when we were in Montreal I understood or I should say accepted a lot of things about his reasons for being away from home at night. There seemed to be many. He was studying at night or attending many functions for ASHRAE or related shows in the industry. I get all of that. What I don't get is why stay out until 2:30 in the morning. I also get that many men, due to their work, such as doctors, travelling salesmen, military and transport drivers have to be away from their families. But why would a project manager in the city have to be away so much and that is in town, at night. I know the answer is staring at me right in the face. I, to this day, can't utter the words. Thinking of it makes me feel so beaten, so defeated.

When he was home he would often have temper fits fueled by excessive alcohol. For instance if he found toys lying around in the living room he would scream and pick them up and fling them across the room. This was followed by a tirade about how lousy a housekeeper I was. My daughter had a plastic horse, from her collection, that lived with a broken leg and a broken tail for many years, a constant reminder to 'Pick up your toys, kids'. We were playing cards with friends one night and I actually won a game, rare indeed. I was so excited. I was yelling and jumping around. He stood up picked up my drink and poured it all over my cards that were spread on the table. We couldn't even tally my winning score. Needless to say that ended up the game and the folks went home. The girls, when they were teenagers, had friends over at the cottage on the weekends. We always had a type of board game going late into the night. During a match of Rumoli, my husband decided to flip over the board game with all of our tokens on it, because he was loosing and didn't want to play any more. There was always such high drama, such a big show. We could never just have fun like regular people do. He was always pouring those drinks and knocking them back and we the family were waiting for the next event to take place. Even if the girls were having a game with their friends, he would interject himself. The friends would naturally say "sure". The daughters would probably think what a way to ruin a party. He just never seemed to be able to know, as a parent, when to keep his distance. He really believed it was AOK to hang out. It was his place after all. He picked up the kids after the dances and took them out to a restaurant for a late night snack. He took them all water skiing. Why the hell not be one of them when he felt like it. I couldn't fight back because there was always somebody around. I would go upstairs and keep my ears open for any trouble. Eventually the youngsters would go outside to the docks and he was passed out, asleep in his captain's chair at the dining room table. I was sad because my daughters and their friends were exposed to that kind of behavior. I would even be more embarrassed because they could go home and tell their parents how awful we were. I had confronted him a couple of times on the following day. His reply to me was

"If a man can't be his real self, at least, when he is at home, then where can he be?"

The younger daughter, unfortunately, was one of his targets. He seemed to like to abuse her and me because he knew we were super sensitive. We were celebrating someone's birthday and the children were asked to come on up to the table and get a piece of cake. Trudy ran to be first in line. The six kids were all shuffling into position. Dick just walked right up to his daughter and screamed right in her face, maybe two inches away

"Get the hell back you pig!"

Trudy and Cher took off like a shot and hid in the rocks by the west beach. He went tearing after them. Maureen and I and her husband went to catch Dick and stop him. He was raging. We had to intervene. Maureen's husband, an army man held on to my husband and my girlfriend and I helped our frightened daughters out from behind the shrubbery. That was the end of that party. Trudy had moved to Toronto after graduating university. My husband used to love calling her

"Ms Hot Shot from the Big Smoke". What was the point of that? You would think a father would be proud about his daughters self reliance. He just had to put a woman down. She would commute for four hours just about every weekend to come and relax at the cottage. Her father would pick her up at the dock late at night. He had been having drinks with the older daughter. He offered to pour one for Trudy. She said "no thanks" she was tired. He went into a hissy fit calling her a tea tottler and chased her out of the kitchen and up the living room stairs. I met her at the top of the landing. Trudy eased past me and I confronted him.

"I swear to God, if you do not turn around right now I will, with all of my might, push you down to stairs and send you tumbling."

He turned and walked back to the kitchen. The last time he tried to assault our younger daughter she was in her 30s. Her husband intervened and grabbed Dick by the neck and hauled him to the side of the house to calm him down. Four of us were on the front porch talking. The first grandchild was sleeping upstairs. Dick looked like he was asleep in a chair, no such luck. He, all of a sudden, jumped up and started kicking at the screen door because the black cat wanted to come in. Next he walked around to the shed to get himself another drink. He came back and screamed at us

"If I had a gun now I would kill you all."

He kept raving, the two sons in law were trying to calm him down but to no avail. Trudy came out of the gazebo and walked over to the gallery. She started to tell her father to stop all of his screeching and at that point he leapt at her. Her husband stopped him, then made sure his father in law got to bed. Dick was drunk the night my sister and my father and I had come back from Montreal for my mother's memorial service. My Dad was supposed to take us all out for dinner but we were too tired. We travelers picked up a large pizza for all of us. I settled my father at the table on the east side of the porch. My younger daughter and my sister and Dick were on the west side. My husband was mumbling about how cheap my father was and so on and so on. My sister and my daughter tried to explain everything to him. Next he turns on Trudy, again, yelling

"You get the hell out of here. You have lived here long enough. You get your own place."

She rented an apartment that very week. It's ironic, you know, our daughter had been away for two years she was just staying at the Island during the two summer months to save on rent money. Then when the cottage was closed she would get her own place. I keep seeing these images as if it were a slide presentation. I feel very nauseated right now and I have a headache. Writing this is probably raising my blood pressure. The cancer pain hasn't subsided this morning even after taking my meds. I just have to finish this. What a mess!

The older daughter's relationship with her father didn't seem as tumultuous. I use the word, seem. This is about me and my recollections of events as I perceived them. I believe the damage Dick did was much more subtle. He took pleasure in putting her down, regarding her studies. He always had to make a wisecrack or devalue higher learning or academia. She was proud about her intelligence and so she should be. It never was enough. I think he was envious that both his daughters were achievers because he had the brains but had flunked out. He berated her about two boy friends for years. He would never let up. What is interesting is her first love ended up very much like her father. He was an addict, insecure, violent and a controlling young man. It's probably more like she modeled my handling of the relationship between her father and me. I was very much the enabler. I thought all of my love could surely fix him. Dick, even though he made derogatory remarks about the young men in her young life, never helped her out trying to find a better way. She left home early. The house just wasn't big enough for the older daughter and the mother. She was in charge of everything in my absence and did a great job. She had a part time job from the time she was sixteen. She started working with her father at the contracting company. She knew more about my husband's whereabouts than his boss and I put together. She even claims she used to doctor his expense account reports so as to cover certain things up. She also mentioned that she used to meet him after work at some bars and hang with him and his drinking buddies. She said two even hit on her. She was only nineteen. Where was her father while this was going on? She has even said she had to drive home because he was too drunk to drive and she wouldn't ride with him unless she drove. I didn't find any of this out until forty years later, after I had divorced my husband. It didn't seem to bother her sharing these stories with me. Maybe she was trying to make a point. Dick and her had become comrades in arms. He never even realized the damage he was doing by setting such a bad example to an impressionable young woman who just wanted to 'hang' with Dad and be appreciated by him. We should be careful about blaming the mother all the time. Some Moms really don't always know what is going on.

When Marie met her future husband who was only nine years younger than her father, then all the past was forgotten. Dick finally approved of her choice. His criteria was simple

"As long as he's strong enough to carry a case of twenty four beer and can fix a motor, the guy is OK in my books."

It wasn't really what he, as a father, could do in finding a good partner worthy of his daughter. It was more what the prospective son in law needed to be like to please the 'old man'. Nothing like setting the bar high. The eldest daughter got to stand tall between her two favorite guys. He really liked her new boyfriend. He was a bartender and lots of fun. He played golf and pool and darts. A son in law sent from heaven. The three of them became amigos. They hung out together and had a great time when I was away in Montreal working my buns off. When I finally got back on the weekend, I became the odd man out. I was the square one, the mother, the wife, the mother in law, the one who didn't want to hang out in a pool hall or a pub. Boring Me!! I would have liked to spend time with my husband alone. All of a sudden after, after twenty one years my husband actually became an interested family man. He really didn't need a wife. He had an ongoing 'bromance' or what they refer to today as a 'man crush' on his son in law. It was the same thing as in Montreal. There was Rod, there was Michael, there was the other Mike and there was Gary. Now a buddy right here in the family. It was that same kind of strange vibe I used to get way back when

"Well if you like him so much why don't you just move in with him?"

They could hang out and bullshit all they wanted. It was family, no harm in that. That is why I think the damage done to Marie was more like an undercurrent, slowly weakening the fabric beneath her. To this day I don't think he ever gave either daughter the confidence of that unwavering loyalty children need from their parents to evolve healthily. But prosper they did! They are in their forties now, brilliant, beautiful and successful women. A Mom does have bragging rights.

Oh what the hell do I know? I'm the wife. I'm the mother that didn't quite keep it all together. I was the one that always said

"The mother was supposed to be the glue in the family". Look who got unglued.

CHAPTER 16

THE GOOD, THE BAD, THE UGLY

POSITIVE THINKING has always been my reprieve. No matter how things went I somehow managed to pull myself up from the floor, stand tall, shoulders back, head held high and believed that tomorrow will be a better day. I credit that strength to my Meme and my aunts Madeleine and Dora. They were women whom I never heard complain and they had a lot of reasons to. I really think I have had a much better life.

I was crazy in love. I never had a single doubt when I walked down the aisle on that wedding day. I had chosen the right man. Dick and I were compatible in so many respects, intellectually, sexually. We were both voracious readers but totally different in our tastes. He relished sci-fi. I buried myself in historical and political epics. I also enjoyed the distraction of quick reads like police and legal 'who done it' novels. We always talked about and listened to each others stories about what we were reading. We never exchanged books though. We could stay up into the wee hours discussing politics with friends and still make it to bed to make love. Is that enough? Then, at the beginning it was. I was in charge of taking care of home and the children. He was to 'bring home the bacon'. The roles of most couples of the middle class were separate and distinct. My husband was a good provider. If there were any money problems I was not made aware of them. I never got any money from him directly except for the groceries. Then again I wasn't working (outside) of the home. In those days that was considering not like 'working' to most men. My needs were few.

He did have a fantastic gift which not too many men had in our gang. His way of giving to me was by enabling my creative juices in home décor. He was the consummate renovation man. I called him my master builder. I came up with an idea. A few hours later, he pulled out his quad pad and with his engineering mind began taking measurements and jotting down notes. Only he could read his squiggles. The first house we bought was a 'fixer upper'. He gave us a brand new kitchen, bathroom, outdoor deck and patio. He built a seven foot high fence. He even made me a raised vegetable garden. At one point, when we purchased house number three, my daughters asked me

"Well Ma what walls are you going to have Dad tear down in this next house?"

I was a freak for space. I had to have a great deal of light. I did not like to be hemmed in. Interestingly enough four houses were on corner lots. I just wanted neighbors on one side of me. That was enough. That is probably a result of what I now know as claustrophobia. I am willing to admit now, for sure I might have been a touch anti social. My work life was 100% geared to client support and services. That was enough people pecking at me. Thank you very much.

That is why the purchase of the Island as a seasonal retreat was the solution to two of my biggest quirks. That renovation was huge. My dear husband used his talents and energy to restore that lopsided turn of the twentieth century house into my castle. He installed new plumbing and new electrical. I do not use the word new loosely here. There was no electricity and no water. We used oil lanterns for light and heated river water on the wood stove. Our cooking was done on the wood stove also. Dick managed to get a holding tank, which is an above ground septic tank. He got a contractor to haul this huge contraption from Montreal on a flat bed truck. It was delivered to the Island by barge. He installed all the piping required to use it. The wire was next to arrive. He drilled holes in all the ceiling beams and walls to install overhead lighting fixtures. He got us a hot water tank. Then "Presto, Abra Cadabra" this old house had power. Over the years he knocked down a few walls. That is, I started the dirty tear down work, board by board and he had no choice but to make everything pretty and functional again. It's more like he cleaned up after my mess. He expanded the little kitchen and changed the windows and added more windows for me and installed a window seat. I had an almost 360 degree vantage point of the mighty St. Lawrence river. The plan was to get to stay there as long as we could. That meant from early spring and to late fall. Eventually it would mean our retirement home for eight months of the year and we could spend winter in a warm climate. In order to facilitate that plan he nailed insulation sheets on every inch of the outside of the house and installed white vinyl siding. He also installed brand new windows and doors to keep out the gale force wind and to retain the heat from the wood stoves inside the house. He stuffed bats of pink fiberglass between all the rafters of the open ceilings and the walls of the rooms on the second floor and covered that with plastic sheeting. Eventually those walls were finished in tongue and groove pine. The only thing left to do was to find an effective electrical heating system that could possibly be controlled by remote from the mainland. We imagined pushing a button when we left the city house and when we arrived at the Island the house would be toasty. He was my genius. I was so grateful to him and proud of my paradise. The amazing thing also was that he always cleaned up after. I was so proud of everything we accomplished and especially his contributions. Those were mostly really happy times for me. We had projects, we were together. I never felt at any time that perhaps he might be unhappy. I guess that's why over time he preferred being on the golf course playing two consecutive rounds of golf. That is thirty six holes! After that he hung out at the club bar with the buddies and the booze. It certainly was a lot less strenuous and a lot more fun. Here I am making excuses again or better yet, in denial still. When I had filed for divorced my best girlfriend said

"Why don't you get another property and get another project going. That was his way of giving to you and you enjoyed it."

I think our problems were a lot deeper than even I could acknowledge. That makes me think of a woman who believes that bringing in another baby in the family could fix what ails the couple. No I don't think so. By then, I had a sick, sick feeling in my gut.

Back to my fantasizing how wonderfully our personalities complemented each other. We were great travelers together. My husband worked very hard and always had several contracting projects going on at once. The suppliers loved him and were usually riding on his coattails waiting for him to order their supplies for his on going contracts. He always spoke of his Friday deal. Something always fell in his lap. He claims most of the deals were made at the bars with suppliers no doubt. He would explain

"That's what they had expense accounts for. Great way to enjoy drinking with somebody and have them sign on the dotted line."

My husband enjoyed that life style. Made him feel really important. He used to refer to them as his friends. I used to call them parasites. His comment on my opinion would be

"You know nothing about business."

I never could have my husband answer his beeper though. In all the years we were married I never called a bar. That's because there were so many. He really got around. What he did do, was manage to accumulate enough bonus points from a major supplier and that awarded us several all expenses paid vacations. The wives got to go on those trips. Some others trips, like golfing or gambling, were exclusively for the men. HA!HA! So Dick and I got to see Portugal, Maui, Hawaii, Trinidad, Barbados, Puerto Rico and had a Caribbean cruise. We also went to New York city for a long weekend with his boss and his wife. We were always with a lot of people but our combined outgoing personalities really came in handy. He would work one side of the room and I would work the other. When we were on our own we toured many museums of art and natural history. We seemed to both enjoy botanical gardens also. We went to the theater. We climbed mountain trails and did some deep sea fishing. My husband liked to play poker so if there was a casino we inevitably always went in for a few hours. I would stand behind him and watch the play. I was a people watcher and did I ever see some fascinating genres. We loved new restaurants. A couple of weeks after one would open, we would go and check it out in the middle of the week to avoid crowds. We would stop going when they became too popular and would try a new 'boite', just for fun. His boss always said

"Take the wife out every once in a while. It makes them feel appreciated"

I can honestly say I really enjoyed my husband's company. I'm sure he did to. Maybe? Surely a man can't fake that. Can he?

Dick was a very kind hearted man. Whether that was natural to his nature or he did good deeds just because he was asked by someone is not relevant. The fact that he did come through was indeed a credit to him. I knew that already. I was there when he had driven eight hours up and back to get his ill father and bring him to a Montreal hospital. A good friend of ours had been visiting and he realized he had forgotten his daughters passport back home in New Hampshire. She had no trouble getting into Canada but to get back to the US she would need her documents. So that night, Dick drove Murray back to his residence which was, there and back, a twelve hour drive. The stamina that man had was incredible. Remember his saying "What me worry". He was always game, the more exciting the better. He was always there to help, anyone who asked, in the home renovation work they had on hand. Many men learned a lot by working side by side with him finishing their projects. Their wives were thrilled. He was proud of his talents and flattered by their attention and gratitude. As he should be.

My dear aunt Madeleine, at the age of 76, had been hospitalized because of a stroke. She had tried to speak but unsuccessfully. She could only manage to garble

"Fis it Fis it!"

It's like she was begging Dick to fix her up also. So sad! She died six weeks later. Even, until the end, she trusted he would take care of things. There was another incident in the Islands. My girlfriend and her husband were to stay home and enjoy a weekend 'sans enfants'. I had offered to take her three along with our two to the cottage for the long weekend. Maureen had warned me that her son, who suffered from asthma, seemed to be having episodes over the last couple of days.

"He should be ok. Here is his medicine. Just make sure he has it every four hours."

I was a little bit anxious about it. The only experience I had had with asthma attacks was when I had been teacher. We were going to be on an island. The nearest hospital was thirty minutes away by car. I did what I do best and invoked the help of the guardian angels. There was that nagging dry cough for the three hour drive to the cottage. We crossed the river at night. I got the kids ready for bed and made sure the boy had his medicine. After a couple of hours he had difficulty breathing. I gave him more medicine. An hour later, after having coughed all of that time, he could barely breathe. I called his mother at her house and described the problem. I did not feel competent enough to wait this out. Dick was going to go across the river now while there was calm and take the child into the hospital in Kingston. She agreed and asked us to keep in touch with her. It was just past midnight. Dick and his very sick little charge took off into the darkness. He called from the hospital around 2am.

"The doctors have had the little guy in an oxygen tent for the last hour and a half. They want him transported to the Montreal Children's hospital where they have a file on him. They will keep him medicated enough to enable me to get him to the city without any incident. I have to do this now." I told him

"I'll call Maureen. She and her husband can meet you in Cornwall. That is half way. They have to assume responsibility for him now. This is very serious business. You can't do this alone and I can't leave the other kids here on the island." My husband said

"I'll call you back in twenty minutes."

I contacted Maureen and they agreed to the 'rendez vous'. If everyone left in thirty minutes they should be able to meet at the 401 service centre at about the same time. The transfer of this wheezing five year old took place around 4:30 a.m. My husband got home in time for early breakfast. Make that with a stiff drink first. The boy was hospitalized for a week and was in an oxygen tent for the duration. I think Dick saved that boy's life that night. The other four children had slept through the whole thing.

The following story is about a river tragedy. Many people have died on the St. Lawrence. The drowning deaths are legendary. Yet every time it happens it seems worse than the last incident. We, certainly in a million years, would not have expected anything to happen to our family. Dick was the 'wild and crazy guy'. He had been nicknamed 'Lightning' by the local fishing guide. My father used to say

"He only knew two speeds, fast and stop!"

Yet the head of our clan was spared no matter what stunt he pulled on that river. His number wasn't up. Our younger daughter Trudy was to be one of six victims in a fatal boating accident. It was a Saturday in May of 1988. My daughter had a guy friend over for dinner after a day of swimming and hanging out. She was seventeen. He was eighteen, another Montrealer. His parents had a cottage on a neighboring island. The parents had all met each other a couple of times. In fact Trudy had asked this lad to be her date at her high school graduation dance in Montreal. She and he had dated in the city a few times over the winter. Rather than have desert at our place our daughter asked

"May we go into the village. We'll call Vicky, she's home and head into the Dairy Queen for some treat" to which I replied

"Sure why not. It's a beautiful calm night. Make sure you are back by 10 p.m. You can hang here or your friends can even sleep over if need be since their parents aren't home this weekend."

The boy had his father's open bow rider boat. That is the kind where you can sit maybe two people in the bow beyond the glassed in area where the steering wheel is. Dick and I pushed the kids off from the dock. We headed upstairs at dark. Dark still came early in May, around 8:30 p.m. I checked the alarm clock on my night table. It was past ten. I went out to the porch. The kids weren't in the boat house. The boat was not at the dock. God how I hate that. Trudy knew better than not give me a phone call. Where were they? The sky was pitch black, a moonless night and it was overcast. I went up to bed and Dick turned off the light. He said

"Don't worry they'll be here soon."

No sooner had I turned over to my right side and had closed my eyes I heard a blood curdling, screaming sound.

"Mommy!Mommy! Mommy!"

It was Trudy's voice, like that of a child. Dick and I leapt out of bed, ran down the stairs, out the front door and over to the dock. There was our daughter wrapped in a blanket being held up by a man from a neighboring island. I took Trudy into my arms. The man said

"Dick I need your help. There's been a crash. One girl is pinned inside the bow of the boat under the cement dock. I can't get her out alone. We have to somehow unpin the boat. She is submerged except for her face. There are three other teenagers in the boat. The driver is crushed against the steering wheel, from the waist down. It's a real mess. My wife has called the police and the volunteers are on their way."

Dick jumped into the boat and they headed out. Trudy and I made our way across the lawn to the gallery. The night was black there was no sound except for the boat leaving the dock. Then I heard them. There was a lot of shouting. The rest of the rescuers were arriving on the scene. I see the lights on their boats. There had to be about six in all. I went into the house and my daughter was crying yelling

"Mom, my teeth! my teeth!"

I couldn't figure out what she was talking about. I came very close and held her in my arms, trying to calm her down. Her face was badly swollen and full of scratches. It was covered in pieces of shredded fiberglass. Several of her teeth had been knocked out or hanging by a thread. She was so upset because she had had her braces removed three weeks prior in time for her graduation dance.

"All that money. It's been wasted, all for nothing. Now all the good work had been ruined."

I consoled her. I rocked her like you would an infant. I told her that her braces and teeth can be repaired. We were lucky that was all that was broken. I didn't even bother asking questions. She was too distraught. All that could come later. Quiet and security was what my little girl needed now.

The quiet didn't last long. A half hour later a police officer came to the door with two other kids, a young man and a girl. The officer asked if they could stay here with me until more ambulances arrived at the mainland marina. At which time Trudy and these two would be driven into Kingston General hospital, thirty minutes away, for a thorough examination. I followed him out to the dock. I asked the man

"Where is Vicky, the little girl with black hair?" he replied

"Your husband and the neighbor were able to push down on the bow of the boat so that one of them could pull her out. She went across the river in a volunteer rescue boat. Your husband was cradling her in his arms. She is unconscious. The driver, Jeff. He has shattered bones from the waist down. He is on his way to the hospital also. There is another guy. He didn't make it. He died on impact. We still have to bring him to the hospital by ambulance of course. We have three ambulances at the marina now. We're waiting for the other three to arrive. If you have the telephone numbers of the kids you do know could you please call their parents and tell them to meet us at the hospital." I said

"The driver's parents live in Montreal!" He replied

"That's ok! the lad isn't going anywhere for a long time to come. They have to get here and sign consent for surgery. I'm sorry to have to put this on you but the news might be easier coming from a parent. I'll be back here in no time for the others."

Trudy was whimpering. The new girl seemed OK. The guy looked older and I was quite sure he was drunk. He was complaining about his shoulder hurting and doing a lot of cursing. He was trying to get up the stairs to the bedrooms. He was arguing with me when I told him NO! that he could lie down on the living room couch. I wanted all of us in the same room. The girls and I can sit in the armchairs. The girl must have been his date because she told him

"Shut up! we're in enough trouble without your trying to pick a fight"

He did listen to her and immediately passed out on the sofa. I just can't think how I would have handled a belligerent thug. Dick and the policeman finally came back. Everyone left the house and got into a boat. I called the children's parents. They took the news calmly and would be leaving their homes immediately. I was sitting in the kitchen sipping on a stiff drink when the phone rang. I must have jumped three feet high. It was Dick. He was coming back home to get me. The police said it could be very upsetting to leave me all alone when all of this mess was going on in town. I would be safer at the hospital with my daughter. I was so grateful someone had the common sense to think of that. While Dick and I were headed back to town he asked me for a cigarette. He had not smoked since his fortieth birthday. That had been four years ago. He then proceeded to tell me everything that he had seen from the first time he left me and Trudy. He also gave me all the information that he had been given by the police. This is very difficult for me to recount. I feel so sad. My eyes have welled up with tears. It was such a terrifying experience. Yet our family was the luckiest one.

We arrived at the hospital. It was past midnight. Trudy's girlfriend was having brain surgery. Luckily her uncle was the surgeon. Dick said

"She had a hole in her forehead and every time she took a breath I could see a bubble of blood popping out. It was really creepy. I kept talking to her when I was cradling her. I don't think she heard me. I just kept saying

"Don't you die on me now, don't you die on me!"

The young woman was in a coma for almost three weeks. The driver of the boat was in an another operating theater. He had a shattered pelvis and hips and legs. He spent four weeks laying horizontally on top of his bed but not on it. He was suspended by what seemed to be a huge skewer. He sure as heck was not going to be escorting our dear daughter to her grad dance at the end of the month. The couple that had been at our cottage were examined and released to go home. The police took their depositions concerning the events of that night. Our beat up Kelly was examined also. The doctors assured us that the swelling of the face would eventually go down and the bruising would disappear after two weeks. I would have to keep a close eye on her in the event that there may be a concussion. I was to be sure that she was able to wake up every couple of hours and answer basic questions, like her name, her birthday etc. Her teeth and gum injuries would have to be looked at by the family dentist in Montreal. A police officer took a deposition from her also. The witnesses in the crash were all interviewed separately by the same officer. They were kept apart and had no contact with each other. That really worried me. What was going on? Where was the sixth passenger? The policeman told us in private.

"The twenty one year old sitting in the passenger seat beside the driver of the boat was killed, immediately upon impact of the boat on to the cement dock."

At dawn Dick and I and Trudy went back to the cottage to sleep for a while. A few hours later we packed our bags and headed back to Montreal. The dentist referred us to a periodontist. Trudy was given dispensation from having to write her final graduation year exams. Her average scores throughout her high school were in the ninety percentiles. She was eligible for her diploma.

The parents of the other young people never contacted us. I certainly would have expected some feeling of gratitude or some expression of appreciation. I found out later why there was to be no contact with anyone. There was going to be a trial. The driver had been charged with reckless operation of a boat. It was the first time in the history of boating fatalities in our area that a, so called, accidental death was going to be tried in court. We were to set a precedent. That was twenty four years ago. Today, it might have been a charge of vehicular homicide. Who knows? Also, the young man at our cottage, the one who appeared really drunk, was suing the family who owned the boat. My Dick did his rescue work well. Weeks later his brain was still conscious of the horrible smell of blood. That was a remnant from the experience at the boat wreck when he was prying the girl form the bottom of the hull. A very good friend who was a transport driver and had also been a British soldier during the civil war in Belfast, Ireland gave Dick some very good advice.

"I've witnessed shootings on the streets of Belfast and have dragged drivers out of trucking wreckage. The best thing to do when that putrid smell comes open you is to light up a match or a candle. It will go away over time. It's called transference. One nice smell will replace the odor in the subconscious."

I was surprised Dick hadn't taken up smoking again. No his resolve was upheld. I stopped working for that summer. Trudy and I went back to the Island cottage full time. Her mission was to visit her two hospitalized friends as often as possible. She wanted to cheer them up. Every single day we got into our boat. She was at the helm. Un frightened, she took us across that mighty river. I would look over to the site of the crash and would get goose bumps all over my flesh. Trudy, my tremendously brave younger daughter had total amnesia. God works strange wonders. She didn't remember a thing from the time she had gotten into that boat to the time right after the impact. There is a lot more to this story. This was just the tip of the iceberg. The whole drama is in a future book of short stories. I'll call the chapter

"The whole truth and nothing but the truth".

This was about most of the times that I can remember that my husband went beyond the call of duty. He was a natural. If your boat had broken down and you needed towing he would get you back to town. If you were lost in a fog and ended at our dock at night, he would open the guest cabin so you could sleep there safely and head back out in the morning. This is why I cannot for the life of me comprehend why Dick distanced himself from me so much when I was battling cancer. Or how a man whose behavior at times was exemplarily could end up doing things that were totally dangerous and ferocious. Actions that would terrify those of us exposed to what I refer to as his fits of momentary madness. It is difficult to categorize what is considered 'bad' as opposed to what is considered 'ugly'. I guess to many it would also be considered relative. Right! Well, personally I do not really give a hoot how someone else would evaluate the extent of the crap I had to put up with. I am telling this story. Memoirs are, after all, personal recollections.

I can best paraphrase by saying

"When my husband was GOOD he was really good but when he was BAD, he was really UGLY."

I know for a fact the signs were all there, early in the game. Yet I was a typical woman of that time. Patsy Cline had a song entitled "Stand by your man!" I, like so many others, truly believed I could fix Dick. All my love and comfort and the secure life we were going to build together would surely help him overcome his demons. He was young. Guys grow out of these bad habits over time. There were heavy drinkers on my mother's side. My own mother was an alcoholic. The drunk was usually given a very wide birth. Nobody talked about it. There were no interventions. Alcohol was a legal substance. Anyways, that would have been considered meddling in somebody else's private business. I can use the analogy that I was handling a live hand grenade. This was trouble from the 'Get Go'.

"Without a word of a lie" I remember when: Some of the following instances have already been touched upon. I guess I haven't purged hard enough.

It was an afternoon in August. We were on a date. Three couples had met at a motel on a lake. The drinking was heavy. It was what I now know to be called 'binge drinking'. I didn't like where the party was heading. By 6pm I wanted to go home but Dick wouldn't take me back. He was totally hammered. Finally his friend said he would. We used the excuse that I would love to have a ride in a convertible. We three headed out to my house. His friend parked his car in my driveway and we went into the house by the back door, as always. He and I started to chat at the kitchen table when we realized that Dick was still outside. I was worried about what the neighbors might see. My boyfriend was hiding under our back porch. I realized he had passed out. We started to talk to him but there was no response. His friend said to give it a half hour and we would try again to wake him. That's when he said

"You know Dick is an alcoholic!" my defensive reply was

"You're a fine one to talk?"

"Look I got you home didn't I! Anyways I'm not wasting my time here any more than I have to. Let's go".

We went out, knelt down on the grass. We each grabbed a leg and started to pull Dick out. He finally woke up and led him to the car and they took off back to the party. The next day, when my then fiancée called, nothing was said by him or me. He perhaps did not remember and I surely wanted to forget. After that incident I made sure I always met him someplace. I always drove my own car, just in case. We were married four months later and I gave birth to our first child seven months after that. Then there was no car for me to 'get away'. I had sold it. Dick's life style never skipped a beat.

There were several passing out incidents.

I remember when:

Once I got a phone call at 2am. Dick wanted me to go get him downtown. He seemed to have forgotten that I did not have a car and we had a baby sleeping in her crib now. That same friend brought him back the next day. They had found him passed out in a phone booth.

I remember when:

We were invited to a supplier's house party on the Lakeshore. I guess I was supposed to be impressed. Another couple, who were business associates of my husband, picked us up. Upon arrival Dick went directly to the kitchen where the booze and the guys were hanging out. I was introduced to the other ladies by the associate as

"She's with Dick"

I was so insulted. I made casual chit chat most of the evening. I hadn't seen my husband from the moment we had gotten there. The time to go finally arrived. The wife of the associate mentioned there was a problem and led me into the kitchen. There was my husband sprawled out in the corner of the kitchen floor, passed out. A couple of the guys picked him up and put him in the car. The associates dropped us at home. The guy helped me get him on the living room couch.

I remember when:

Oh Ya! this was so embarrassing. One week before Christmas, Dick's boss and his wife had invited my brother in law and us to dinner at the Hilton Hotel. I was so excited. Dick finally got home, late that afternoon after doing the usual rounds of office parties. His boss and wife arrived. More drinks were served. Everything seemed really pleasant. The babysitter arrived to take care of the four children. The five adults travelled in two separate cars. I thought I looked gorgeous. The dinner was fantastic. It was a real treat for me. Dick's brother and I were having a conversation with Dick's boss when all of a sudden a huge crash was heard. My husband had passed out right into his desert plate. I was mortified. I tried to shake him awake but couldn't. The boss signaled to the Maitre D, who came over with a wheel chair. That man and my brother in law ease Dick into it. My brother in law wheeled him out to the lobby doors and to our parked car. He drove us home. The boss and his wife stayed to finish their coffee. Nothing was ever said by anyone. I sent my usual hand written thank you note. Dick's boss was a big drinker. They used to drink at the office or mostly at his house after work. It's OK if the boss is a 'drunk' but not the employee. In fact when the position of General Manager came up, the boss gave it to his son in law instead of Dick. My husband resigned a year later. He said it was nepotism. Let's face it! Who can you trust your business too? A very competent, loyal employee who has a bad reputation as a drunk in town or a not so competent but trainable, loyal, quiet family member.

I remember when:

We were on a cruise, again with another boss and his wife. There were eight of us at the dinner table. Dick was his usual charming, funny self. After dinner we all retired to the lounge, all except my husband. The boss's wife was getting very anxious for his whereabouts. I tried to reassure her. I went into the other lounges and bars and the casino. He was nowhere to be found. I was trying to be discreet. I said

"I really don't care. I just want to have fun. I don't want to be having to chase him down. He'll show up eventually." then she says

"What if he keeled over the railing and fell off the ship?"

I had never thought of that. It was very late. We three were tired and I really felt bad for the boss's wife. She was a lovely lady and was very fond of Dick. She was just anxious. So we headed out to my cabin first. There was my husband passed out on the bed. Well at least, for her sake, he was not out in the ocean somewhere.

I remember when:

We were on a suppliers bonus points award trip to Trinidad. Seven days of constant open bars. It was my first time away from our baby girl. The couples were all very nice. We got to see a lot of interesting things. There was a carnival night. I won a limbo contest. I was thrilled. The party's over. You would have thought it would have been enough. No! not for Dick! We went back to the room. Five minutes later he said

"The band had invited him to hit a few local spots with them downtown."

I thought this could be very dangerous. He did not. I heard him come in around 5 am. I ignored him and went back to sleep. At 8 am I awoke and tried to get into the bathroom. I could not. My husband had passed out and his legs were pushed against the door. I kept pushing and eventually gave myself enough room to get by. Heck! I really had to go bad. This was a first. Imagine having a pi and a poop sitting on the throne with my husband at my feet. Not the Queen's act I had envisioned for myself. You see how I can still play the humor card. It is disgusting to me how I, to this day, can still deflect everything. I think that's why I'm still alive!

I remember when:

My brother in law and I and Dick were at our best friends' party and my husband was found by her children on the second floor landing, by the bathroom door. He had probably passed out. To avoid any trouble we all decided to leave him there. He spent the rest of the night in that spot. Max and I went on home.

I remember when:

He used to sit at the head of the dinning room table in the 'captain's' chair. He had a habit of folding his arms at the elbows and crossing his hands together under his chin. He would let his head rest there as in a cradle and go to sleep. The dinner guests used to think it was cute. How rested he looked! My daughters and I were relieved he was going to take a drinking break and was sleeping some off. He inevitably always woke up soon enough. I used to keep track of all the drinks and hope that the next one was going to be the one to put him out. That was the only advantage of having a drinker pass out. You didn't have to worry about him anymore until tomorrow. It was much safer than watching him drink himself into an out of control, aggressive, screaming banshee. Some of the examples of aggressive behavior have already been described. A few others were monumental for me because it was I who had to take the brunt of his madness. In each instance I should have been better prepared but I was never expecting bad things to happen again. I seem to have this naivety that all the incidents were random. Interestingly enough, the circumstances that led to his outrageous behavior were all unique. Nevertheless, his drunken tirades were pretty much the same every time.

I remember when:

Our friend Raj had been married that afternoon. The reception was in a hotel. He and his bride had left on their wedding trip to scout out places in San Francisco where Raj had managed to get himself a new job with a pharmaceutical firm. Luckily they were not there when Dick got into a screaming match with his other good friend Murray. He had been trying to calm him down but to no avail. I was just hoping Murray would have punched him out. Instead he and his Stella turned around, got into their car and sped out of the parking lot. He started to chase after him but we got lost. We ended up on an 'on ramp' of a turnpike and ran out of gas, no less. I was surprised the steering wheel was not damaged for all the pummeling it took. Better it was that than me, is all I can say.

Next thing my husband gets out of the car and heads out on foot into the cornfields. I did not go after him I was much too afraid. I kept yelling at him.

"Come back, you're going the wrong way. The gas station is down the ramp, right behind us."

What the heck did I know? Imagine trying to talk sense to a raving lunatic. I could hear him yelling about

"Raj getting married and leaving him alone like that. It just wasn't right!" After a while there was no sound. Where was he? Had he fallen asleep in the field? What if the State troopers showed up? Would we get arrested? He had taken the car keys with him. I couldn't even walk down the ramp to get some gas then go home by myself. I know I would not have done that. I loved poor Dick. He was really upset. I realized he had not passed out when I started to see the flicker of his lighter every time he started a new cigarettes. He came back eventually. I saw him, through my side view mirror, walking back with a young gas station attendant who was carrying a canister of gas. He was giving the kid the height of shit, as if it was his fault. We got home at 4 a.m. I had learned a long time ago not to bother talking with a drunk. He'll either punch you out then and there or he will take 'the fifth'. I was just relieved to finally be safe.

I remember when:

We and our girls were spending the weekend at my dear aunt Mado's house in celebration of her birthday. Meme and her son were over night also. Sunday lunch came by. The cake was ready. The girls and ladies were all in a festive mood. The men, Dick and my cousin Gerry, had gone ice fishing in the early morning. We expected them back shortly. The guys didn't show up until 4:30pm and they were drunk. I was so angry, I yelled

"This is an insult to my aunt's birthday. Lunch was supposed to be four hours ago and now we have to rush around because we still have to head back to Montreal soon before dark"

My auntie and grandmother took the kids into the living room while my husband and I went at it. Next thing I know Dick came running at me with his hands extended out to throttle me. I squeezed myself between the stove and the counter and covered my face. He came in so close that I took my foot and hit him in the face to slow him down. My cousin was pulling him off of me. He sat him down at a kitchen chair. Dick was furious. I had broken one of the lenses of his glasses. Well that ended the fight! We had an early supper. The ladies and I chatted with the girls to keep everything calm and fun. We had birthday cake. I started to pack our suitcases. Dick was busy making a cardboard cut-out with a tiny hole in the center to replace the missing glass. He blamed me for this terrible inconvenience to him. I was mortified that we had ruined my auntie's birthday party.

I remember when:

Our friend Raj was spending the weekend with us. We were coming back from a party on the South shore. It usually took about twenty minutes to get home. Dick was driving eighty miles an hour. I started to ask him gently to "Please slow down".

There was no response, just faster speed. I became louder and more insistent and kept repeating myself.

"Slow Down!!"

I even asked our friend to please reason with him. Raj said to me.

"Let it go, were almost home."

Dick took his right arm reached out and started to shove me up against Raj and trying to reach for the door to push me out. I think Raj being the obstruction was the only thing that saved me. God only knows what could have happened had we been alone. I probably would have jumped into the back seat. We got into our town and he took a left turn. At the corner of the park, my husband abruptly stopped the car and put in park. He opened the driver's door and walked around the car to the passenger side. Our friend and I looked at each other confused. My husband opened the car door and he asked Raj to get out. He then grabbed me by the arm and pulled me out of the car and threw me on the grass. He then told Raj to get back into the car. They drove home. I walked home. It was two o'clock in the morning. I got home thirty minutes later. The house was dark. Everyone was asleep.

He was prone to violence when I challenged him. Most of the time I tried not to and kept quiet hoping the incident would end quickly and we could talk about it in the daylight. Fat chance of that, he never remembered anything. So he would say

"You're exaggerating! As usual!"

I remember when:

He had a bonfire going at the burning pit on the Island which was just twenty feet from the house and under a tree of all places. We had a hose that I always had hooked up at the ready. After the parties, when the guests had all gone to bed I would go out and hose the whole area down and the ashes in the pit so that the fire was truly out. We had horror stories in the Islands about winds picking up during the night and stirring sparks of a fire that could fly onto grass and buildings and burn areas down in no time at all. Trudy had a couple of friends over for the weekend. I was watching them play a board game in the dining room and I decided to go and

"Check on Dad!"

Low and behold there Dick was stoking the fire which was already reaching heights of five feet. I asked him politely, than less politely, to get the hose and water the tree branches above. This fire looked dangerously high. He wouldn't. So I did! A verbal fight ensued and then he started to shove me. I shove back a couple of times. I gave up and was walking away when he tackled me to the ground. My face was buried in the grass and I had trouble breathing. He was sitting on me and kept pounding my back. Our daughter came out to the back porch, after hearing all the yelling. She pried him off of me. We both went upstairs to our separate rooms, thank God for big houses. Kelly and her friends put the fire out.

I remember when:

The now married daughters and their husbands and one grandchild had been over for the weekend. The eldest was also six months pregnant with the second child. Our daughters were in their thirties by then. Dick and the two sons in law were to go golfing on the Sunday. We were all sitting on the front porch. Trudy had already retired to the gazebo. Dick seemed to have nodded off. Then all hell breaks loose just over a black cat. That animal had a habit of sneaking into the house. He was the eldest daughter's cat and she didn't mind him coming in but we did. As she was trying to let the animal in, her father kept kicking the door shut on her hand so that the cat couldn't get in. So much yelling always over so little. (Just like with my mother). Next thing you know Dick leaves to go get himself another drink. He comes back then says to all of us

"If I had a gun right now, I'd shoot you all!"

We all started to argue with him. Trudy heard the ruckus and walked over to the gallery. She told him to

"Shut the f'up! Everybody on the river can probably hear you!"

Next thing you now he takes a flying leap off the porch with his arms extended seeming to want to throttle her. Her husband, by this time, had been standing beside her at the bottom of the gallery. He was able to grab

Dick by the collar as he jumped. He led him off to the side of the house and brought him upstairs.

The following morning. Dick and the older son in law went golfing. Kelly's husband chose not to go. He said

"I can't go and pretend nothing happened last night. This has to be cleared up."

I had asked the eldest daughter

"How could your husband do that? Ignore it all?" He had told her that he felt "Dick would do what ever he damn well wanted. It wouldn't do any good. People don't change."

Both girls told me they had to reconsider coming to the cottage in the future. They did not want to expose their children to all this negativity. Dad didn't seem to be letting up. In fact, it seemed more to the contrary. The two golfers came back and I did try an intervention but to no avail. Talking to Dick was like talking to a stone wall. The look on his face was of total indifference to me. The daughters and their families left early that day. I, to this day, think my daughters wanted me to fix this that day. I do believe they were disappointed in me. I truly didn't know how. I remember the couple of times I mentioned alcoholism to him and the need for counseling for him and me, he replied

"I don't have a problem. You have a problem!"

My husband continued to drink and I continued to count and watch and wait. I have even contemplated homicide. I made up a plan in my head. I would help him get really drunk one night. We would go out for a boat ride and when he passed out I would push him off and swim home. The boat would be found the next day drifting in the Forty Acres and my husband missing. It is really pathetic how a gentle person can become diabolical due to special circumstances. I understand that person completely. Looking back I feel such pain for myself. Recounting these stories is making me very, very sad.

I remember when:

One night, in the second year of our having bought the cottage, Trudy came running into our bedroom screaming

"Dad is on the roof of the house. He's flying a kite."

I thought she might have been dreaming but low and behold, there he was laughing his head off like a mad man. This only happens in movies right. Hell no! Her father had snuck into her room, opened the small window and squeezed himself through to the roof of the kitchen then crawled up to the attic roof, three stories high. I quickly woke Maureen's husband and a male guest in the hope that they could help me get Dick down. By then the whole house was wide awake, all eleven of us. It was three in the morning. The men were not going on the roof, for sure. It took us an hour to talk him down. He came in so excited, bragging to the guys. He went to bed and fell promptly to sleep. I don't understand this. How oblivious can a man be about his own safety or all the anxiety his beloved family and friends have to endure because of his craziness? The following day his friend took him into the work shed and gave him a very serious talking to. He was the only male, his friend and a city neighbor that I can recall, who actually ever said anything to him. That did not seem to phase my husband either.

Trouble with the police wasn't even a deterrent.

I remembered when:

Dick had gone to an exhibition in Montreal. He had arrived back into our hometown of Gan and realized he had run out of gas. He was running on fumes when he pulled up to the gas pumps at the donut shop. It was 11:05 pm. The pumps were closed. He walked into the donut shop and asked for a couple of liters of gas. The waitress said

"The pumps are locked at 11pm and the attendant goes home. I can't do it." to which he replied

"You can sell God Damn donuts twenty hours a day but you can't even give me gas in an emergency."

He started to berate the poor woman. A couple of local guys said

"We'll take you up to the highway gas station and you can get a jerry can full and bring it back here."

He stopped picking on the lady and went with them. The lady called the local police while they were gone. A police officer met my husband at the highway pit stop. She appraised him as being intoxicated and told him to phone somebody to come and get him because he was not going to be allowed to drive. So he railed on her. She said

"Make that phone call or you will be arrested for drunk and disorderly."

He called me. I headed out around 11:45pm. I had to wake up Trudy and tell her where I was going. I got to the donut shop and found my husband sitting in the back seat of the police cruiser. The lady officer told me what had gone on and let him out of the car. She told us

"Move the car away from the pumps and put it in the parking lot away from the entrance."

He started to scream at her and I saw her speaking into the shoulder thing they carry. She was calling for back up. I told her we would get it done. My husband was furious. We moved the car. I pushed in the back. He pushed from the driver's side steering the car. Back up came. The men stood by. Nobody helped. That infuriated Dick even more. I drove us home. He never said thanks. Not a word was exchanged between us. The next morning Trudy and I drove him back to the gas station. He got gas and went on his way. My younger daughter and I headed to work and university. I was exhausted.

I remember when:

The first formal arrest was in Montreal on our fifth wedding anniversary. The charges were for drunk and damage to private commercial property. He spent the night in jail and the company took care of legal fees. The second arrest took place about fifteen years later, in Orange County, California. He had been on a business trip and was staying with our friend Raj. The convention was quite a distance from where he lived. Dick did the commuting. He had attended one of the shows and partied after. His friend had recommended he spend the night in his hotel room. There was another single bed available and he wouldn't have to drive the distance at that late hour. Dick refused said

"I'm fine!"

Two hours later he was stopped by two motorcycle cops of the California highway patrol. He had been weaving. He was arrested and spent four days in jail. Judges don't do court hearings on weekends. Because he was a Canadian he was fined. He had to register for a correspondence course on Safe & Sober driving and let go. Raj bailed him out of jail and my husband flew back home. This took place in late fall. I found out, about it, in March of the next year. I was going through the correspondence on our desk. I opened an enveloped addressed to my husband from the Orange County legal offices. It was an invoice for $4000. This was the third and final request for payment. I stood in shock. You could have pushed me over with a feather. I confronted him. He explained everything. Of course he spent most of his time describing how frightening the black men who were in his cell seemed. He used to have this saying he would tell our girls

"If you can't do the time, don't do the crime!"

He should know. Yes I paid that bill! I spoke to my friend Raj years ago and asked

"Why didn't you call me and tell me all of this stuff. How could you take his side and not warn me?" He answered

"I thought for sure Dick would have told you when he got home. I was pretty annoyed with him also for all the inconvenience he caused."

The third arrest was in our local town. It was what is referred to as a 'Ride Program'. Police officers cordon off an area and stop all the cars and check for drunken drivers. Dick had driven back from Ottawa and stopped into a hotel for their local businessmen's Christmas party. He was tired so he did not stay late. The hotel did provide shuttle transport for the guests. The bus had headed out to another town with several men. Dick was not going to wait around for it to come back. He saw the line up of cars in front of the entrances to the mall. He tried to duck into the parking lot. There was no way out without going through the police cordon. He got back in line. He was given a breathalyzer test. He was arrested and brought to jail. He was five minutes away from home. It was only 8 pm. The police car delivered him to our home at 11pm. They had impounded his car. The next morning he had to call his boss and tell him. That company car was the only vehicle we owned. An employee went and got the car. I offered to his boss that I could quit my job and be my husband's driver for the next thirteen months. There was no reason why the company should fire him and rehire. That would have been too much disruption for everyone. The only problem was that his auto was a standard. I pleaded with the boss to get us an automatic as a trade in. He agreed. I had to go to the court house when his trial came up. I would sit in the waiting room and read. My eyes buried deep into the pages of a huge volume. I was so ashamed. The legal fees were $4000. I didn't have that kind of money anymore. He got a loan from the bank. I cleared up that debt and many others of his a year later with some inheritance money my father had left me. My husband had to take courses run by the government. He had to attend one AAA meeting. He claimed to 'get it all'. As he once said to me

"I never promised you I would not drink anymore. I never said that!"

A year later in 2000, his boss gave me a check for $100. along with a Thank You letter. My husband gave me a $100. bill that Christmas.

A few years later I was saying to him, hoping to get some sign of appreciation and validation from him

"I had to quit my job to help you!" his reply was

"Well it wasn't like it was a big job!"

I really began getting numb. It must be like a paralysis of the heart. You could stick all these painful needles in it, like you would a voodoo doll, but a person just doesn't respond anymore. I compare it to emotional flat lining. I do understand every single feeling a woman or a man, who have walked in these shoes, experiences. People would ask me.

"Why did you wait so long to finally get divorced? Why didn't you fight harder? You should have stood your ground. You gave him way too much leeway. Why didn't you stand up for yourself?"

Those very same questions are being asked today to people who are walking over the very same hot coals. I strongly suggests that GOOD FRIENDS stop asking those questions and start offering solutions and support now. Like I said it is a form of paralysis so friends or family have to take the individual, who is being victimized, by the hand and walk them into a shelter or to a counselor and get help. We can't do it. We are drowning. Our lungs are filling up with our tears. Short of killing our partner, which some have and been arrested for, there is no solution but our own isolation and despair. Than there is the other option which also occurs often enough, our partner kills us. What should a GOOD FRIEND do? Help now or bury us later.

Dr. Phil McGraw wrote a book in 2013. He seems to have done a turn around regarding specific deal breakers. Thank God! I thought he used to be a little bit too soft on the 'bad guys'. It's about identifying the perpetrators of harm and the ways and means to avoid them. I liked it because it's like getting a professional blessing to do what's right for you. Better yet how to develop the smarts to steer clear of toxic people and the baggage they bring. It's about learning to protect oneself from miserable experiences now and in the future.

Writing this chapter was extremely painful. I often think what a waste of time for me and of a human being with such great potential as my husband. I'm not embarrassed anymore. I understand it is OK to protect one's self from danger. All the love and forgiveness and patience in the world does not heal a person in need of psychological help.

"Better be safe than sorry and 'get the hell out of Dodge'!"

I do believe in love. It's truly rewarding. But if it is not reciprocated in kind, it is useless. I'm old now and my chances of having the right partner are next to nil. But for those out there with many years left ahead of them, I say

"Go for it! but Be careful this time!"

CHAPTER 17

CANCER, THE WAITING GAME

CANCER WARRIOR is the only way I could describe myself. I'm not a cancer survivor because I still have the disease. Cancer has dictated my life's comings and goings for over twelve years now and I am, truthfully, really fed up. My earlier writings would seem to indicate that I was very stoic, back in the day. Check this out written on August 19th, 2000.

"My soul has 'arrived', solid, dug in. It concentrates finally on the finer, more gentle things of human life. I feel no need to compete, to show-off, no need to prove anything. There is no need to 'make-up' my exterior, no need to distract or entertain my mind with useless activity. I hover like the osprey on a current of air, wings outstretched, eyes keen on the 'world that is my family'. My purpose is to avail myself to them and to others, encourage and share the thrills and upsets of their lives. I am entranced and enthralled." Holy Moly that is good even if I do say so myself.

I do believe in the premise of positive reinforcement and consistent optimism for all of us who are struggling to stay alive. Nevertheless I also know the depths of despair a survivor wallows in every once in a while. My writing of the arduous path I am on, is not to discourage anyone. It is actually a no nonsense approach for all of us to better tolerate our lives while we are ill. You notice I don't say accept because having cancer is unacceptable. Yet there are ways and means available to us that make our having cancer just slightly more manageable. Cancer patients, be it of three days or three months or three years or in remission, or no longer around after ten years, are heroic individuals. We walk the corridors of 'death row' praying every night for a reprieve. Yet every morning we swing that beat up old body, regardless of our age, out of bed. We put one foot ahead of the other and walk step by step to the bathroom and then to the kitchen to have ourselves a cup of coffee. Cancer patients are known for their enthusiasm at trying to stay alive. It pains me to write my own truth because it reminds me of things I would much rather eliminate from my mental archive. My ups and super downs are similar to that of so many other people. I hope to be able to give cancer patients an opportunity to be kinder to themselves. I hope to give their family and friends and physicians an opportunity to get a glimpse into the psyche of we remarkable fighters. What really annoys me so much is that we have to accept nuclear, toxic medicines in our system in order to try to stay alive. Nevertheless there are thousands of individuals out there, as we speak, who are willingly polluting their bodies with excessive consumption of bad food, alcohol, prescribed drugs and street drugs. So far they get to do whatever they want and without any negative recriminations. A fellow patient, once, said to me "It's the luck of the draw".

Let me begin this odyssey. In 2000, the results of a annual mammogram indicated questionable tissue found in the left breast. A biopsy was done. The diagnosis was tubular carcinoma in the left breast. The surgeon said this was a 'well behaved' kind of cancer. It would require surgery called a lumpectomy and was to be followed by sixteen rounds of radiation. The last round was on December 28th. I walked out of the chemo center and said to myself

"Self! That whole thing went rather well. No problem. This has been taken care of. Anyways what's the big deal? I can slip on this icy sidewalk and crack my skull open and be dead."

I returned to my usual routine with the additional and beautiful assignment of having to take care of my first grandchild, a girl, while my eldest daughter worked. I used to hold her close to my chest while giving her a bottle and think her positive, healthy body and spirit were protecting me from any more cancer. What a superb distraction! I felt useful and had purpose. She and I were together Monday through Friday for four years, until she started school. I was very fortunate during these last twelve years because four grandchildren were born whose lives I have been able to closely share. We all lived in the same town so Nana was 'on call'. Having their beauty and cheerfulness around me, so often during the week, helped me stick to the plan. Their energy forced me to focus only on the positive. These little people kept me alive. I was not going to allow myself to be any less than what those grandkids deserved from a grandmother.

In 2004, after returning from a road trip south to visit family and friends, it was determined that another cancer in the same area had developed yet again. This time the surgeon said

"This one is aggressive so the breast has to be removed. Oncology will be in touch with you after surgery for a consult on the probability of a chemo regimen."

It's interesting because there are something like forty different kinds of breast cancers. I'm not 100% sure of the number, and as close as I can recall this new invader was breast cancer +estrogen/progesterone receptor. I looked everything up on the internet in the hope of educating myself. I went through all of the guilt trips. I was responsible for having cancer. I had been a smoker since I was twenty. I was on the contraceptive pill for four years after the birth of our first child. I used hormone replacement medication for ten years after I had begun menopause. My family had a history of cancer deaths. My maternal aunt died of breast cancer at the age of forty six. My maternal uncle died of liver cancer. My paternal uncle died of lung cancer. My mother died of colon cancer. My father died of pancreatic cancer. My younger sister had breast cancer in spring of 2000 which required surgery but no radiation or chemo. She had a reoccurrence ten years later but is now cancer free again. Then most of the other siblings on my father's side and his parents as well as my mother's elders lived into their late eighties, early nineties.

Why in hell did I get stuck with this? I didn't deserve it. I was a good girl all of my life. Well not quite all of my life. It took a long time to understand that the doctors themselves didn't have any specific explanations for the existence of certain cancers, let alone the re occurrence. As my husband would say "Shit happens". I finally began to question less when the ninety year old Dutch mother of a dear friend of mine said

"Some people are born with good bodies and some people aren't".

It has always amazed me how the women I knew who dug themselves out of war torn Europe after WW2 had a propensity for pragmatism. I still haven't acquired that skill. As a cancer patient I spent a lot of time thinking, pondering. In retrospect, I think, perhaps too much time. I, probably, would have been better served watching 'Walt Disney' movies. The date for the surgery on cancer two was in early March. Our youngest daughter had just moved into their first, new home and invited the whole family for dinner. It was to be a combined house warming and 'good luck Mom' party. Dick and I left around 8pm. There was a drizzle going on. That meant black ice. Already I was getting nervous for the drive back home. I said to my husband

"You'd better get off the driveway and walk on the lawn with me. It looks slippery where you are."

No sooner had I said that, he took a flying leap off the ground and landed on his knees. His forehead was down on the pavement and his arms extended out ahead of him. I rushed over to him. I thought he might have broken his glasses. The grandkids were standing at the front door waving goodbye. I yelled

"Get Mommy and Daddy out here."

My sons in law came out. Dick, while trying to break his fall by extending his arms, had shattered his left wrist. 911 was called and the ambulance was there in less than ten minutes. I went into the ambulance with him. The emergency room doctors put a temporary cast on him and he was scheduled for surgery the next morning. We took a taxi back home and had a few hours of sleep. He was super brave. No crying or cursing. All went well on the Monday. He had a stainless steel metal contraption on his arm, out to this hand, being held together by several screws. It looked like a bridge.

Only two days later it was my turn. Remember! I was scheduled for a mastectomy of the left breast. OH YA! We were so busy worrying about Dick that I, well of course, was only an after thought. I'm tough, I can deal with all of this happening at the same time. I was a multi task specialist 'par excellence'. No time to cry or feel sorry for myself. No time at all. Surgery was Wednesday morning. All went well except that I broke my right front tooth when I bit down on the rubber tubing at the time of anesthesia. I stayed the night and one of the nurses, another Montrealer, was kind enough to keep me company when she wasn't busy. I couldn't sleep for the life of me. Too much excitement I guess. Recovery at home seemed to be going well. I did have a build up of fluid under the scar which eventually had to be drained. It is not unusual. The Homecare nurse said

"It's not common to have both husband and wife requiring care at the same time."

She would take care of cleaning the studded, drilled holes in Dick's arm and hand at the dining room table. After, she and I would head upstairs to my room where she would clean my eighteen inch wound and put on a new dressing. She said

"You haven't had a chance to grieve yet, have you?" I asked

"I beg your pardon?"

"The removal of your breast. It's not uncommon that the patient feels a loss, a sadness, even some depression may occur. You have been very busy making sure your husband is all right and keeping up with the daily chores and so on. How are you feeling? You can talk with me anytime you need to confide"

"My husband can't do anything. I'm OK I don't think about it much. Like you said I'm too busy."

I even had prepared a cute little bedroom for myself, very 'French' country. I had painted the walls bright daffodil yellow with white trim. I had a white whicker night stands and a white whicker chair. Of course let's not forget shelves full of books. The reason why I wanted to have my own room was because I didn't want to have to worry about Dick and I bumping each other in bed during the night. He had a beat up arm and I had a beat up chest. Three months later, Dick's wrist had healed well, no complications. The metal gadget was replaced by a light cast. He was pretty normal. I was doing alright also. Now it was time to plan for the chemo sessions. I went in fully informed and ready. I had read all the relevant pamphlets and was sure what was referred to as 'following side effects, blah!blah!blah!, may occur' was not going to apply to me. After all I was made of 'strong stuff'. Well, my conceit was in for a mind altering shock.

My oncologist was the tiniest, cutest lady from Indian descent and very intelligent. She was probably about the same age as my daughters. I am so proud of the women today. They have made such huge advances in the fields of medical sciences. Good for them. As a woman, I felt more reassured because I truly believed and still do that a woman can better understand the complexity of female illness and their psychological as well as physiological impact. I was able to connect with my lady doctor immediately and in my usual manner never let up when it came to asking questions and expecting answers. The only thing wrong with that is, in so far as cancer outcomes are concerned, the doctors often answer

"We don't know!"

She prescribed a six month chemo program. The purpose was to ensure that the possible presence of any undetected cancer cells would be destroyed. There are several types of what we, in the trade, refer to as 'chemo cocktails'. I use the word we because I believe that the patient is a member of that team of medical experts. The sooner the patients accept the fact that they manage their health care, the better. The type prescribed to me was the 'numero uno', the strongest, the toughest one used to do the dirty deed. The IV drip was put in my arm and I lay there for an hour watching the bright red liquid slowly pour into my vein. I called it 'my little red devil'. I sat in a recliner in a room with at least a dozen other patients who were doing the exact same thing. Sometimes I couldn't look up because I wanted my privacy respected. Sometimes I killed time by chatting away with the person on either side of me. I found the chemo room to be a cornucopia of human personalities. I learned very quickly to read the negative or positive vibes and behave accordingly. Blood work was done every month, (more needles), the day before transfusion was to take place. It was a precaution in order to ascertain that the white blood cell count was conducive for the treatment to take place. My count was below norm just once. The treatment was to be postponed by a week or longer. I was so ticked off. You see cancer patients have an agenda. That is to kill the bloody rogue cells and to do so as quickly as possible, without delay. We want to get this damn part of our life over and done with. We have places to go and people to see after this. At one point I even had the audacity to tell this very fine professional, who was caring for me, that I had decided that

"I was not going to pursue my treatment anymore. I found it too arduous. Everything was just a 'crap shoot' anyways."

This pint size person looked me straight in the eye and said

"Have you been to school for a total of ten years just to study medicine and major in oncology? I did not think so. Well I have, and only I will determine how many treatments can be used in the hope of killing this cancer".

I had been told. She might have been tiny but she was mighty.

My husband, though physically present was psychologically and emotionally absent. I, as usual, learned the hard way. I was at the kitchen counter preparing our dinner plates. Dick was sitting at the dining table, watching the news, waiting to be served. That's was our M.O. I guess I must have had one of those weepy moments. They occur often. I happened to say, as I was lifting the two plates

"Well the least you can do is show some empathy" to which he replied

"How in hell do you expect me to give you sympathy. I've never had cancer, how the hell am I supposed to know how you feel?"

I kept walking to the table. I placed the plates down, one for me and one in front of him. He kept watching the T V. I picked up his fork, lifted it up high over my shoulder and stabbed him in the arm. He screamed and asked

"What did you do that for?"

I sat down and we ate our dinner. Years later, when the legal separation papers had been filed he claimed

"That was the reason I didn't come home until late in the day. I was scared you would attack me again."

An old friend of ours, from Florida, while visiting me after we had been legally separated, had gotten in touch with him for a luncheon date. During the meal he had asked

"Why did you stop loving her?" to which my husband replied

"Every year there were operations and recovery and more treatments and more surgery. It never ended. It went on and on. It was too much!"

Poor baby boy! It was all unbearable. His once strong woman, his 'tough old broad' was too needy. There is a saying, that I unfortunately cannot remember the source of

"Never fall in love with a narcissist. You will forever be lonely!"

It was only years later that I learned divorce is not as unusual as it seems in cancer family trauma. One gentleman, fellow patient, had mentioned his first wife had left him. He had a recurring prostate cancer. This time around his live in girlfriend couldn't cope. He wanted sympathy. I gave it to him. I think that sometimes some of us can actually feel the vulnerability of our fellows better than most people can. Then there was that infamous scandal about the North Carolina senator who had sired a child with his mistress while his wife was waging her own cancer fight. So at least I know I am not alone. Marital tensions are just another road hazard in this bumpy experience. Family counseling certainly can help.

Cancer, in my opinion, is a humbling experience. Chemo, on the other hand, is a humiliating experience. Some of my notes recount

"My bowels are screwed up. The diarrhea is impossible to control. Staying in close proximity to a toilet is a necessity. Better yet, the constipation is very painful and can only be relieved with stool softening pills. I, to this day, have not figured out which is worse. The cankers in the mouth make even swallowing painful. I'm shedding like a cat. I'm washing my hair with the balls of my fingertips because my scalp is amazingly super sensitive. I cannot scratch my head. It hurts. When I dried my hair, clumps of it fell into the red towel like leaves falling off the trees. Even the pubic hairs were disappearing, to be found in the panties or the toilet paper. I plugged the drain in the upstairs shower, YUCK! so much hair, fistfuls. Now! I'm really getting angry. This is incredible and very messy. It is really starting to get on my nerves. The next day I made an appointment with the hairdresser to get my head shaved."

The second time I needed IV chemo, which was five years later, I elected to get my buzz cut done the week before so I wouldn't have to put up with the mess again. Now comes all the questioning.

"Self! How do I love thee?"

Am I confident enough to deal with the total differences in appearance? Can I go out proud of being alive? Or do I cower behind sunglasses, scarves and wigs? Can anyone notice that I have had a breast chopped off on the left side? Will those that know me notice that I have gained another thirty to forty pounds? I look like a Blowfish without the spikes. This treatment is so demoralizing, so discouraging. I feel ancient. I walk by the mirror and think

"Shit! I look like old uncle Johnny, bald and rotund, better yet Alfred Hitchcock."

Everything I undertake or think in order to keep a positive spin on this experience is proving useless. It takes every ounce of strength just to keep from weeping all day long. I must try and like myself enough to realize

"ME! cannot just be defined by breasts or hair or bowels! That, surely, I am more than any or all body parts and body functions combined. ME is something from within that cannot be mutilated by surgery or disease or treatments. My Lord this is hard! Please God in heaven help me. I'm drowning! Better yet, dear God stop me from going mad!"

Within three weeks my vanity won out. Better yet, I was adamant about my need for privacy. I didn't want anyone to know my business. I did get a buzz cut, which I liked. I was comfortable with the look as long as I was with family and very close friends. I did buy a wig, grey hair. I wore it when I went out in public. I did not like it because it was bloody hot and itchy in summer and kept creeping, ever so slightly, up my skull. I did buy a fake left breast. A prosthesis consisting of a bra with a side open seam in which you stuff a rubber booby. I found it very heavy and hot and sticky in the summer also. With all of this paraphernalia I still had a complex. My younger daughter would say to me

"Mom don't worry. Nobody knows. Nobody is looking at you. You look normal."

I have the greatest admiration for women today who choose to go public about their fight with cancer by sporting the buzz cut. They are really pulled together women. That makes them good looking in my books. They portray confidence which is very helpful to all of us who watch. I'm proud of them. Oh! by the way the hair starts to grows back quickly a couple of months after the treatments are over and for most of us it was curly for a year or so.

My notes seem to indicate that there was a great deal of sleeplessness. I should say that I slept a whole lot but at many different times of the day and night. Perhaps the fact that it was so inconsistent and seemingly unnatural proved to be frustrating to me. Everything that you know as 'supposed to be this way' is altered when undergoing chemo. I have something in my dairy that mentions sleeping pills. I chose not to take any barbiturates for sleep or even mental stress and anxiety. That was my experience. Another person's might be different. That is why I so believe in psychological counseling to help diffuse that anxiousness in patient and families. My phobia about drugs was due to the fact that my mother had been a pharmaceutical drug addict for forty years. Doctors explained to me that it takes a couple of weeks for the anti anxiety medicine to start taking effect. I could only be on it for a few weeks. The coming down was quite hard on the body and the psyche. I did not want any chemical dependency. I had to have my wits about me to deal with this. I would just have to talk myself out of my anxious moments.

Because of my experiences of the last twelve years I truly believe in 'mind over matter'. I spent a great deal of time having conversations with myself like I would with a best friend. Some of the nights were pretty spooky. Simple things like going to the bathroom became scary. As soon as I would put my feet down on the floor, there was such a hot tingling sensation all over the balls of my feet. It felt like they were being zapped by continuous electric shocks. A couple of times I had to crawl to the bathroom on my knees because walking hurt so much.

Remember my husband and I did not share a bedroom. He would go to bed much later than I and fall into a deep, deep sleep and proceed to snore. He didn't seem to have a care in the world. How I envied him. Perhaps it was more 'passing out' than falling asleep. I know I wouldn't want to bother him. He had to work the next day. He couldn't help me anyways. He was definitely not one to hold your hand and listen to tales of woe. The worst thing for me was what I refer to as 'night terrors'. To this day the doctors, or nurses or my counselor cannot explain those occurrences. I still have them occasionally. I sometimes wondered if I was being haunted by ghosts like at the Island house. I can just imagine what chemo does to the brain! It has so many devastating side effects on the body why not study the effects on the brain. I would volunteer for that kind of a study. My chemo must have fried millions of particles and synapses. I wonder if it causes early dementia. It doesn't really matter to many because the patient is usually dead within three to five years. I'm still alive after twelve years of treatments of some kind or other. The long term use of nuclear medicine has damaged my heart. Why not my brain? I wouldn't mind having a brain scan to find out for myself. There are so many unanswered question. Such as, are the apparitions caused by chemo and a combination of barbiturates like morphine based meds or steroids? It would be so much easier for me if there were other patients who shared these same experiences or doctors who had done studies in these areas. I was and still am a staunch supporter of 'Knowledge is Power'. This is how the visions occur.

I would be minding my own business, sound asleep. Then WOW! A huge, ugly face would appear to me. This was not like a dream where you see a large screen performance. This was just the immediate vision of a face sometimes a man, sometime a woman, a totally dispossessed, looking person. The image was never the same. It was instantaneous and lasted a split second. It would come either to the right or the left side of my head, right 'in my face' if you will. My response was always the same. I would immediately wake up and sit bold upright in my bed, wide awake. I remember being quite shaken every time. I would then have to talk myself down and try to get settled in for the rest of the night. I would even tell the ghostly creature to

"Leave me alone!"

This might seem dopey to many, especially non-believers but I did have a trick then, that I use all the time now. It seems to work. When my Meme had died, my auntie Mado had given me her rosary beads, as a memento. They are about a hundred years old now. They are made of solid wood and the carvings on each bead have actually been worn by her fingering them, as she said her daily prayers. I started to use her rosary and would place them at the edge of the pillow on my right side. It was as if the presence of her beads were actually warding off the evil spirits. The concept of good spirits protecting we mortals from the harm of evil ones is still prevalent in many world cultures. My Meme's rosary acts as a shield. They are close to my head and when I get anxious, which is most nights, I hold on to the crucifix as it lays there and say my prayers. I don't care if you believe me or not. Your opinion at this juncture of my life is not really relevant to me. It does work though. I do not have apparitions when the beads are at the side of my pillow.

I have had two very positive sightings of spiritual significance to me. One was actually during the day while I was napping. Chemo had a way of enhancing color for me. Everything thing seemed super bright, reds were redder. Yellow was yellower. I could not have been awake during a nap, not possible. In fact I don't think I dream during naps. I can only try to make sense of this. I think I saw through, my mind's eye, that huge angel wings had surrounded my shoulders. I was sitting up in bed staring at the unadorned, bright yellow wall across from me. I can feel the wings surrounding me like a cape. The only thing left is the top of my face, my forehead and my eyes which are wide open staring out from this sanctuary. I can see, as I turn my eyes to the left then to the right, the top feathers of the wings. The calm and intense feeling of serenity was awesome. I know there are guardian angels. I literally physically felt one. I carry that feeling with me when I am close to despair. I am not afraid as long as I maintain that belief. Call me crazy! like I said

"I don't care!"

In 2006, I chose to have the right breast removed. Two consecutive mammograms indicated some questionable tissue. I was not going to put up with anymore crap. I was much more comfortable also, no longer uneven. The recovery did not go well. The surgeon had to do some cosmetic work on the left side also. Now I had a combination of scars that ran from under my left armpit straight across to under my right armpit. I guess that would be about thirty six inches. An infection set in below the scars and I had to go to the clinic to have the fluid drained out. The surgeon Dr. G. said

"We might as well remove all these forty eight stitches while we are at it. It's almost fourteen days since the surgery which is when this procedure would normally occur."

He proceeded without giving me a local freezing. He was right at the center of my chest, when I begged him

"Please stop! I can't take it! Let me catch my breath! I think I am going to pass out." To which he replied

"No can do. I'm almost done, half way there. Hang in there! It's going to hurt no matter what. Dick was sitting on a chair in the corner. The nurse was on my left side, holding one of those small, useless, turquoise vomit trays. I took a deep breath then passed out. I came to and my forehead was resting on her shoulder. The doctor had completed the procedure. The good thing I learned from this exercise is that when things really get horrific, the brain has the power and common sense to shut the body down. The doctor left. The nurse gave me a drink of apple juice. My husband and I headed down the hallway to the main doors. Dick stopped. He turned to me and said

"Boy! Are you ever tough!"

More than anything I really needed a hug. I was so fed up of being 'tough'. The following five years I was placed on several oral chemo drugs. Nothing seemed to work. The cancer had found it's niche, along the chest wall. I could actually see the 'mets' everyday as I showered. Apparently regardless of how thorough the cutting and scraping of all the cancerous flesh is, residual tissue remains. There was to be no surgery for this. Surgeons do not remove ribs. The whole rib cage, as I understand it, would cave in. They cannot be replaced.

IN 2008, the doctors went back to the drawing board and determined that even though radiation had been used eight years prior, there was a slight chance it might work. There were no guarantees of course. Oncology is not an exact science. I started a radiation regimen consisting of a morning treatment and a late afternoon treatment. There were forty six rounds in all for twenty three consecutive days. Each dose was a mini zap so as not to risk burning the sensitive skin and causing ulcerations which would lead to blood poisoning and death. Well that did not work either. The chest wall cancer persisted. The new male oncologist said, in French

"Ca sa magasse!" which means "This is bugging me!"

I felt like saying buddy if you think you are ticked off can you just imagine how I feel. So just "Shut the F' up". I found working with this doctor very difficult. He left me cold. Mind you we started on the wrong foot a year prior. I was in for the usual three month consultation. I was told by a new nurse that Dr. P. was no longer with this hospital. She was in Toronto doing research. My usual nurse of four years Ms. L. was working another division. I was so upset I screamed

"I just got divorced after forty years and now, you have taken the only two people I can trust in my entire life away from me. How could you do this?"

I then threw myself to the floor in a corner of the room. I curled myself up into a fetal position and proceeded to weep uncontrollably. That is what the new doctor came into for our first appointment. He gave instructions to have my former and best nurse Ms. L. brought to this examining room to soothe me. He then had a psych counselor meet me there also. I finally calmed down after a half hour. It was shortly after that I began to take part in a weekly one on one counseling program. I would walk into the therapist's office and she would ask

"How are you?"

I would then proceed to bawl my eyes out. She would pull out the box of tissues and then I would begin trying to speak. I could stay as long as I needed to. Then all of a sudden, about an hour into the session, I would announce.

"Oh! I'm really tired now. I was totally drained. I would start giggling, then laughing. We would hug 'Goodbye' and I would be on my way. My youngest came to a few sessions with me. I truly believe that therapy is one of the best ways for the patient and the family to grieve this frightening circumstance. Ms D. and I have been together on and off now for about four years. I can say, without any reservation that, there were things that I confided in her that I could not have shared with anyone in my world. I find it much easier to share inner thoughts and feeling with a stranger. A professional makes no judgment and has no expectations. I can express myself without any fear of recriminations or guilt. I owe my maintaining my sanity to my sweet Ms. D. Words can hardly begin to describe the depth of my gratitude.

In 2009, after experimenting with several new types of drugs, which proved to be ineffective, that same oncologist ordered up a super strong chemo treatment. It had horrific results. My opinion is, not medical fact, that a combination of side effects of steroids, the cocktail made in hell, diarrhea and constipation and my usage of laxatives and whatever, were actually so severe that my insides blew out through my rectum. I had been legally separated for a year and a half. I lived in my own condo. I was alone and after forty eight hours of unbearable pain I called 911. My eldest met me outside my building. I remember arriving at the emergency admission's desk of the hospital. I remember a nurse's face on my right side. She was young, maybe mid twenties. She had blond hair put up in a pony tail. I was clinging to her hand so hard I'm surprised I didn't break it. I remember the priest and my friend praying at my bedside. I cannot see my daughters which makes me sad. I remember my voice saying

"I'm crossing over now. I'm crossing over"

I remember looking up and, in my mind's eye, seeing my three most favorite people in the whole world looking down at me. Well, they were not of this world. They had all died ten and twenty years before. The spirits were standing on what seemed to be a theater stage. My Dad was first, behind him stood my Aunt Madeleine whose chin was resting on his left shoulder and behind her was my dear Meme whose chin was resting on Mado's left shoulder. I did not see the bodies of the women just their faces. They were looking down at me with a puzzled expression on their face. They were not smiling. They were not frowning. They just seemed to be so serious. It was as if they were following the proceedings taking place around me. Three days later I woke up in the ICU. I had an IV in each wrist connected to two poles on either side of me from which four bags hung on each. I could not move. I was in the hospital for forty two days. I had suffered a perforated colon, septic shock and a perennial tear of ten centimeters. I had had surgery and two transfusions. I was plugged in everywhere. There was a catheter for three months, a colostomy bag for two years and feeding tubes. There was even a tube stuck in my nose that was supposed to drain the fluids from my intestines. I hated that tube. When it was removed after several days I ended up vomiting for hours. Finally the nurse called up a resident at 2am and he reinserted it. Oh what a mess! I was only allowed to have chipped ice. I did manage to loose thirty pounds. I couldn't move so when I would slip down in the bed, the orderlies would have to grab each side of the bed linen and give me a boost back up. I had doctors, nurses, and residents examining and caring for body parts that are called 'privates' for specific reasons. It was all very embarrassing. I was there for forty two days. By the end I was calling daily rounds of my examination 'Showtime'.

The professional stated, in so far as my visions were concerned that
"You were probably hallucinating on morphine."
I beg to differ. These critics, I believe have zero imagination. I had almost died and probably had a near death experience. My younger daughter saved something, for me from the event, which I still have. There are two sheets of paper on which I had printed, in red ball point ink, the following
"SH ME DOWN", "NURSING", "I'M CROSSING OVER", "HEAVEN",
"GUARDIAN ANGELS SAVE FOR THE KIDS", "DATE NANA PLEASE STAY"
My daughter, she is such a kind soul, said I was actually still trying to communicate and I had asked for paper and pen. The words are written with a very, very, very shaky hand. This is saved for prosperity. I can honestly say I was more than ticked off when I awoke in ICU. My daughter said the disappointment was written all over my face.
"Oh shit! I'm still here."
Now I was going to have to try and live when I would, much rather, be dead and in heaven with Dad and Mado and Meme."
Some people have said that God kept me here for a reason, for inspiration for others. I don't try to figure it out anymore. That puts such an onus of responsibility on me to excel at something, yet again. I don't want to. BEING! is enough for me now. If 'passers by' in my life learn from that, ok so be it. I think of my father's saying
"When your number is up, your number is up"
I had a hard job ahead of me. Thanks to the gentleness and friendship of many home care nurses, I was finally going to make it. It was going to be a long recovery. With all of that, my most important priority was to still keep my sanity. My daughters, my grandkids, my best friends, my nurses and my counselor all took care of my body and soul. I am reserving a place in heaven just for them. Are we ever going to party! YET, unbeknownst to all of us, the battle was to be far from over.

I'M

CROSSING

OVER

HEAVEN

GUARDIAN ANGel

Save for the kids

IN 2010, the annual CT scan found that the cancer had metastasized and was now in some areas of the spine and the left hip. A new oncologist, a lady, the head of the oncology division of our hospital was now going to be in charge of my case. She was pleased to report

"That the cancer was not yet in any vital organ, that is the lung, the brain or the liver. They would not have expected it to go to the bone but all things considered that could be a good thing. There was to be no prognosis of time. Previous doctors had said twelve months?, thirty two months? You have proven them all wrong. Because you are still in recovery from the previous chemo debacle, we will wait until the new year and use a much milder treatment. This is chemo but only a half hour infusion every twenty one days. The known side effect is damage to the heart. This medicine actually goes to the core of the cancer cell and breaks it in half so that it cannot multiply."

I used Google for info on this product and looked up answers to my concerns about breast cancer metastasis to the bone. Things like spine compression and bone breaks with poor possibility of healing and eventual life in a wheelchair sure upset and frightened me. My daughter and I thought that perhaps it was time for me to shop around for a retirement complex where, overtime, long term nursing care would be available. I found just the place, just before winter arrived. The top, second floor, had private suites for people who were self sufficient. A section of the first floor was reserved for full time long term nursing care patients. I sold the condo in late October and moved into residence. I did not have to cook. I did not have to clean. I did not have to launder my clothes. I didn't even have to make my bed if I'd rather not. I drew the line at that kind of service. That was much too decadent for me. We numbered thirty four. I was the youngest in the gang. All the seniors were old enough to be my mom or my dad. I was the live in resident volunteer and was put to good use. I lived there for nine months. I have concluded I am not a conformist. Why did that surprise me considering I had thought of myself as a 60's flower child? None of the symptoms suggested, regarding bone cancer, had occurred. The new medicine, I had been on for eighteen months, was doing a hell of a good job. There were heart scans every few months to ensure that the damage to the ventricle of the heart were non existent. I decided to move. I bought a new car and started to search the internet and drove to different locations to check out buildings. I had everything planned out. I was going to move July 2nd

The most annoying thing to me, since the turn of the new millennium, century 21, was that whenever things were going fairly well for me and I would make plans, something inevitably screwed me over. The carpet was always pulled out from under me. There was a residents and administration meeting held at the 'home' in the middle of June. It became very heated. I was the spokes person and as usual my passion for the rights of all the clients was extreme. The members had voted me interim president a few weeks after I had arrived. The criteria was simple. I was the only one there who could walk without a walker and could speak without forgetting what the topic of discussion was. The few of us who could get that joke always had a good laugh. The meeting was difficult but finally successful. I was exhausted. There were many health care service providers in the main floor lounges who had set up information booths. I was circulating when a lady approached me with a great idea. I introduced her to the manager and the chef. I had just left them in the dining room when I started to feel woozy and nauseous. I told the head nurse how I felt. He took my blood pressure and it was a roaring 210/ 110. I had such an ache in my jaw that I could hardly speak. I just nodded to him when he suggested

"You just go upstairs and lay down. You probably got way too excited at the meeting. It went well. You did a great job. Now it's time to rest."

I rarely used the elevator. I used to use the stairs to and from the second floor. When I got off the elevator, I leaned against the wall for balance as I made my way down the hallway to my room. It seemed to be the longest walk in my entire life. Dinner was served at 5:30. I could not get out of my recliner. The nurse came by to check on me.

"I can't go down. I am so tired. No! I don't want to eat anything. I feel so sick."

This went on for three days. On the Friday I woke up with such a pain in my back and in my chest. I phoned down to the office to try and get a lift to the hospital. I knew I could not drive myself. The head nurse and the director of nursing came up. They asked me questions, then they called 911. I called Marie, my eldest daughter and she met me at emergency. My youngest daughter, Kelly met us also. She had just gotten off a plane from California, where she had been working all week. After several hours and an x-ray, it was determined that I had pneumonia. The eldest drove me back to the residence. She tucked me in and she and I made plans for her coming in next week to pack my books and paintings and dishes. There was not very much. She did a superb job. We definitely knew I was in no shape to do it. Moving day arrived. I still felt very weak. I told the guys that I was going to lie in bed and that they could work around me. After the van was filled, the truck left and I followed in my car. It's amazing that I could drive. I was fatigued but determined I was getting out of residence. It was great because it was on a Saturday so there was minimal staff. The administrators were not there. The residents, many of whom, couldn't figure out what I was doing or care less waved good bye. I drove into my new underground garage. I parked in my designated spot, no 84 and took the elevator up to the seventh floor. The boys came in with the bed first and set it up in my new bedroom. They continued the work with me laying on the bed. Marie arrived and gave the men instructions. She put all the dishes away and placed all the books on the book shelves. She even connected the T V and sound system. She had purchased some groceries for a couple of days which she placed in the fridge. She was a very fast worker. I used to be like that. She kissed me

"Aurevoir, A Bientot Ma!".

I kissed her back and thanked her profusely. She left and I promptly went to sleep and napped for a couple of hours. That was the second time I had moved in nine months. I liked my new place. It was a secure building and it was on the waterfront. I was on the street side so there was lot of commuter traffic noise. I was really happy to have my freedom. I rented a cottage by a lake for a week in August. Other than my not being able to swim long distance out to the raft, everything seemed normal. I had obviously recovered. I had put my name to reserve a lakefront unit in our building. I was very fortunate to get that eleven months later. Since June 2012,

"I have been Living, near the water's edge, happily ever after"

I think this is where my litany of memories began so many pages before.

CHAPTER 18

WHAT NOW?

WHAT'S NEXT is totally unknown to me. I can't even begin to speculate. I have no idea, as in the past five years, what to expect. I don't even go there anymore. I love the AAA prayer that reads this way. It is framed on a wall of my bedroom. I wake every morning and use it as my prayer.

"GOD grant me the SERENITY to accept the things I cannot change the COURAGE to accept the things I can and the WISDOM to know the difference"

We all know what we perceive serenity to be like, quiet, calm, no stressors. We all know what courage feels like. Wisdom though, I am not sure of? It is intangible. I will describe to you what it feels like. To me, it is that gut wrenching feeling of fear. It is the message you hear from the inside of your brain that says "Beware". It is what you see through your mind's eye, "Danger". I and so many have lived these occurrences. We still remember them as vividly as if it were yesterday. I waited way too long to act.

I find it fascinating when people are asked "Do you have any regrets?" and they reply

"NO regrets ever."

I wonder if they were living in a cocoon. I have a couple of regrets but I'm not ashamed of myself. My life could have taken a different course for sure. Yet I chose not to listen to 'Wisdom'. One is, I should never have reconciled with my husband after a ten month separation in the mid-eighties. I was content. I was no longer walking on egg shells. I no longer had to wait for him to show up. I had a decent job and the girls and I were managing fairly well. I cowered under family pressure and those traditional social and religious standards that dictated that a woman's role was to uphold the semblance of family life rather than cater to her own selfish needs. I am very happy to see that our western society is more accepting of the measures needed to protect family, women and children, from the atrocities of bad marriages. The second regret I have is that, in the early nineties, I moved to another province a year after my husband. This time there was no pressure. I willingly left my parents, my friends and my job, moved away from a city I loved to be with him. There is a French Canadian saying

"Mon mari c'est mon pays", translated "My husband is my country".

My grown up daughters were university students and living in the same town as my husband. We had established roots in cottage country. I stayed behind in Montreal. I had the better job and was earning a higher salary. The relocation cost us dearly financially. He and I were still young enough to get decent jobs again. I was so looking forward to he and I having a healthy future together. I realized in short order that he really enjoyed our being apart. He had the single life style he always craved, no wife to account to during the week anyways. The situation was perfect for him. He could still have fun and yet keep the guise of conventional married life. His social life was expanding, mine was non existent. I was kept at arms length. I was the outsider coming in for the weekend. I became the fifth wheel. The connection I had hoped for between my husband and myself as we built a new life together became a chasm that grew wider and wider as years went by. Aloneness can exist even when another person is in the room. I was such a romantic. I was so naïve. I was so blind. To protect myself from severe emotional bruising I used the path of least resistance, denial.

Some readers may surely be thinking
"Really you must regret having had cancer for so long".

Not really! That is something that comes under the 'accept but cannot change part.' Remember the saying

"God deals the cards. It's all in how you play the hand. In my opinion cancer is not about dying. It is about living. That is learning how to truly live life."

I have met so many professionals and so many good, genuinely kind hearted individuals. I learned so much about medical sciences. There was a whole world out there that I never knew existed until I did get cancer, and the treatments for and the serious, life threatening ramifications when things go bad very quickly. I am really proud of who I have become. A thoracic surgeon said to me

"You shouldn't even be sitting in my office across from my desk right now." He continued in his report, and had stated

"We discussed the aneurysm and likelihood of the dissection in her ascending aorta. I outlined the natural history of the disease stating that most people do not survive an untreated type A dissection, although she is in the minority that has"

The cardiologist said, of me, in his report.

"Her case is absolutely fascinating".

I had asked him

"Do you think I am going to live" he started to laugh and answered

"Live, look at you! You have a stage four cancer that should have killed you three years ago. You recovered from a near death experience two years ago. You are now walking around with an ascending aortic aneurism which defies most scientific data. YA! So far, you are going to live."

To many this sounds like I'm trivializing the issues. Honestly, that was the first time I had been complimented by a couple of men in a very, very long time. I have always wanted to be famous. Now somewhere in the patients archives are those two reports. I had copies made for me. My family especially my grandkids can see that a person should never say "die". You might need to say "uncle" a couple of times in life but no matter what it is, we have to have the guts to see it through. That is the 'Courage' part. I have read several biographies. A few of my favorite heroes would be Golda Meir, Condoleezza Rice and Nelson Mandela. These individuals went above and beyond the call when it came to personal achievement and fulfillment.

I have no regrets about having married my husband. At the time he was a young man with great potential and we were well matched. The fact that he did not have the guts to rid himself of his dark side sooner than later has nothing to do with me. I see that now. My husband, like my mother, had what I refer to as a huge hole in their hearts. They were so needy. The more you tried to fill the void, the more they required. The irony being nothing was ever enough. I have done a great deal of research in the field of behavioral psychology and have come to a couple of conclusion, amateurish perhaps but awfully close to my past reality. My husband was probably suffering from a borderline personality disorder. He certainly did experience bouts of depression which would account for his ever present negativity. He self medicated daily with large amounts of alcohol. I'm quite sure he was probably bi-polar. He would be such a 'devil may care' bon vivant to everyone on the outside but a raging bully to the women in his house. He, a few years after our being separated, described himself as a chameleon. He claimed he took on whatever personality was required of him at the time. My daughters have often wondered about what childhood trauma might have warped his sensibilities. Other than his mentioning to me a long time ago that he had been sodomized when a teen, I really have no idea what happened to him. He, to this day, would not talk about anything very personal about his youth or our life. I am of the opinion, that his frontal cortex which stores the information and experiences relating to emotions such as empathy, feelings, an awareness of right from wrong, conscience if you will, has never reached the full potential expected of most human beings by the time they are in their mid twenties. The weekend binge drinking which started in his mid teens killed brain cells during their infancy. Those two factors combined led to a less than psychologically stable man. All of which were not of my doing. I am over trying to figure it out. I am relieved to say I don't care about the 'why or where for' anymore. I am no longer in denial. It's as if a huge yoke has been removed from my shoulders. The 'albatross 'is finally off my neck. My former husband had proven himself to be an imposter, a fraud, a phony, a hypocrite, a pathological liar.

Dr. Phil McGraw, in his new book 'Life Code' describes the type as a 'baiter'.

I have no regrets whatsoever about having children. This is my reality, of which I am very proud. I have two kind and generous, intelligent, industrious and caring daughters. I have four wonderful grandchildren who seem to be emulating many of the traits of my girls. I truly believe my elders' legacy is being passed on. That makes me feel accomplished. I am alive and, for all intents and purpose, am fully functional. No one could have told me, a year ago, that I would have written a three hundred page book. I learned to let go. I finally got a handle on using each moment offered to me to the best of my ability doing what I had to get done. It's amazing how some things become so urgent such as getting a hug from someone I trust, or listening to Barbara Streisand songs and weeping like a baby or laughing out loud, so hard at a television comedian's joke that I can actually startle myself. I have even taken up a childhood hobby of mine. I do large 'paint by number' sets. My body has a mind of it's own but this pleasure allows me to control the beauty of the picture, slowly but surely. Everything falls into place as it should. There is order. The results are always uplifting!

If you have made it to the end of this tale you will notice one thing. I have proven we are masters of our destiny. Choices good or bad make up the landscape of our tableau. Life is a work in progress. We, every once in a while very much like a vehicle, have to get some realignment done. I had a couple of sayings.

"Three strikes and you're out" or

"You are allowed many mistakes in life but never the same one twice."

If you are fortunate enough to have been spared severe drama in your life than help another poor soul wake up from the horrific nightmare they may be experiencing. Help them get up on their own two feet again.

If you're one us who was kneeling in a submissive position, forehead on the floor, arms raised over your head protecting it from the next blow say to yourself. We, your sisters will help you whisper it

"This is the last time, EVER, I allow myself to be debased."

If it doesn't feel right, then it isn't right. Every human being has a right to peace of mind and soul. If it is taken away, then you must get it back. We must learn to believe that we are worthy of love. It is a huge mistake to equate the living with a man as the be all and end all of our total well being. We are surrounded by a kaleidoscope of affection. There is the love of children, of family, of friends of colleagues and neighbors.

There are many ways to be bullied. Mental cruelty is one of the worst because the wounds cannot be seen by the naked eye. No one has a right to willfully and willingly try to destroy another human being, hurtful word by hurtful word and indifferent gesture by indifferent gesture. It is sheer torture to the partner. When you have finally freed yourself, sooner than later, from bondage do send me a note and I'll help you write your book. Each one of us has what is needed to alter the course of our lives. Each one of us knows it. We just have to do it! Having myself for company is pretty good. There never are any arguments or disappointments. I actually like myself which is a wonderful, gentle, rewarding feeling to have. I had finally learned to love myself more than I loved my husband.

So in the end I am a winner.

"I GET IT! I FINALLY GET IT! It is a lot easier to allow oneself to slide into mediocrity than it is to force oneself to struggle up the treacherous path to self fulfillment."

Trust me the view is spectacular from up here. Oh gosh! Looking forward, I see there is another crest to climb. That's OK! Day by day!

This is not THE END, it is more like

PEACE! (to be continued).

CPSIA information can be obtained at www.ICGtesting.com
Printed in the USA
LVOW09*1837071114

412566LV00001B/5/P